THE TRUSTEES OF THE PUBLIC LIBRARY
OF THE CITY OF BOSTON
EMR

A MASTER CARVER'S LEGACY

essentials of wood carving techniques

Le peu de soin, le temp, tout fait qu'on dégénére,
Faute de cultiver la Nature et ses dons.

Jean de La Fontaine (1621-1695)
Fable XXIV Book VIII

In fond memory of Monsieur Louis Bouchet of Dinan, Brittany, in whose establishment I learned, and of his son Paul who was my teacher.

A MASTER CARVER'S LEGACY
essentials of wood carving techniques

Brieuc Bouché

TAB BOOKS Inc.
Blue Ridge Summit, PA 17214

FIRST EDITION

FIRST PRINTING

Library of Congress Cataloging in Publication Data

Bouché, Brieuc.
A master carver's legacy.

Includes index.
1. Wood-carving—Technique. I. Title.
TT199.7.B67 1986 736'.4 85-27614
ISBN 0-8306-0329-8

Cover photographs by Patty Martin.

Contents

Acknowledgments

I am deeply indebted and grateful to the many people, friends, pupils, and family, whose encouragement, reviews, and criticism have made this work possible. I am especially thankful to my wife, Lucile, and my daughter Anne-Marie for their suggestions and corrections of the text. A special mention goes to my daughter Nicole for her indispensable help and patience in organizing and typing the material.

Foreword

As manufacturing processes and equipment design evolve under the pressure of social change, technology, and merchandising, old working traditions have had to adapt or be discarded. Professional wood carving has not been spared, and pessimists even lament what they see as the vanishing of the wood-carver's craft.

After many years of absence from Brittany, I had occasion to visit the site of my training. Previously, at least three shops of artistic furniture making gave dependable employment to some 150 full-time, skilled cabinetmakers and wood sculptors, not counting the work contracted out to a few independent artisans. Upon my return I could not find a single professional carver in the town. The centuries old and very successful apprentice system had all but disappeared.

Far from courting oblivion, however, wood carving is indulged in by increasingly more people. This craft, once the monopoly of a few beautifully trained professionals, has become, at least in the United States, the property of a proliferation of hobbyists and small artisans. They may lack the quality and depth of training of old, but they are nonetheless in love with their chosen craft and aim at a remarkable perfection of skill. In addition, new tools and better art education have encouraged experimentation. The exquisite execution of the old-fashioned ways of carving and the extensive knowledge of classical forms have been exchanged for more freedom and individual artistic expression. The screaming electric router and exploding chain saw show that, as long as there are wood, tools, and people to guide them, wood carving will flourish.

In offering these notes, I hope to be of service to the hobbyist as well as to the student, the furniture maker, the restorer of past splendors, and the teacher of art, crafts, and industrial arts. To those who are attracted to woodcarving but have doubts of their fitness or natural gifts, I offer these words of encouragement: In the past, as well as now, all over the world people have been and are being trained in industry or schools to perform various kinds of crafts, with little regard for special gifts. After many years of learning and teaching, I am convinced that, while only some may reach truly professional standards, practically anyone can acquire a degree of proficiency that will procure deep satisfaction. The gift is there, dormant, a "Sleeping Beauty" waiting to be awakened. It is up to each of us to cultivate it assiduously. The prerequisites are faith, a stubborn will to overcome a few minor difficulties, and a little patience.

Et, si de t'agréer je n'emporte le prix,
J'aurai du moins l'honneur de l'avoir entrepris.

La Fontaine, "*Fables*" *à Monsieur le Dauphin*

Photograph 1

Introduction

In assembling these notes I had two main purposes in mind: first, to present to the curious and scholarly a tableau of the wood-carver's equipment in general use in the shops of Western Europe early in this century; second, to offer the would-be carver deprived of a qualified teacher and unfamiliar with shop equipment and practices a few graduated problems and notes as guides for their efforts. To this end, I have presented in detail the equipment as well as the step-by-step description of techniques. All the material described is of professional quality. If some of the equipment is not available today, suitable substitutes can be found.

It is suggested, and hoped, that students will complement this necessarily limited outline by making full use of the many and often excellent books on carving, art, decoration, and related subjects available on library shelves.

Part I

The Equipment of the Wood-Carver

Before beginning work you must prepare an appropriate work area, and acquire an assortment of basic carving tools and drawing equipment. You must also become somewhat familiar with the function of the various types of carving tools. Both inadequate working space and lighting, and an insufficient selection of basic tools will only hinder you along the way as you attempt to complete the various exercises that follow.

SHOP, STUDIO, OR WORKING CENTER

In choosing a working center you should be aware that wood carving is a clean craft, so much so that some people practice it in the living room, where tools, equipment, and work become a center of interest and beauty enhanced by the fragrance of many varieties of wood. Wherever it is located, the working space should be as comfortable as possible—airy and cool in summer, warm in winter. If there is a cement or stone floor, your feet should be protected from the cold, humidity, and hardness of the floor's surface.

Proper lighting is of the greatest importance. Both natural and artificial illumination are acceptable. The best daylight comes from the north. When you are using this natural light, the bench should be placed next to the window, with the base of the window close to the level of or below the top of the bench (Plate 1, fig. 1). Avoid direct sunlight on the bench top. Artificial lighting should create strong, sharp contrasts on the carving. Your eyes, however, should be protected from the glare of lights. To achieve this end, lamps of adjustable height are very convenient (Plate 1, figs. 1 and 2). Finally, regular electric bulbs of 100 or 200 watts are better than fluorescent tubes, which give a diffused light and destroy light and shadow contrasts.

THE BENCH

Carvers work standing up to guarantee freedom of movement. As a consequence, the bench must be built high enough to avoid painful backaches. The top of the bench should reach some 10 cm. to 12 cm. (3.9 to 4.7 inches) below the elbow of the standing carver. The measurements suggested are for an average bench.

The bench should be sturdy and well braced so it is stable. If a workbench is already available, it can be brought to the proper height with a removable vertical extension fastened to the top (Plate 3). If a discarded table is to be used as a bench, reinforce it and condition it so that it will have as much strength and stability of a regular bench as is possible.

The ideal bench top is made of hard, close-grained wood, such as maple or beech, and should be thick enough (6 cm. to 8 cm.) to stand pounding. It can be made of a solid piece of wood or of pieces glued together and fastened to the base with heavy screws countersunk and covered with wood plugs (Plate 4, fig. 1). The trough at the back of the top keeps tools from falling and their cutting edges free of dust and grit. An opening in the top permits chips and dust to drop to the floor, facilitating cleaning (Plate 4, fig. 2).

The bench setup would not be complete without an auxiliary low stand, which will help when carving on particularly high pieces (Plate 2).

THE HOLDING EQUIPMENT

To protect yourself against personal injury and to avoid damaging your work, the piece you are carving must be securely fastened to the bench top. There are many possible ways of fastening it.

Many bench vises are available, but the metal jaws are deadly on the carving tools. In addition, the jaws must be covered when in use or the raw metal will mar the softer woods. The old-fashioned vise with wood jaws garnished with cork and thick hide is not available for purchase, but it would be worth the effort for the professional user to build one (Plate 5, fig. 3).

The carriage clamp, or *C clamp* (Plate 5, fig. 1), with an opening of 15 cm. and a depth of 75 mm., is readily available in hardware supply stores. The "Jorgensen" type, quick-action clamp #3706 (opening 15 cm., depth 75 mm.) or the #3712 (opening 30 cm., depth 75 mm.) is lighter and more practical. The "Wetzler" type #712 (opening 31 cm., depth 20 cm.) is heavier and more expensive, but a must for the professional (Plate 5, fig. 2).

The carver's anchor screw (Plate 6), standard equipment in Europe, has yet to make its appearance on the American market, although a toy-size version minus the most important part, the anchor, is available in some catalogs. A substitute can be made as suggested in Plate 6.

THE SHARPENING EQUIPMENT

Much depends on proper sharpening of tools. Appropriate materials must be used and careful attention paid to correct sharpening procedures. Sharpening techniques will be discussed in the next chapter. Here I am concerned with the equipment needed in the main steps of sharpening: grinding, whetting, honing, and stropping. These steps permit you to shape and refine the cutting edge of your tools.

Three types of equipment can be used to grind the cutting edge, or bevel:

- ☐ The rough face of a bench stone is easily available and inexpensive, but slow going (Plate 7, fig. 1).
- ☐ The electric high-speed dry wheel is readily acquired but costly. Its use demands extreme caution and substantial body protection. Because this method tends to burn the tool, you must also have a container with water on hand to cool the tools often (Plate 7, fig. 2).
- ☐ The slow-turning, water-lubricated sandstone is an old standby. Although it is costly, the sandstone cuts moderately fast and presents little danger either to the tools or to the operator. For these reasons, it is the best choice for grinding the bevel (Plate 7, fig. 3).

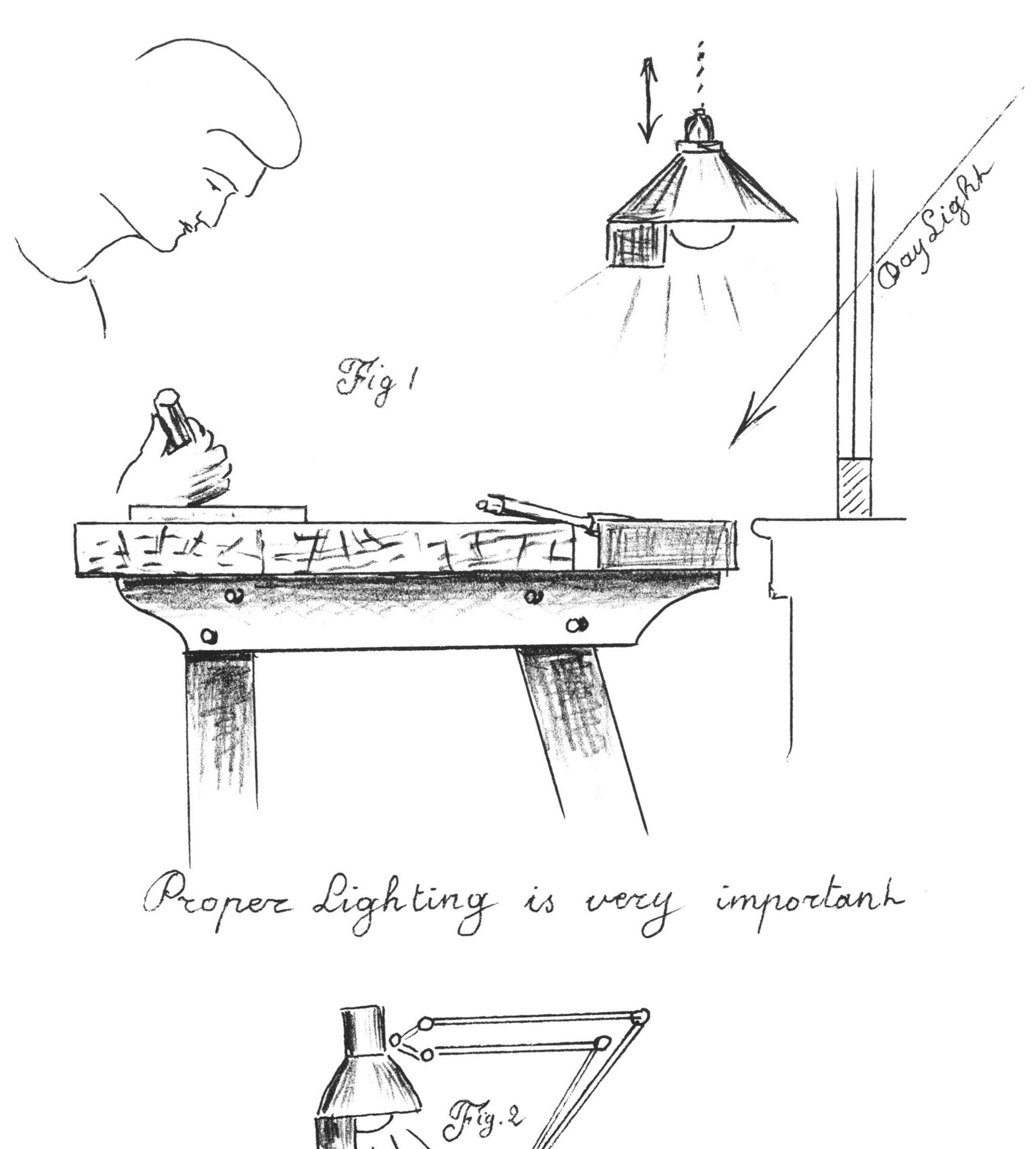

Proper Lighting is very important

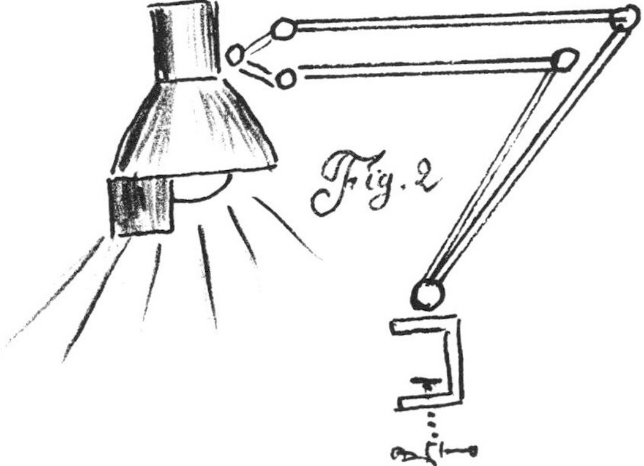

Plate 1

Whetting and honing are often handled in a single operation with one stone. The old-style carver used a set of mined, natural stones known as "Pierres du Levant," or Middle Eastern stones, lubricated with water. Many stones of varied origins and composition are on the market today. The mined natural stones are significantly more expensive than the artificial kinds. Most dealers carry only a few varieties of stone, but you can obtain other types by special order.

Generally the heavier grains are used for whetting, the finer for honing. Many carvers use only the finer honing stones, however, which lengthens the sharpening process. The hard Arkansas is about the finest slipstone you can get. Used for surgical tools and the like, it is not essential for materials such as wood. Carvers will get full satisfaction with the artificial medium-grade India for whetting, and the fine-grade India for honing (Plate 8). There are also excellent fine Carborundum stones. They are fast-cutting but may also wear faster. Stone shapes and numbers that are recommended for purchase are shown in Plate 8, fig. 1.

Stropping can be done on a thick piece of hide dressed with a very fine Carborundum powder. The hide is bent to strop the inside of the gouges. The stropping block is more practical and equally effective (Plate 8, fig. 2). It is made of a box, carved by each apprentice, in which is packed a warm mixture of melted suet and Carborundum powder #100, minimum grit. Too fine a grit has little effect on the edge. In the past, emery powder was used. If the paste is too greasy, you can add powder on the surface to make it hard and shiny. The stropping mixture takes the shape of the inside and outside of the gouges.

THE CARVING BLADES

Blades come in a great variety of shapes and sweeps, or widths (Plate 9). The best tools are not necessarily the most fancy ones in shape or presentation. Only the working qualities should matter. A numbering code, regrettably not strictly adhered to, is used to designate the shapes of blades.

When you are purchasing tools you can rely, at first, on the selected shapes shown in Plates 10 and 11, rather than on the numbers. The slight variations in sweep or width are not too important when you are just learning the craft. About a dozen straight tools are needed by the beginner (Plate 10).

THE HANDLES

The simplest handles will do very well and are less costly (Plate 12, fig. 1). Octagonal and round shapes are used. The top of the handle should be wide with a gentle convex surface; narrow pointed tops cause blisters (Plate 12, fig. 1). A slight curve or swelling in the length is also recommended. Use a few drops of salad or linseed oil to season new handles and provide the raw wood with a patina. (See also Plate 13.)

THE CARVER'S MALLET AND CARVER'S ROLL

The mallet is an indispensable part of a carver's equipment. Although mallets can be obtained in a variety of styles, a rounded shaped mallet is best for carving because any part of the curved surface can be used to strike the handle of the chisel (Plate 14, fig. 1).

The professional mallet is made of wood, metal, or of late, urethane. Metal mallets are most commonly made of cast iron or bronze. They are indestructible and space saving when compared to those made of wood. However, metal mallets can be somewhat cumbersome to use, weighing as much as 1 kg (about 2.2 lbs.) (Plate 14, fig. 1).

A good wooden mallet can easily be turned on the lathe. The wood should be

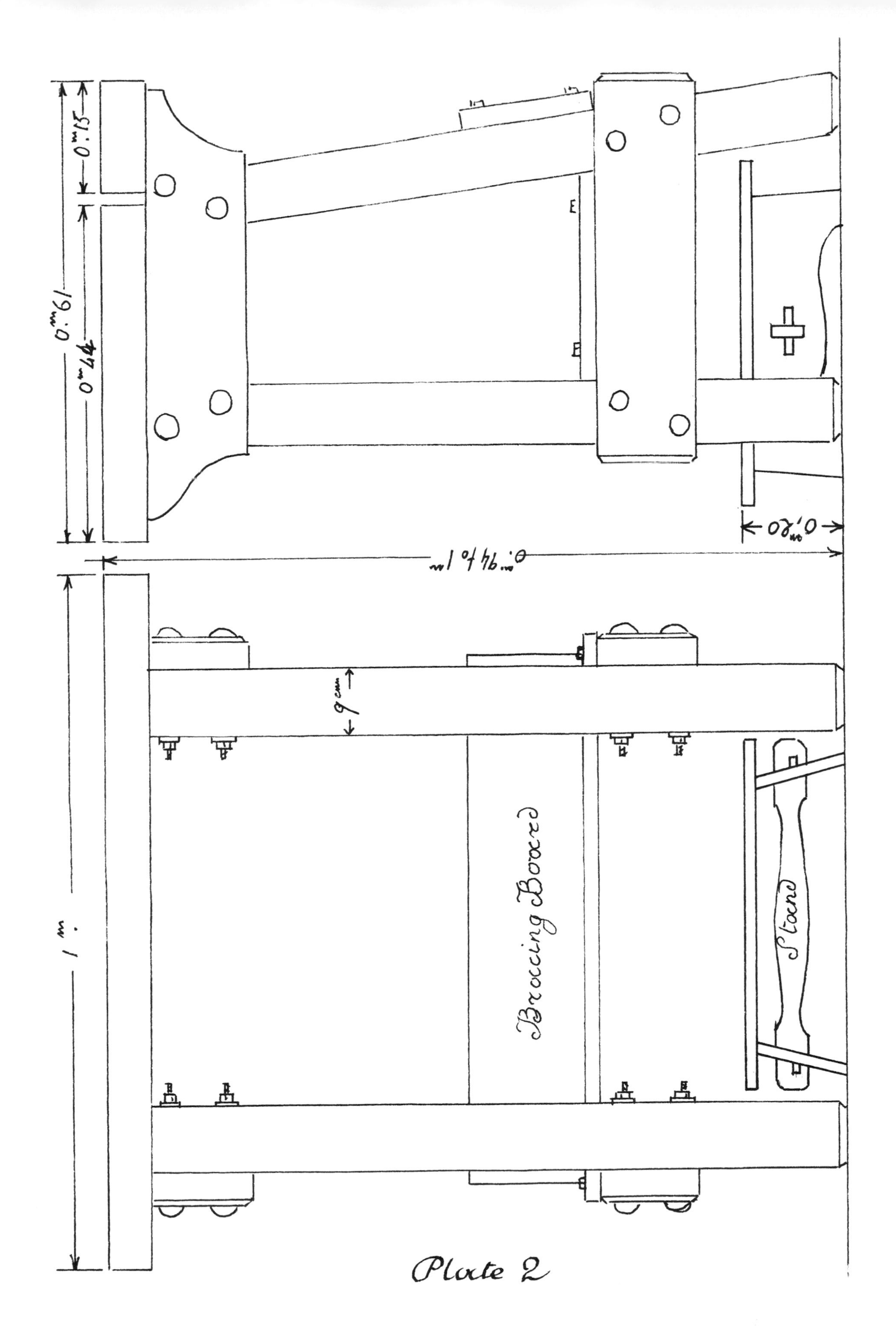

Plate 2

free of defects, well seasoned, heavy, and of a close-grained variety, such as maple. Lignum vitae is especially favored because of its weight and durability. Wooden mallets for carving can weigh up to 500 g. Any heavier and they become cumbersome and awkward to use.

The roll is a most convenient, light-weight, and easily made device to protect and transport your tools. Make it out of a fairly substantial fabric, such as light canvas (Plate 14, fig. 2).

RASPS, FILES, AND RIFFLERS

Rasps and files are almost a necessity when you are carving in the round. The rasp should be half round, medium, or fine, and 20 to 25 cm. long. The file should be half round, bastard, and of similar size. See Plate 15.

Rifflers, rather small and fine, can be of use for fine finishing on advanced carving. When you are purchasing curved rifflers, select ones in which the cutting, bent heads are curved from the handle to the tip. Acquire enough varieties of this tool to fit all details—concave, convex, narrow, and wide. Rifflers with a rasp-type cutting surface are used on wood and should not be used on other materials.

Great care should be taken to avoid ruining the cutting surfaces when you are using or storing rifflers, files, and rasps.

STIPPLING AND STAMPING TOOLS

Stippling and stamping tools may be difficult to obtain. Generally they are made by the apprentice carver out of mild steel.

Stippling tools are indispensable for finishing a background so it accentuates the carving (Plate 16, fig. 1). The stippling face can be made easily with the help of a three-cornered file (Plate 16, fig. 2). The almond-shaped face is no more than 1 cm. long from point to heel.

Plate 16, fig. 3 shows a variety of stamping shapes. The larger bead would be about 8 mm. wide. These tools are used to give a clean effect in spots that cannot be reached with a cutting gouge.

THE CARVER'S ROUTER AND SCRAPERS

Routers and scrapers are easily made. Each carver constructs them as the need arises. The router is used to make deep test cuts on large panel work (Plate 17, fig. 1) to ensure an even depth of background. Scrapers can be made of old, broken band saws (Plate 17, fig. 2).

THE GAUGE

The gauge is a tracing tool used to inscribe lines parallel to the dressed edge of a panel. They can be readily obtained in hardware stores. A simple and economical model can be made of three small pieces of scrap wood and a nail. (See Plate 18.)

THE TARABISCOT, OR SCRATCH TOOL

The tarabiscot is an adjustable tool used to cut, by scratching long **V**s parallel to the edge of large pieces generally on straight lines or very open curves. It will not cut across grain. The tarabiscot will be of greatest interest and use to the professional carver who handles large jobs. They are not available in stores and must be built by the carver. The cutting blade is held between two metal plates. See Plate 19.

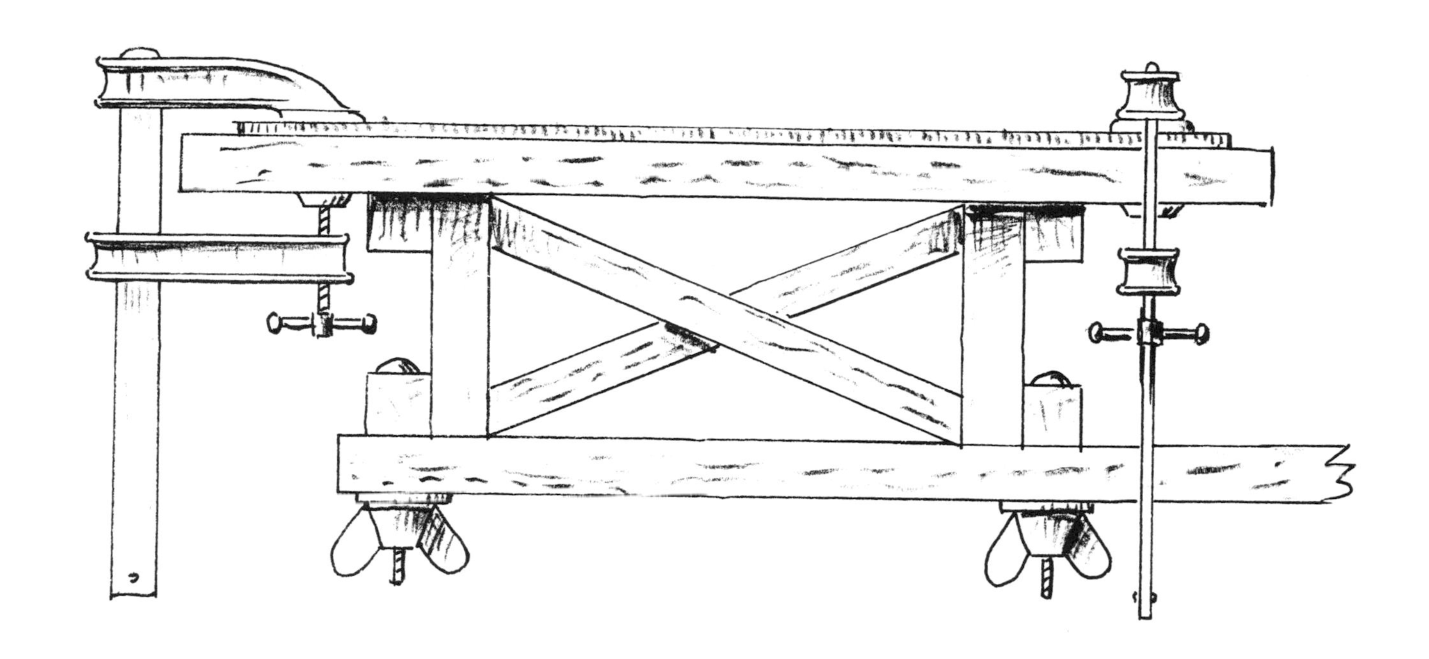

The Bench Extension

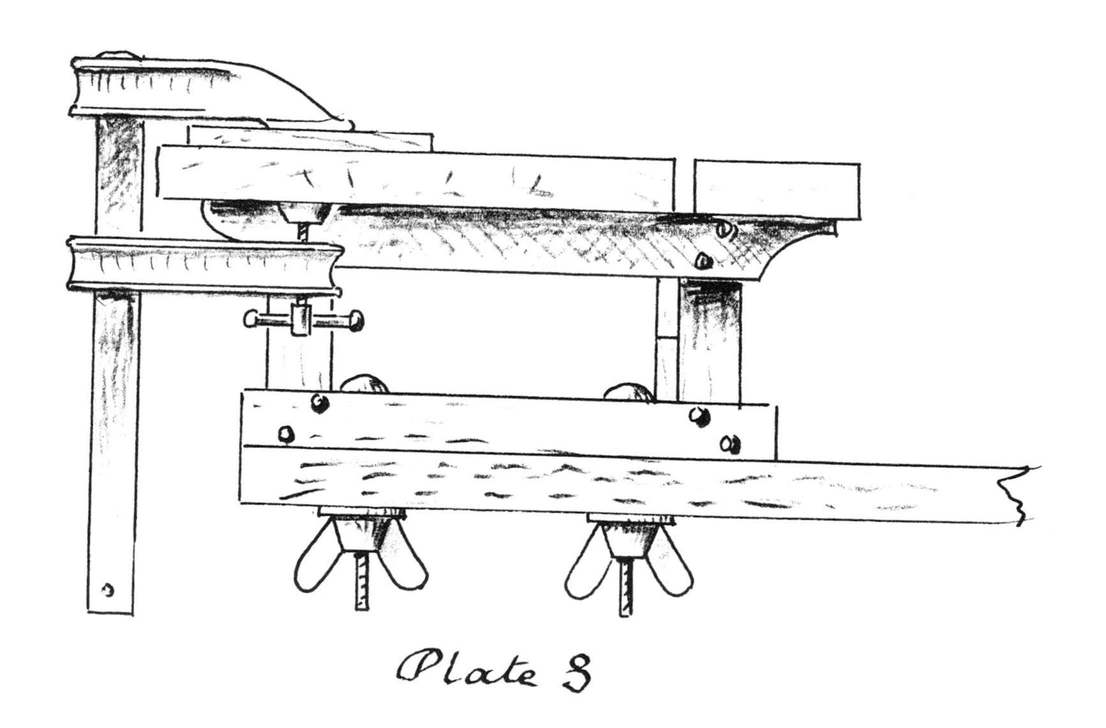

Plate 8

DRAWING TOOLS, WORK CLOTHING, AND OTHER ITEMS

Drawing tools are indispensable to the carver for planning his work. I recommend that you obtain two compasses, or *dividers*. One should be equipped with a pencil for work on paper. The other, more solidly built for inscribing in wood, has two dry points and is about 18 cm. long. Squares and rulers made of wood or plastic are preferred to reduce the chances of harming the cutting edges of gouges. The squares, one 90° and the other 45°, should have heels to slide against the dressed edge of the wood. A T square would prove very useful for larger works. Good rulers, small or large, graduated or not, can be made easily (Plate 20, fig. 1).

Old-time carvers wore a smock to protect their clothing when at work. This garment was made of pure white material so that it would act as a reflector, directing light on the shady side of round carvings. The smock was made quite simply, without features that could catch, tear, or otherwise interfere with the work (Plate 20, fig. 2).

The list of additional accessories is long and includes:

- ☐ #2 pencils, sharpener, erasers, sketching pad of paper.
- ☐ Tagboard to cut out patterns, carbon and tracing papers, thumb tacks, and scissors.
- ☐ A can of light oil and a cleaning rag for use in sharpening tools.
- ☐ Sandpaper #2/0 (100) and #4/0 (150), sometimes used for finishing. Finer grits have little effect on wood but are useful for sharpening pencil points.
- ☐ A counter-type brush with soft bristles for dusting and cleaning carvings and the bench.
- ☐ Finishing and gluing equipment and supplies are treated separately in Part IV, *The Finishing Touch*.
- ☐ Finally, but of great importance, you should always have on hand a first aid kit equipped to handle minor, as well as deep or large, cuts.

SUPPLIERS

The three addresses listed here offer an extensive variety of gouges, chisels, and stones for both the professional carver and the serious carving student. Write for catalogs and price listings.

Frank Mittermeier Inc.
3577 East Tremont Ave.
Bronx, NY 10465

Sculpture House
38 East 30th St.
New York, NY 10016

Woodcraft Supply Corp.
313 Montvale Ave.
Woburn, MA 01801

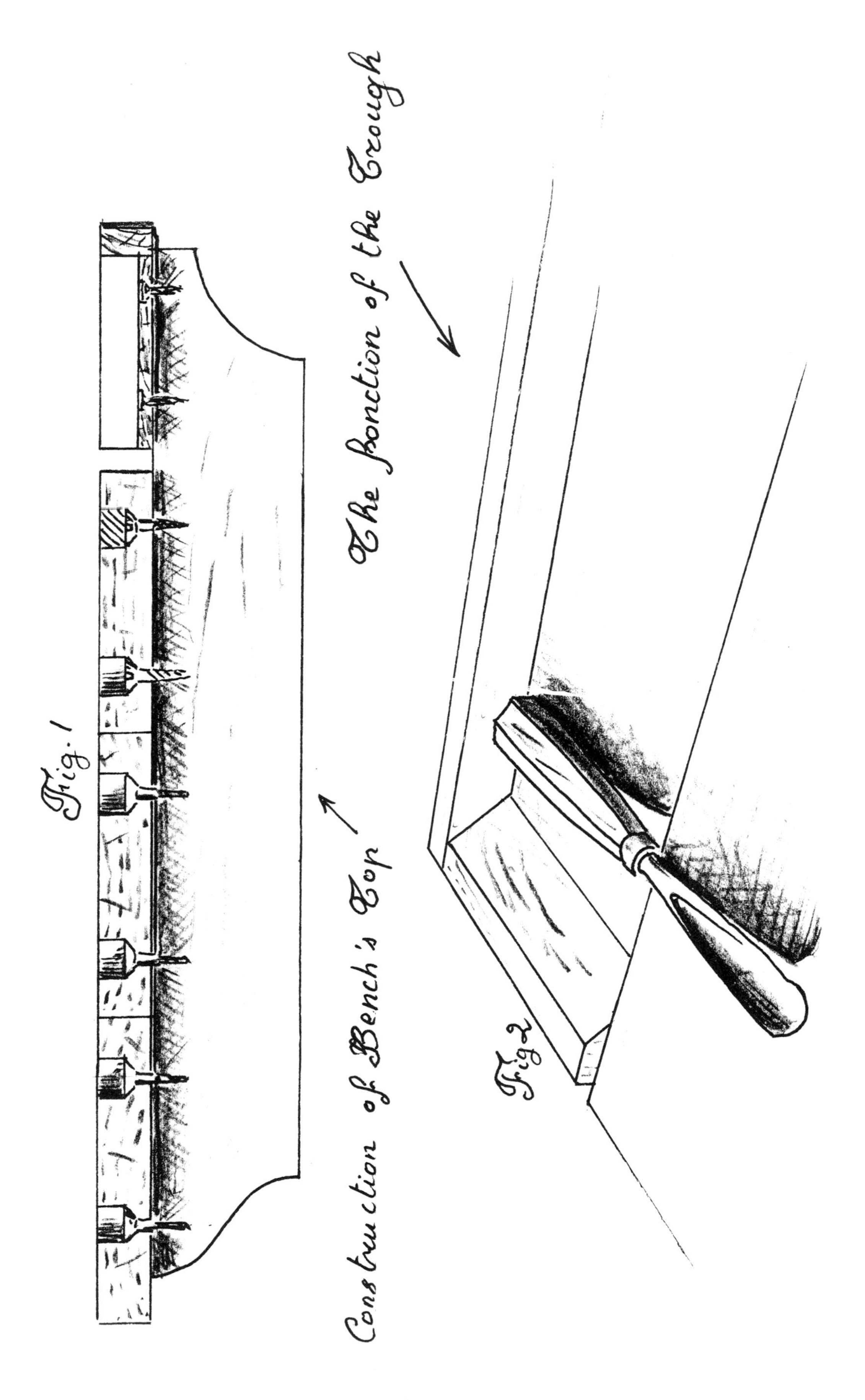
Fig. 1
Construction of Bench's Top
The fonction of the Trough
Fig 2

Plate 4

SUMMARY OF SUGGESTED EQUIPMENT FOR THE BEGINNER

The Shop or Work Corner: Bench & good lights (Plates 1 - 4). Two clamps (Plate 5, preferably fig. 2).
Dress: Choice of white shirt, smock, or apron.
Sharpening: Grinding facility (Plate 7, first choice fig. 3, second choice fig. 1).
Slip and honing stones, India fine #22-#42 and #44 (Plate 8).
Stropping box, suet, and carborundum powder #100 or #120.
Can of light oil, clean rags.
Carving Tools: See Plate 10, and for proper handles Plate 12, fig. 1.
Mallet, 500 grams (Plate 14).
Carver's roll (Plate 14, fig. 2).
Stippling Tools: Two almond-shaped, 1 cm. long, one wide and one narrow (Plate 16, figs. 1 - 2).
Repairing and finishing supplies and equipment: See *The Finishing Touch.*
Drawing and Tracing: Ruler, squares, compass (Plate 20, fig. 1).
#2 pencils, erasers.
Drawing pad or paper, carbon paper, transparent tracing paper, tag board.
Emergencies: Simple first aid kit, including bandages, disinfectant, tweezers, and clean, sharp needles.

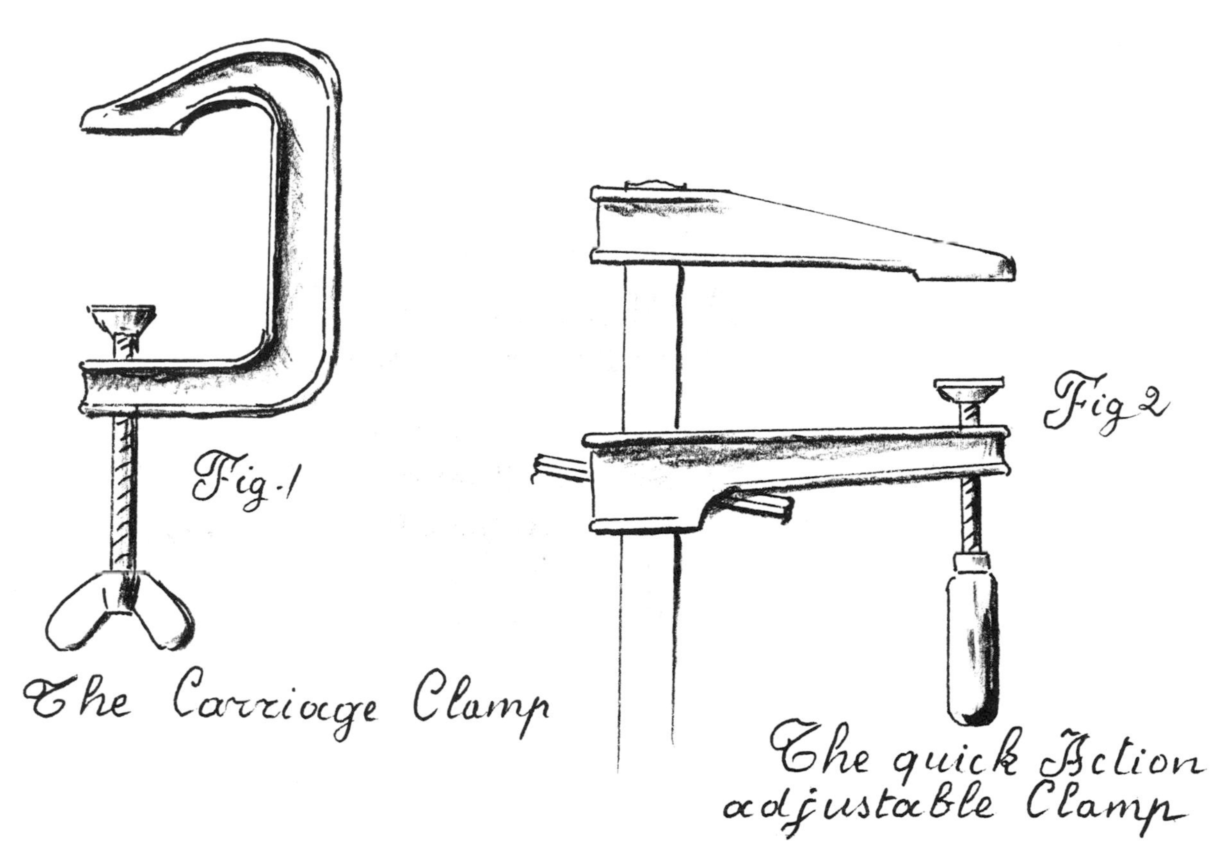

The Carver's Vise

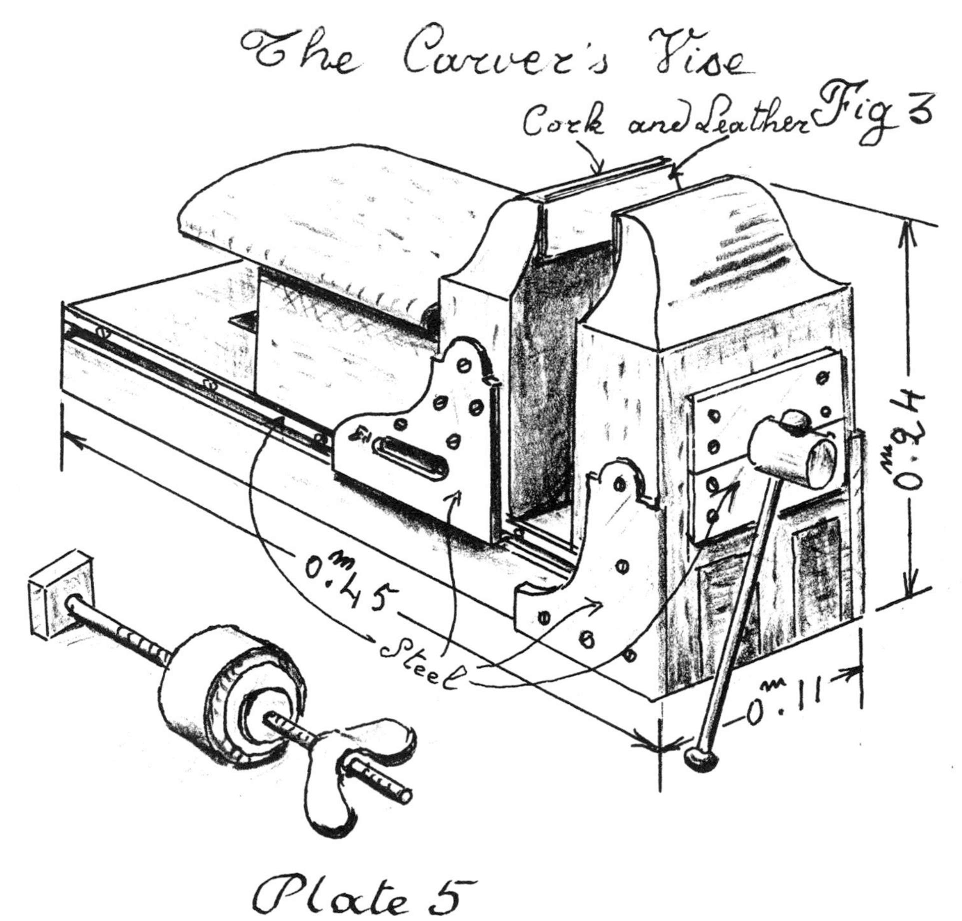

Plate 5

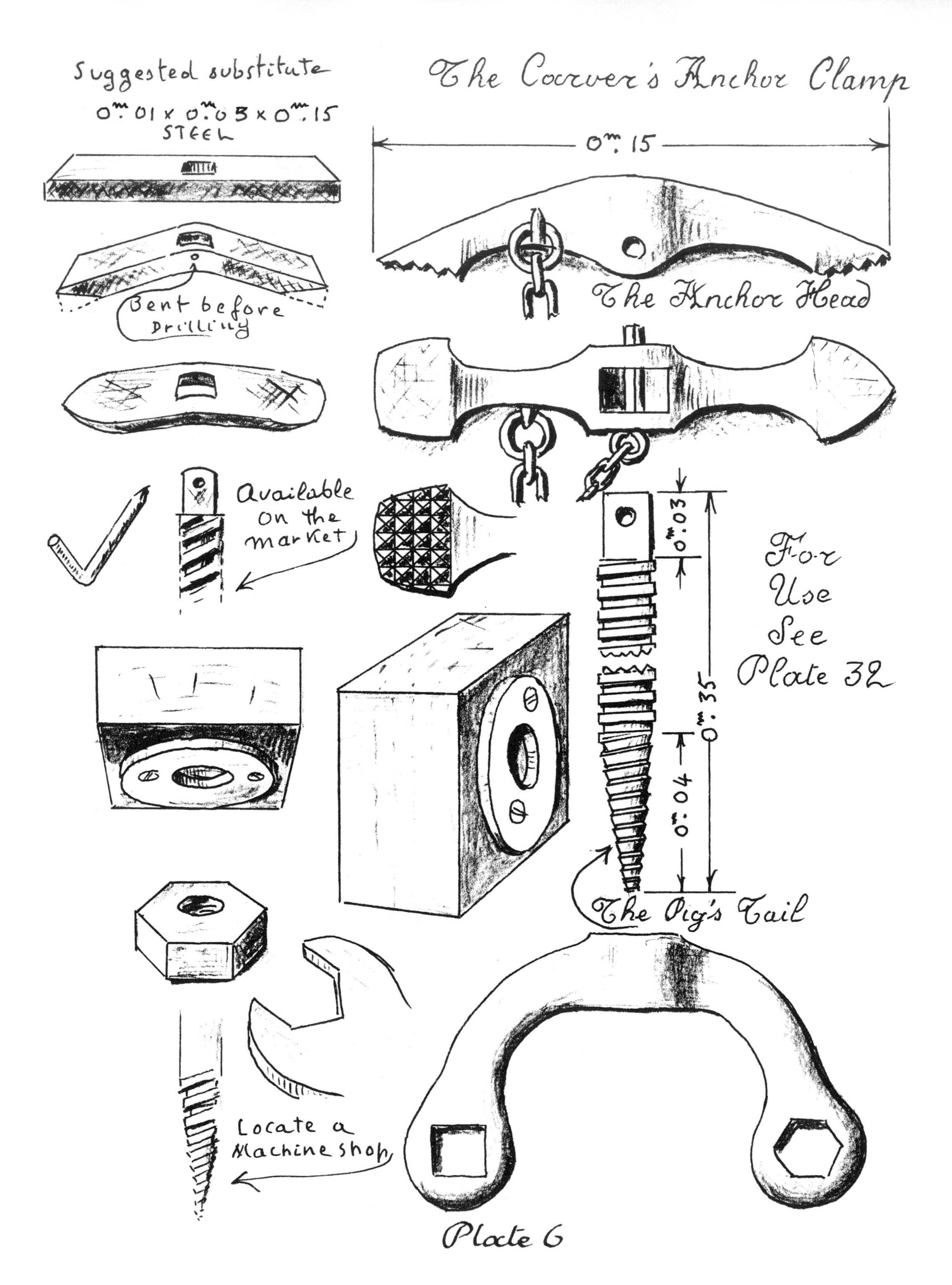

Suggested substitute
0m.01 x 0m.03 x 0m.15
STEEL
Bent before Drilling
Available on the market
Locate a Machine shop
The Carver's Anchor Clamp
0m.15
The Anchor Head
0m.03
0m.35
0m.04
The Pig's Tail
For Use See Plate 32

Plate 6

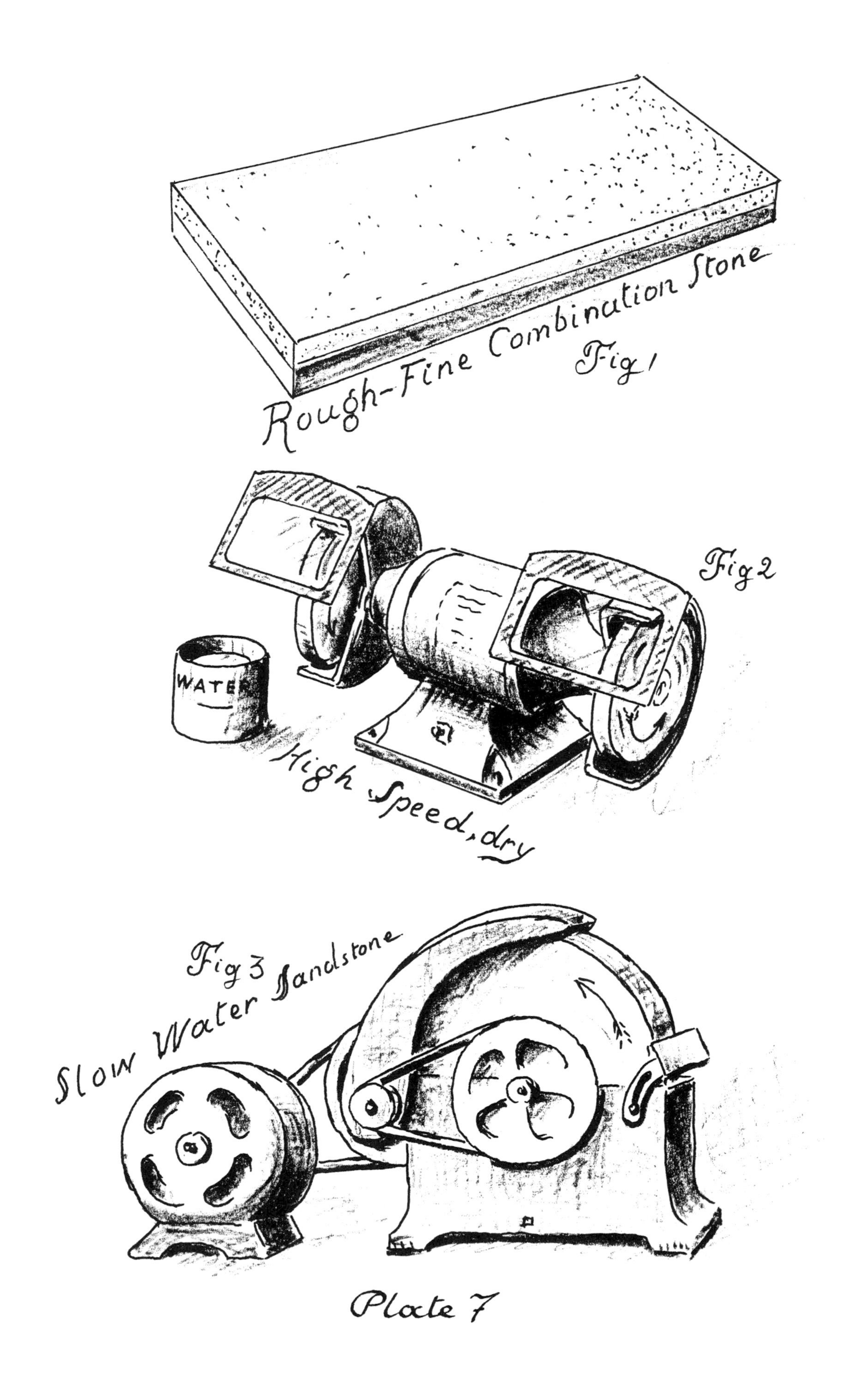
Rough-Fine Combination Stone
Fig 1
Fig 2
WATER
High Speed, dry
Fig 3
Slow Water Sandstone

Plate 7

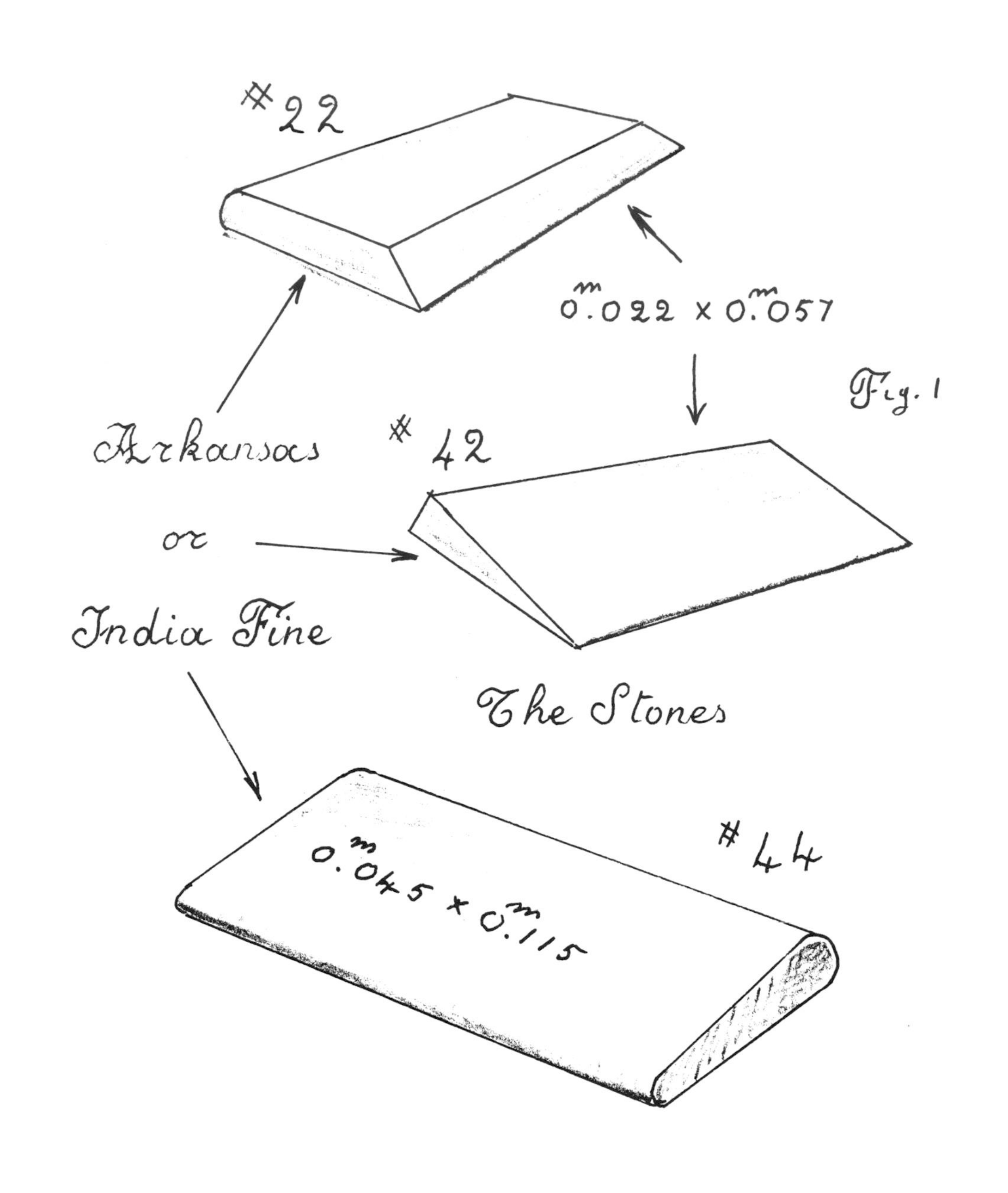
#22
0.022 x 0.057
Fig. 1
Arkansas
#42
or
India Fine
The Stones
#44
0.045 x 0.115

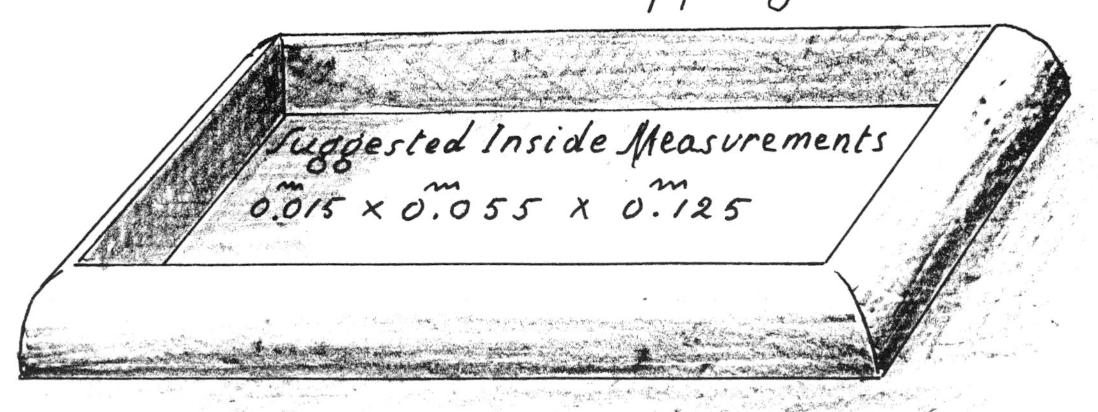
The Stropping Box
Fig 2
Suggested Inside Measurements
0.015 x 0.055 x 0.125

Plate 8

CARVING BLADES AND BEVELLING PROFILES

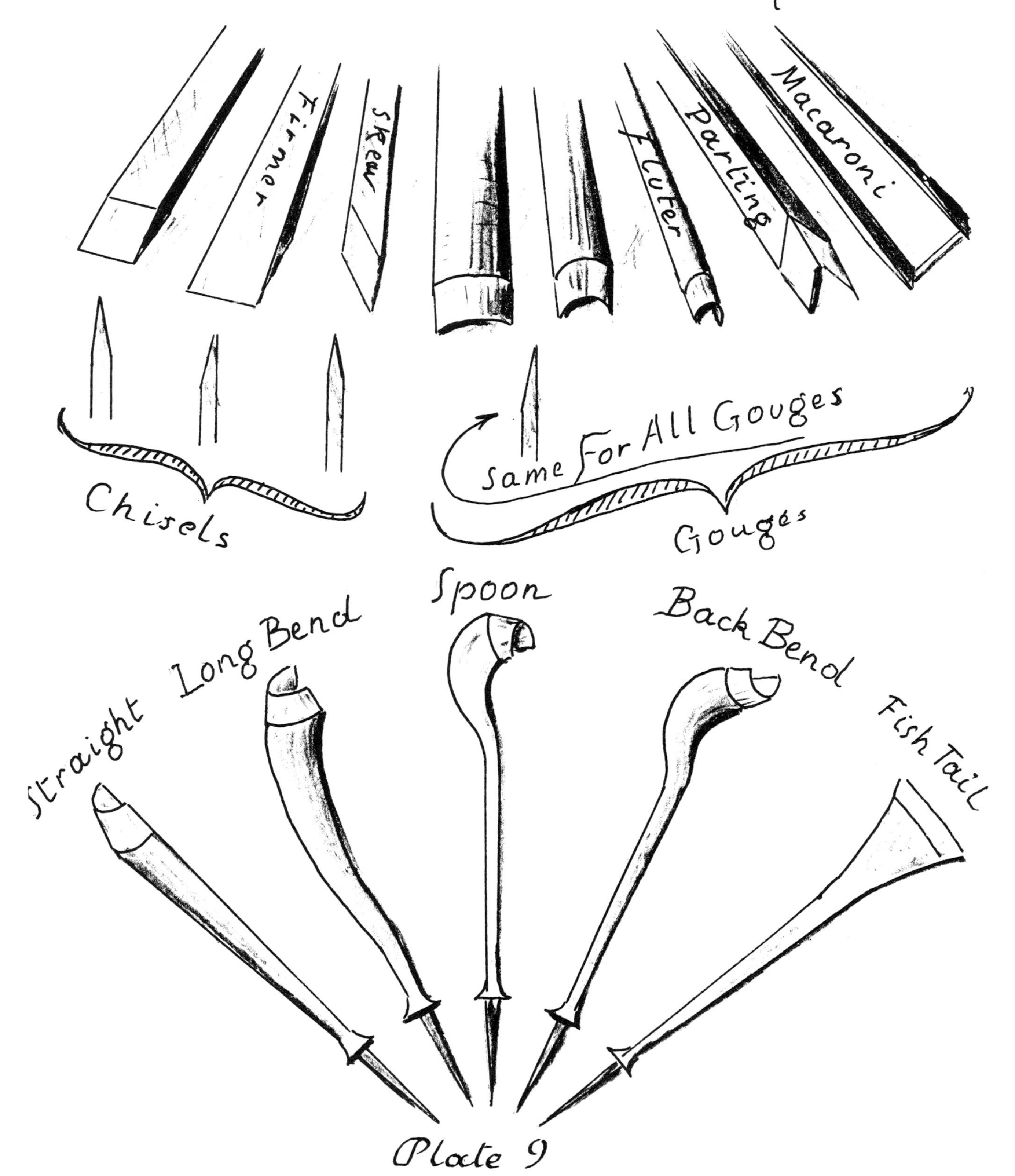

Plate 9

Tool Selection #1. (Sculpture House NY)

Numbers	Metric Sizes	Old Style	Shapes	Remarks
45	$0^{m}.01$	$\frac{3}{8}$		Parting Tool 70° Opening (#39 Sheffield Style) (Mittermeier Catalog, NY)
1	$0^{m}.016$	$\frac{5}{8}$		
2	$0^{m}.005$	$\frac{3}{16}$		For Skew
3	$0^{m}.005$	$\frac{3}{16}$		Very Shallow Curve
3	$0^{m}.016$	$\frac{5}{8}$		Very Shallow Curve
4	$0^{m}.016$	$\frac{5}{8}$		
5	$0^{m}.008$	$\frac{5}{16}$		
5	$0^{m}.016$	$\frac{5}{8}$		
6	$0^{m}.005$	$\frac{3}{16}$		
6	$0^{m}.016$	$\frac{5}{8}$		
7	$0^{m}.012$	$\frac{7}{16}$		Or Slighty Larger
9 or 10	$0^{m}.003$	$\frac{1}{8}$		Fluter

Plate 10

Tool Selections

#2

Numbers	Metric Sizes	Old Style	Shapes
1	$0^{m}.005$	3/16	
3	$0^{m}.01$	3/8	
3	$0^{m}.025$	1"	
4	$0^{m}.003$	1/8	
5	$0^{m}.023$	7/8	
6	$0^{m}.008$	5/16	
7	$0^{m}.006$	1/4	
7	$0^{m}.008$	5/16	
8	$0^{m}.01$	3/8	
9	$0^{m}.006$	1/4	

#3

Numbers	Metric Sizes	Old Style	Shapes
1	$0^{m}.01$	3/8	
22	$0^{m}.006$	1/4	R Skew
23	$0^{m}.006$	1/4	L Skew
24	$0^{m}.003$	1/8	
24	$0^{m}.006$	1/4	
27	$0^{m}.008$	5/16	
29	$0^{m}.01$	3/8	
31	$0^{m}.003$	1/8	Fluter
43	$0^{m}.01$	3/8	Parting
52	$0^{m}.006$	1/4	Fish Tail

Plate 11

The Handles

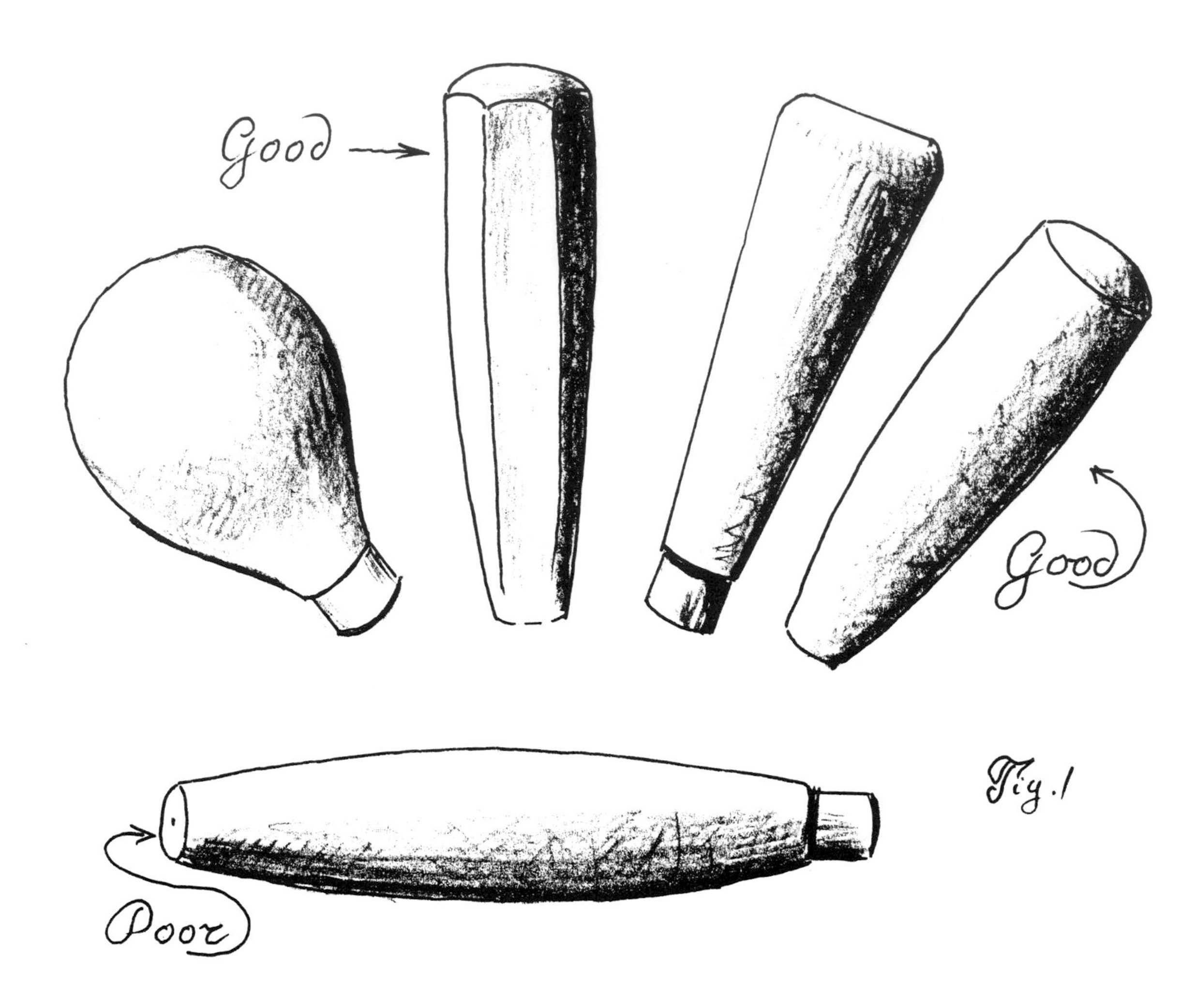

Preparation for setting Handle

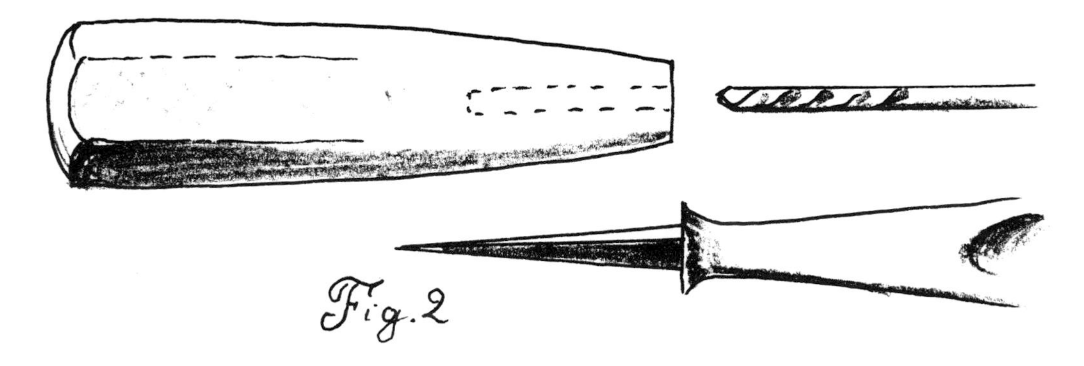

Plate 12

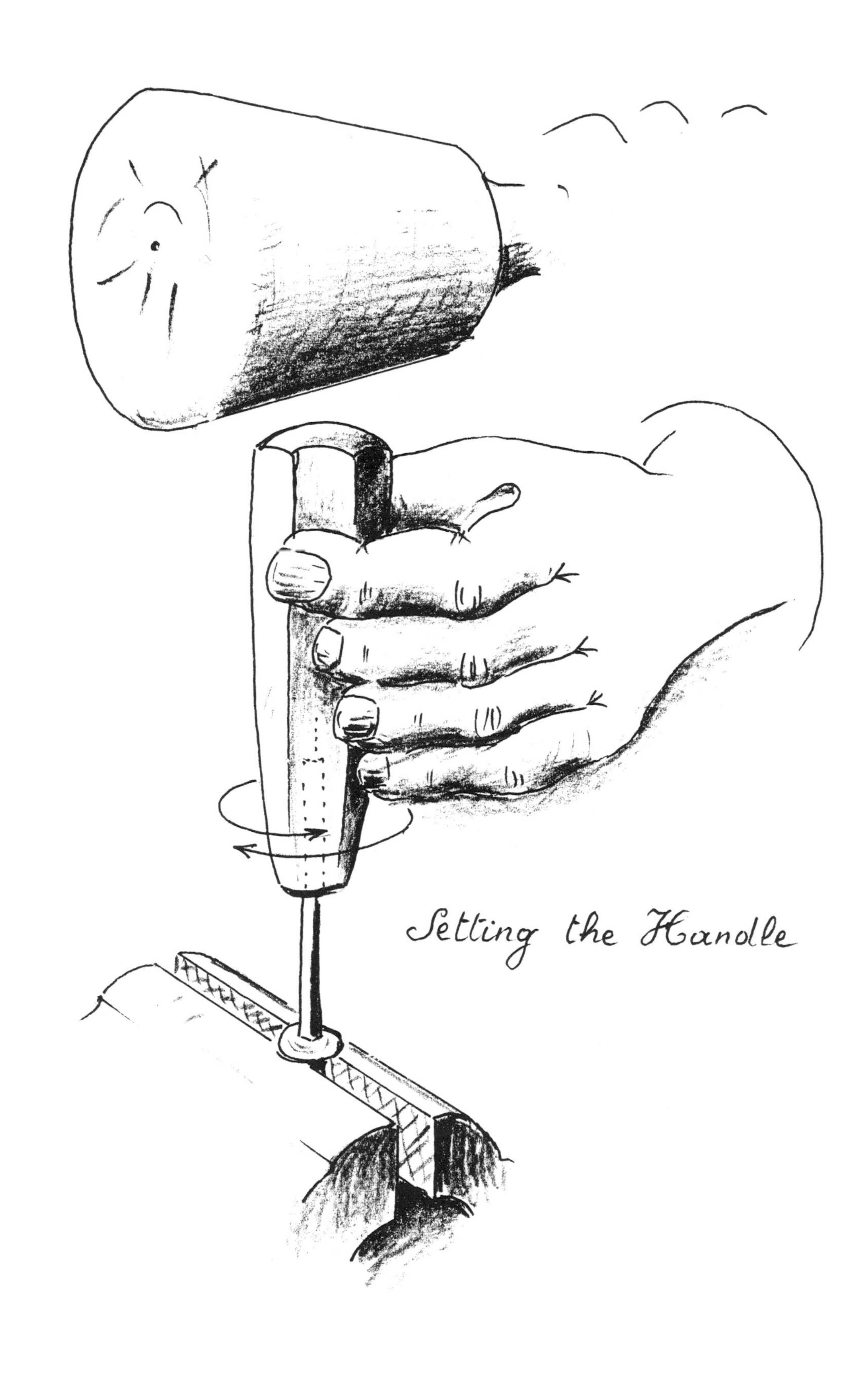

Plate 13

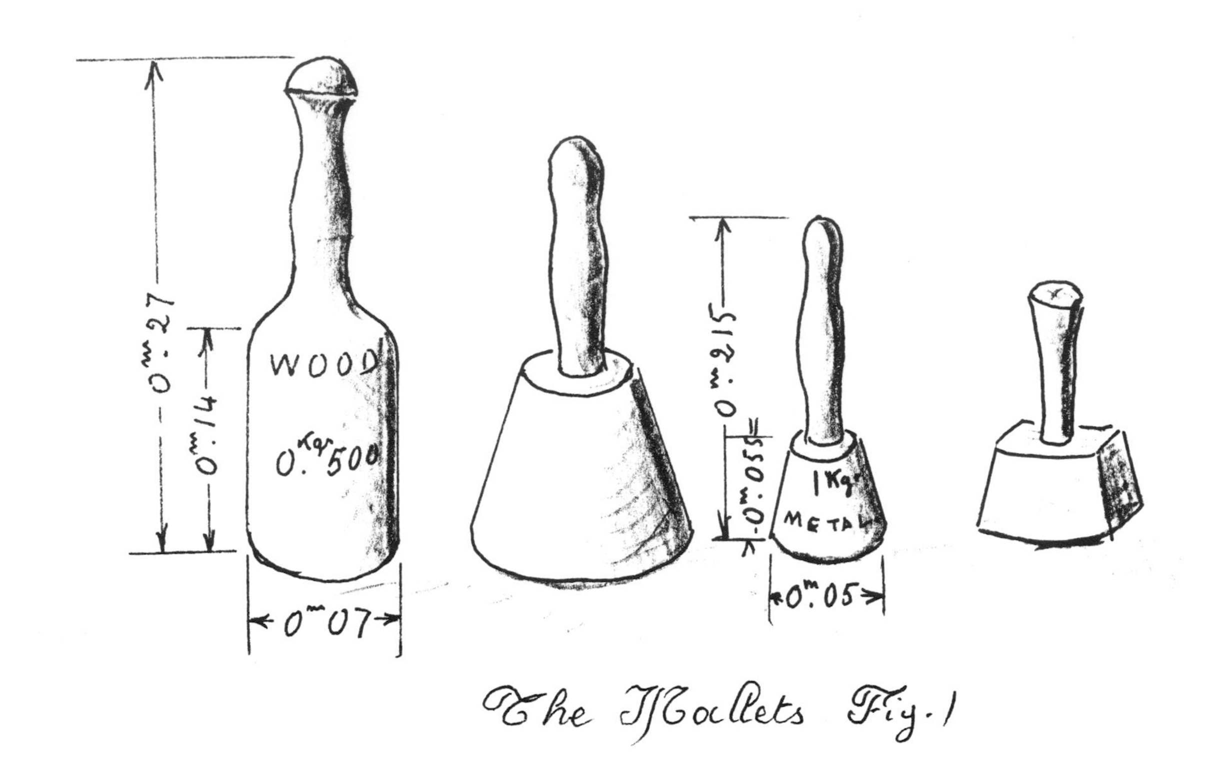

The Mallets Fig. 1

The Carver's Roll Fig. 2

0m.60
0m.12
0m.12
0m.12
0m.05
Fold over

Plate 14

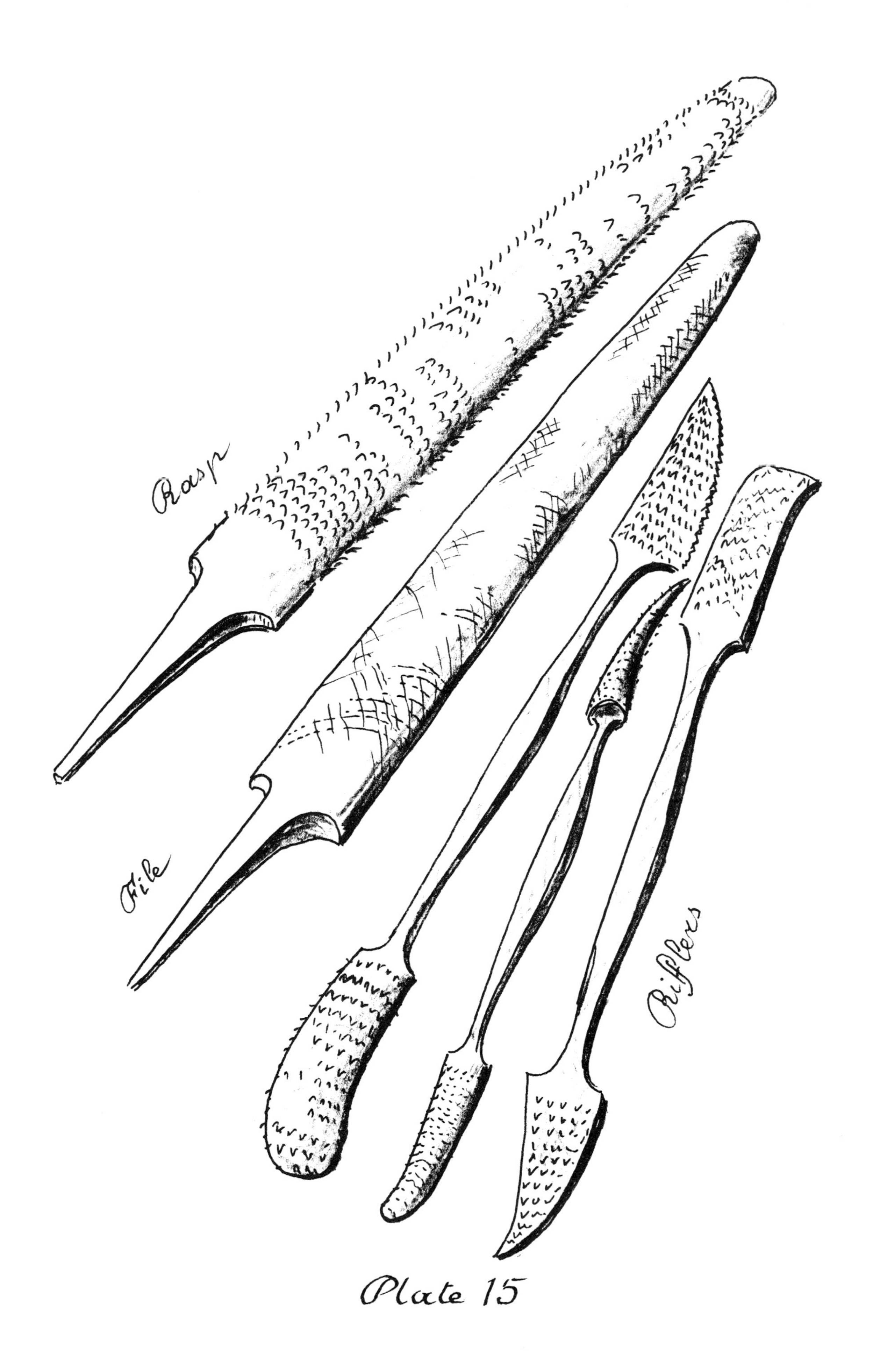

Plate 15

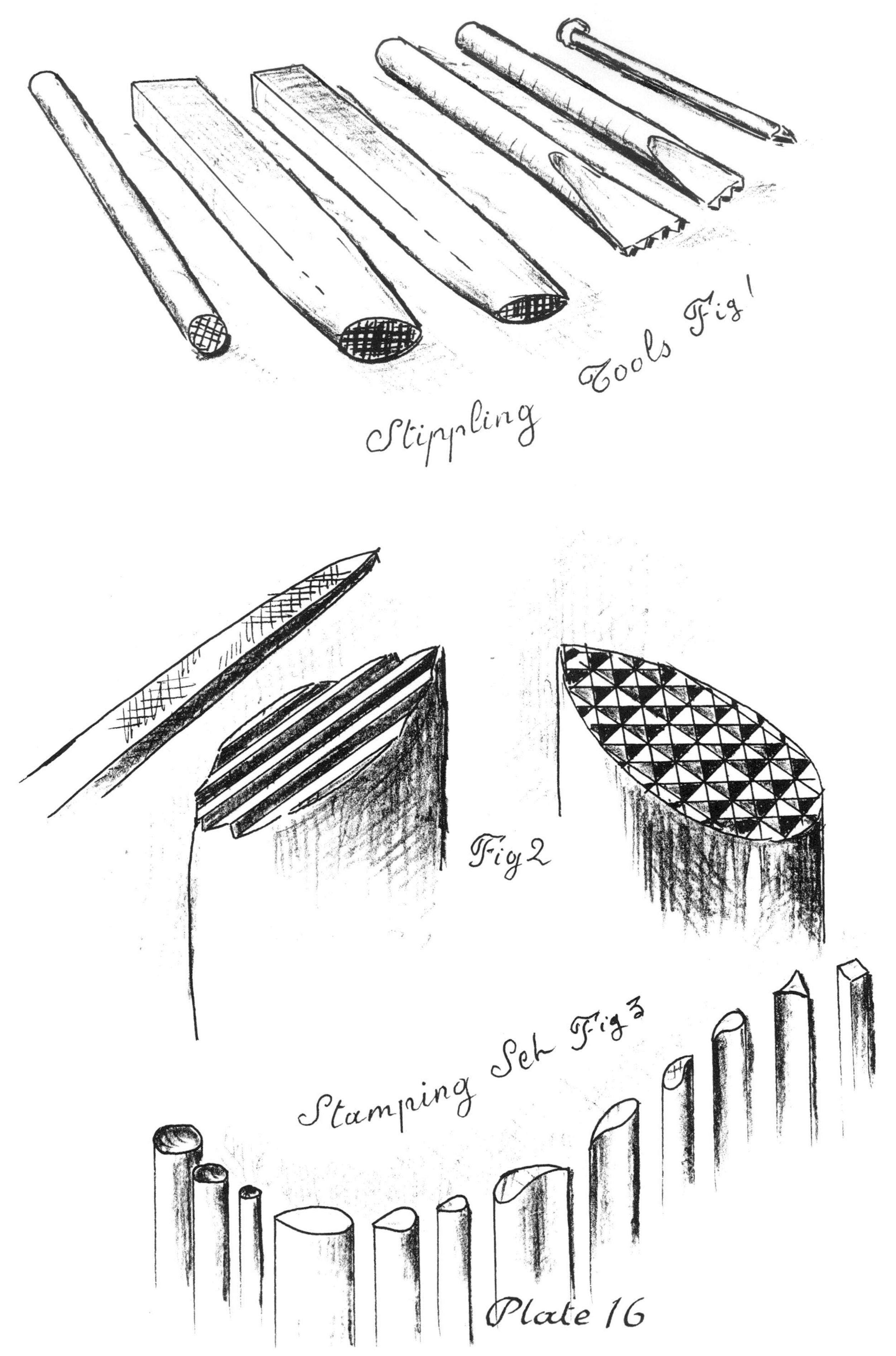
Stippling Tools Fig 1
Fig 2
Stamping Sch Fig 3
Plate 16

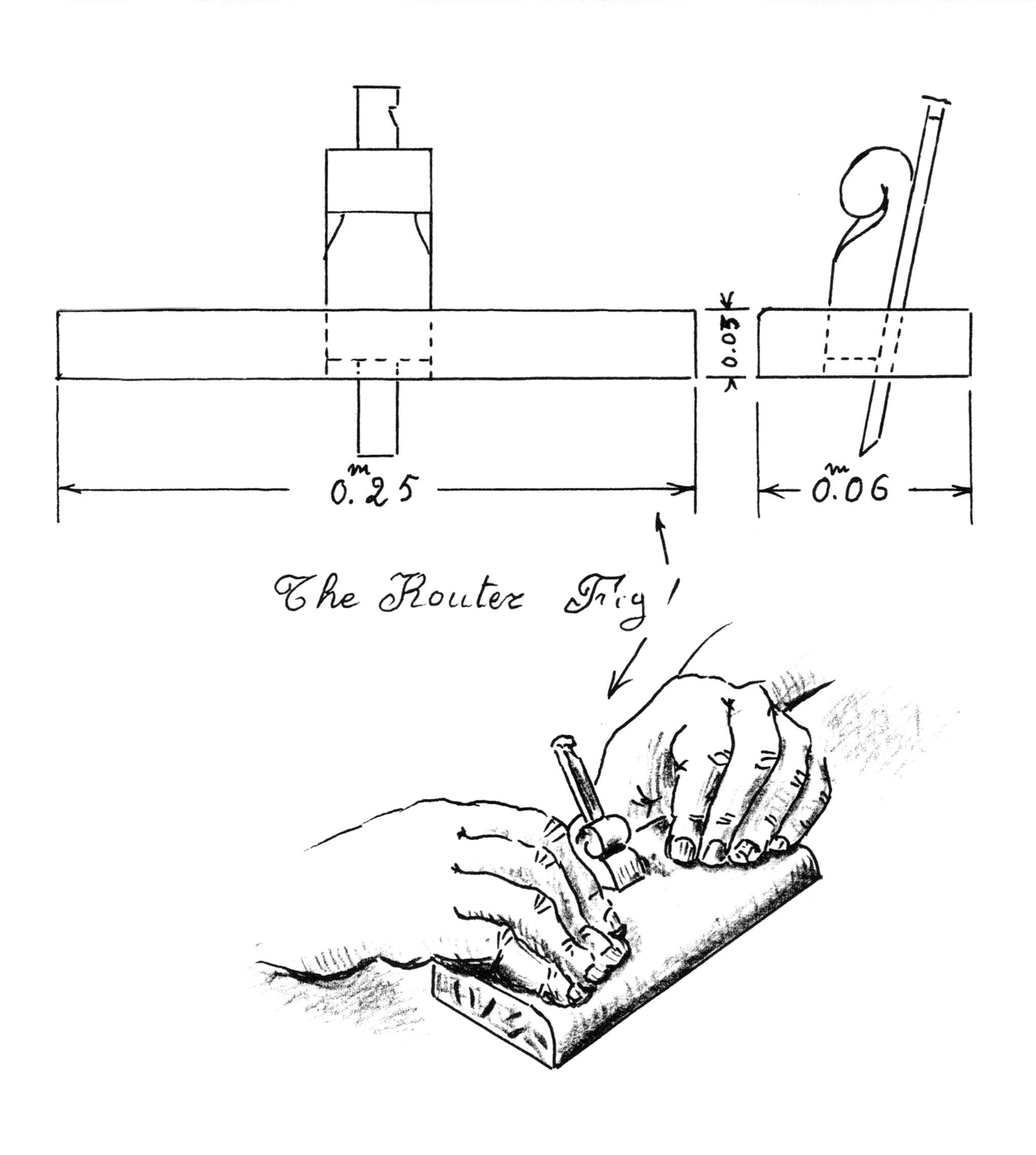
0.03
0.25
0.06
The Router Fig 1

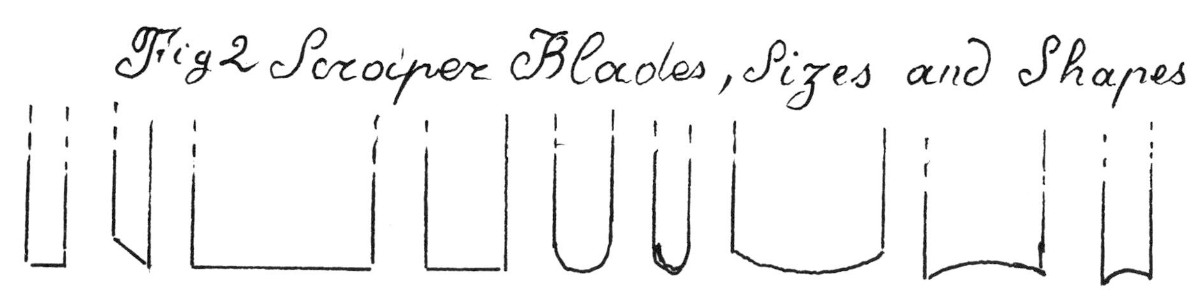
Fig 2 Scraper Blades, Sizes and Shapes

Plate 17

A simple Carver's Gauge

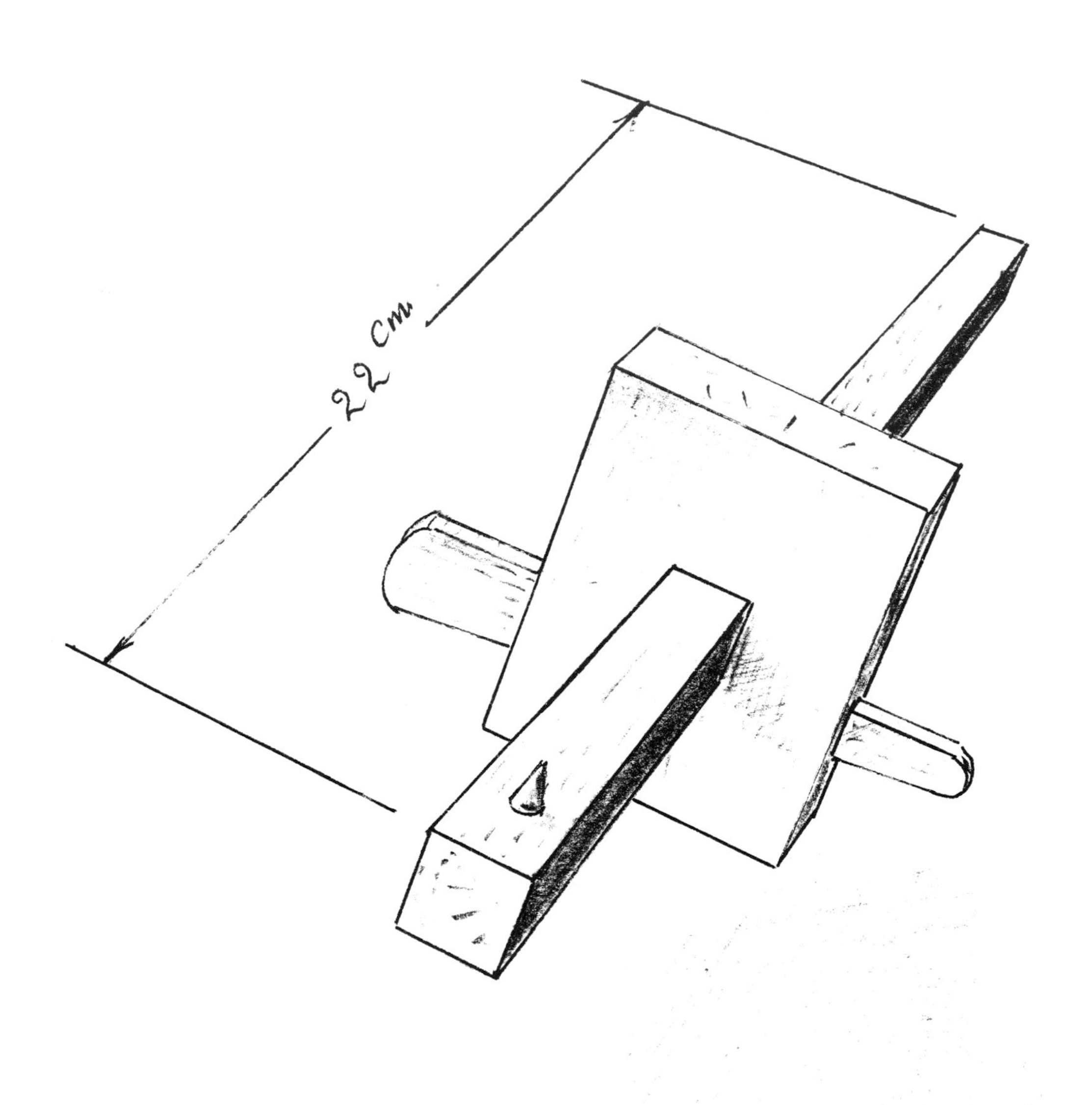

Plate 18

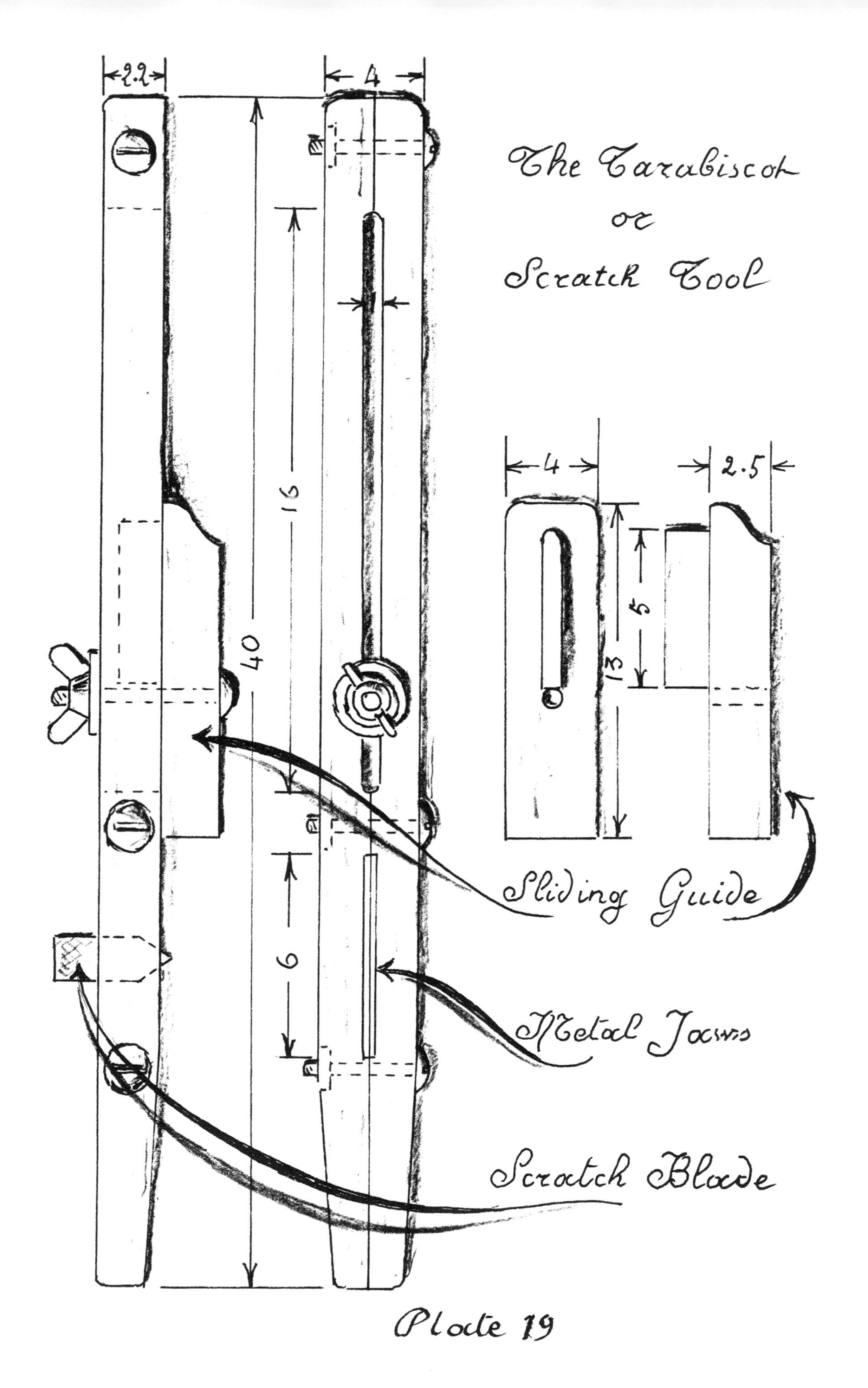
The Tarabiscot
or
Scratch Tool
2.2
4
40
15
6
4
2.5
13
5
Sliding Guide
Metal Jaws
Scratch Blade

Plate 19

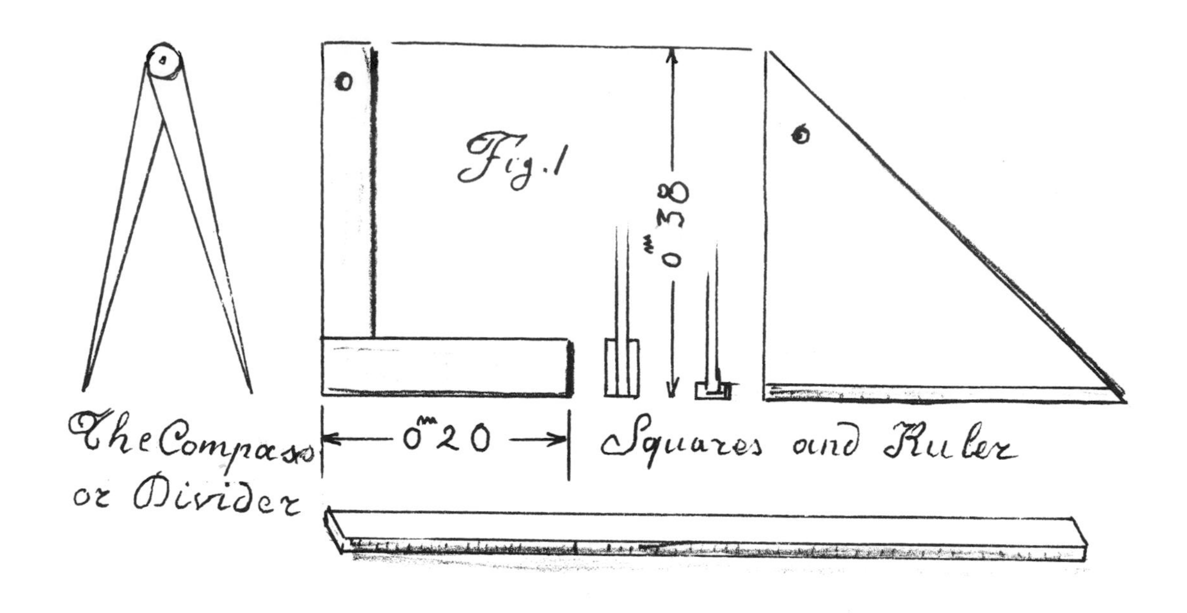
Fig. 1
0m38
0m20
The Compass or Divider
Squares and Ruler

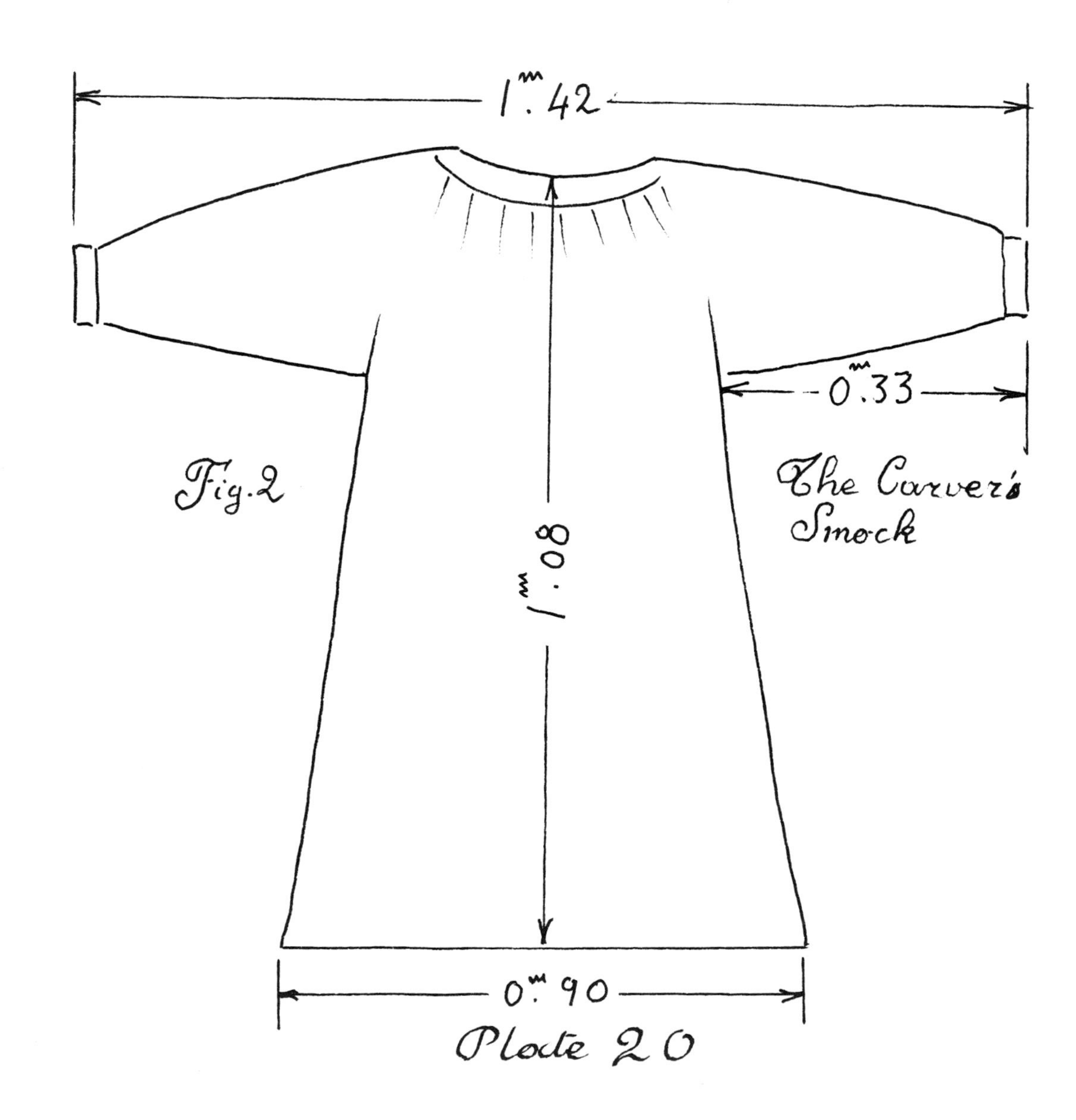
1m.42
0m.33
Fig. 2
1m.08
The Carver's Smock
0m.90

Plate 20

Part II

Use and Care of Carving Equipment, Wood Selection, and the Problems of the Grain

Proper use and care of your carving equipment is essential, both in terms of the success of your efforts and personal safety while carving. Similarly, you must understand something about the properties of wood generally, and of specific wood types, in order to make appropriate selections and to use your carving equipment effectively.

THE SHARPENING TECHNIQUES

Although every step in carving requires care, the proper sharpening of tools is of critical importance. The process is time consuming and tedious. A good half hour may be needed to put the average tool in cutting order. To add to your woes, you are dealing with the quasi-microscopic action of the finest stones on the cutting edge. You are not, as yet, trained to see and feel the results of your long efforts. Nevertheless, the understandable desire of the beginner to get at the wood should not distract you from the necessity for a high degree of concentration, precision, and understanding. If the sharpening is not properly handled, you will soon meet with difficulties and disappointments.

As mentioned earlier, there are four steps in the sharpening process: grinding, whetting, honing, and stropping. These steps permit you to first shape, and then gradually refine, the cutting edge.

- ☐ Grinding the cutting bevel is done on a coarse-grained stone and leaves a flexible burr, or feather, on the cutting edge (Plates 21-26).
- ☐ Whetting is done with a finer stone, such as India medium. Whetting removes most of the feather edge but leaves a very fine hairlike burr on the cutting edge (Plates 27-28). Many carvers omit the whetting step, at the cost of a much longer honing time.
- ☐ Honing is done with the finest-grained stones. Honing eliminates any remaining metal particles on the cutting edge. If need be, use a magnifying glass to make sure the cutting edge is completely clean.
- ☐ Stropping finishes the cutting edge by giving it the quality of a razor blade.

A piece of wood, such as soft pine, balsa, or even cork, can be used to test the edge. If it is properly sharpened, the tool will make clear cross-grain cuts easily and without a trace of tearing. The cutting edge should be razor sharp and remain so, or you will need to go back to honing.

Grinding on the Bench Stone

Lubricate the rough side of the stone with a few drops of oil to prevent particles of steel from embedding themselves in the surface and interfering with the proper cutting of the stone. One hand holds the tool by the handle; the other presses on the blade (Plate 21, fig. 1).

Grinding on the High-Speed Dry Wheel

The wheel rotates toward the carver. For this reason, great care should be taken to guarantee the safety of both the operator and the tool. The high turning speed will quickly heat the tool; so you must have a can of water on hand in which to dip the tool's edge frequently to cool it. When the edge burns it will show a blue discoloration that must be completely ground out; burned steel is worthless (Plate 22, fig. 1). Each time the tool is to be replaced on the wheel, it should be positioned at the same angle so you do not start a new bevel.

Grinding with the Sandstone

In contrast to the dry wheel, this type of stone is water-lubricated and will not burn the tool. In addition, this wheel turns away from the operator and presents no danger to the tool or the operator (Plate 22, fig. 2 and Plate 23). Be careful to use the whole grinding surface so that you keep it flat and free of grooves.

Grinding tips are shown in Plates 24 and 25. Grinding exceptions are given in Plate 26.

Whetting and Honing

After selecting the proper slipstone (Plate 27, fig. 1), add a few drops of light cutting oil to lubricate it. The stone should be held in such a way as to avoid cutting your fingers (Plate 27, fig 2). The slip is held below the cutting edge (Plate 28, fig. 2). The stone moves but the tool is still, except for a rocking action to cover the whole surface of the bevel while the stone moves up and down against it, taking care not to round and blunt the edge.

When the feather edge is all "turned in," the round edge of the stone is used to work on the inside (Plate 28, fig. 2). As the feather edge goes, a wire edge, thinner than fine hair, is left. *Honing* is the removal of this edge with the finest of stones.

Stropping

You are now on the last step in the sharpening process. Stropping should not take much time; a few strokes will suffice if the previous operations have been carefully done. If not, however, the stropping will have no effect whatsoever. Furthermore, mishandled stropping can be disastrous. It will dull, rather than refine, the tool's edge (Plate 29). After stropping, wipe off any possible grit left on the tool with a clean rag. The tool is now ready. Set it down with the others and cover them with a cloth until you need them.

When you have finished for the day, dust your bench and cover your tools to protect their edges from dust and humidity.

Grinding

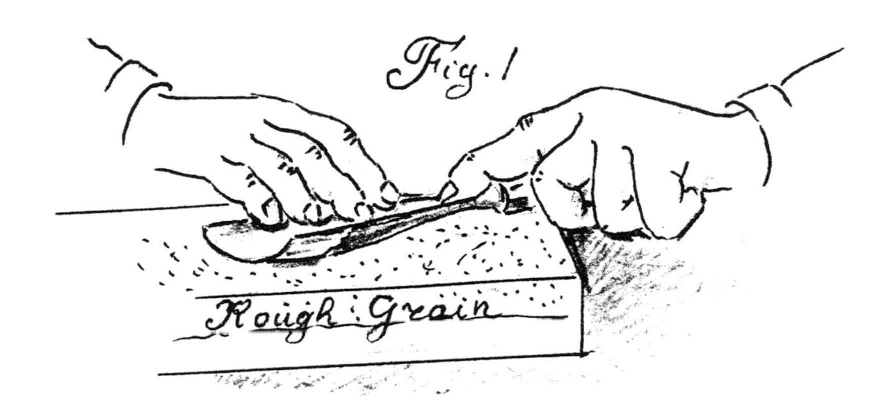

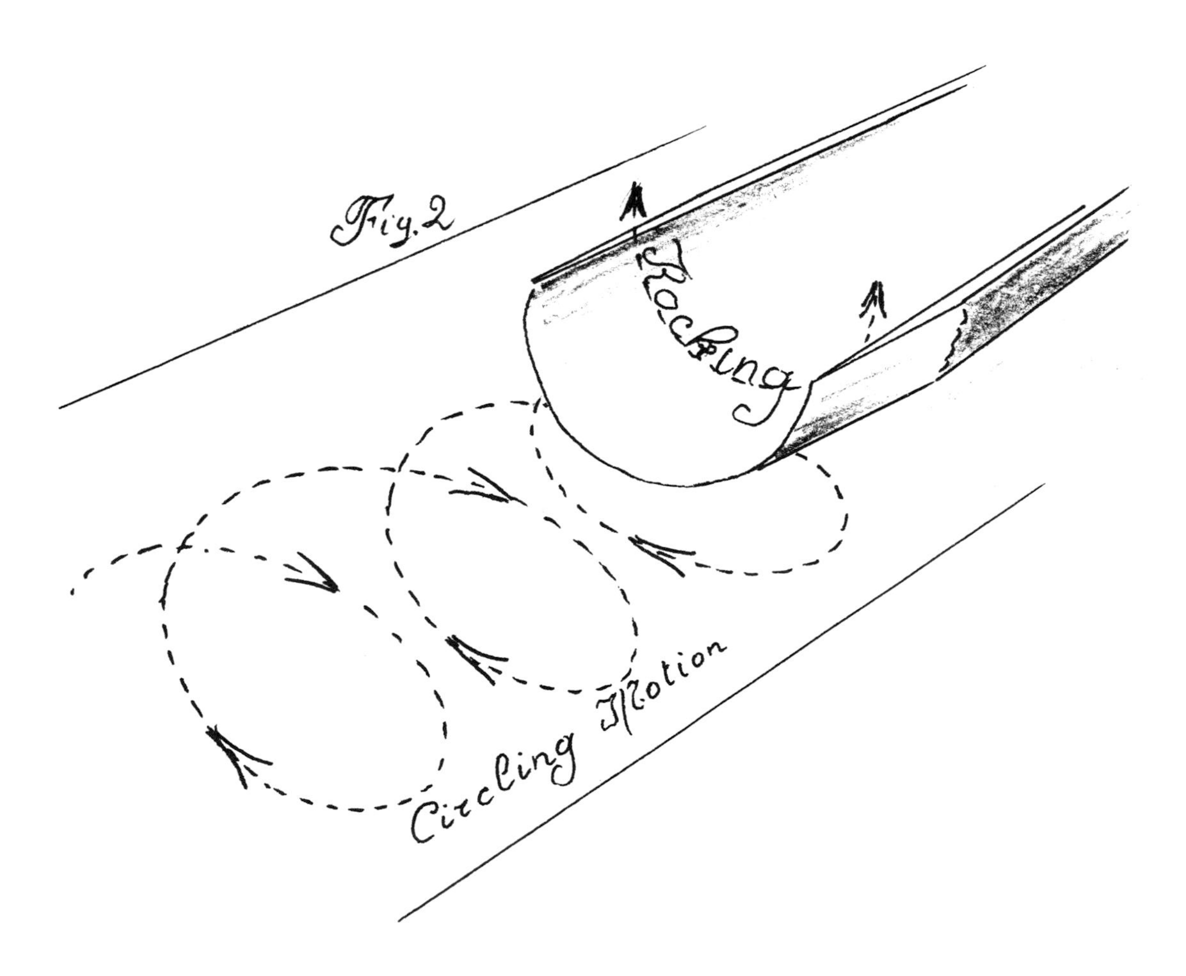

Plate 21

FASTENING TECHNIQUES

The way you fasten the work to the bench will vary with the shape of the wood. In general, you can nail flat pieces or panels, or hold them down between cleats or under clamps. For round carvings you may use large adjustable clamps, vises, or bedding pieces that fit the shapes involved (Plate 33, figs. 1 and 4). Each problem will suggest its own most practical solution. For example, drawers can be held with two boards and a few nails (Plate 33, figs. 2 and 3).

Using nails to fasten panels (Plate 30, fig. 1), a method widely used by professionals, presents no hindrance to the carving movements but does prevent you from turning the work around. Nailing also mars the bench surface, as will cleats held by screws (Plate 30, fig. 2).

Cleats held by clamps diminish the hindrance to movements, but tend to hold the work somewhat loosely, which can be a problem, especially when the carving requires the use of a mallet.

On small work, direct clamping may hinder your movements. In any case, the clamps should be placed with the screw below the top of the bench (Plate 31, figs. 1 and 2). A small piece of thin wood or cardboard should be used to protect the wood's surface.

If you use the carver's anchor screw, you will need to drill holes in the bench top, but it is ideal for most flat work and for some carving in the round or half-round (Plate 32).

CARVING TECHNIQUES

For greater efficiency and safety, carving tools are placed on the bench with the handles in the trough, the cutting edge facing the carver. The flat tools are on one end, and the extremely curved tools occupy the other end. This disposition of tools helps in locating and selecting the proper instrument when you are working (Plate 34).

When you are carving, observe the following critical rules for handling tools, to ensure a safe operation for you and accuracy for your work.

- ☐ Never hold the wood with one hand and the tool with the other (Plate 35, fig. 3).
- ☐ The cutting edge should face away from your body, out of your arms' circle (Plate 34).
- ☐ Any cut, large or small, must have meaning; it must be planned and executed under perfect control. In this way, you will greatly diminish the possibility of an accident that will injure you or damage your work.

Three basic ways of holding and directing your tools provide for safe tool control and accurate cutting. They are:

- ☐ If you are holding the tool with two hands, one hand takes the blade with the thumb on the lower part of the handle. The other hand holds the handle with the palm on the top of the handle (Plate 35, figs. 1-2). The arm and wrist of the first hand rest steady on the bench or work (Plate 34). A number of short (1 cm. to 2 cm.) scooping cuts are taken. The arm and wrist are shifted as work progresses. To satisfy the grain demands, the tool can change hands indiscriminately (Plate 36, fig. 1).
- ☐ The tool is held and guided by one hand on the blade, thumb on the handle as just described. The palm of the other hand, cupped to avoid vibrating fingers, taps on the handle top to produce the cutting (Plate 36, fig. 2). The tool may change hands as necessary. Vertical cuts may be taken in this manner.

Grinding

For high speed grinding protect the eyes with Shield

Keep water handy for frequent cooling of blade to avoid burning

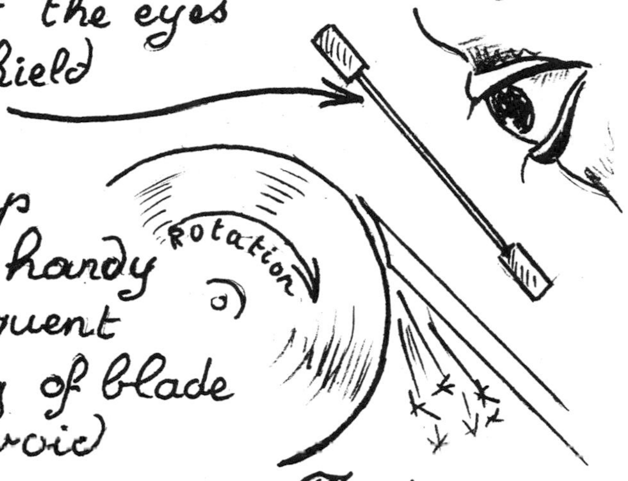

Rotation

Fig. 1

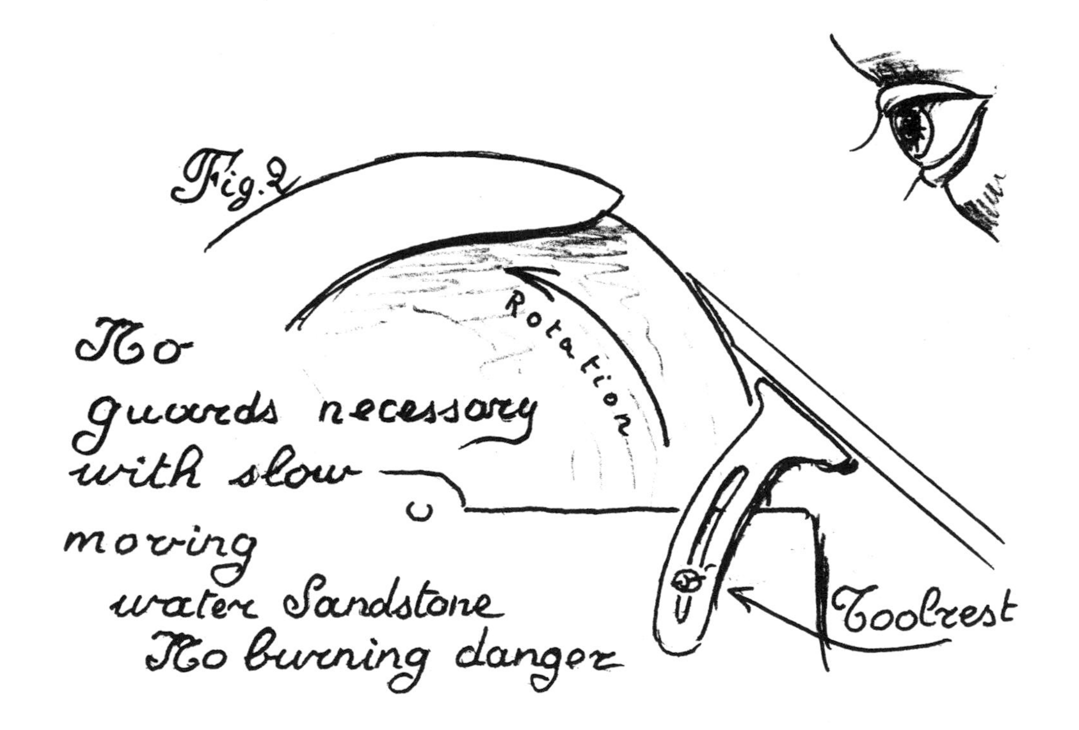

Plate 22

- ☐ The dominant hand takes the mallet, the other holds the tool as before; no change of hand is convenient. When you are taking vertical cuts, the tool is often held by the handle only (Plate 37, figs. 1 and 2).

It is poor practice to hold the gouge between two fingers (Plate 37, fig. 3) close to the cutting edge. In this position, the tool is unsteady and a slight off-balance hit by the mallet may result in a split handle or a broken blade.

Push free chips out of the way by blowing on them or with the help of a clean brush. Avoid using your hand or fingers. You may get splinters, and oil or dirt on your hand will spoil the freshness of the work.

SELECTING THE PROPER WOOD

In the past, the carver seasoned his own wood. However, this is a delicate, tedious process that may require years and the use of heavy equipment. Today you can obtain a variety of properly aged woods from your local hardwood lumber dealer.

Wood density and hardness vary from compact and close grained to open and porous, and from very hard, as in rock maple, to very soft, as balsa. A beginner should avoid both extremes, as well as exotic materials, which may be costly and prove to be unsatisfactory. It is best, at first, to settle for some domestic product of medium hardness, a little bit on the soft side. As a general rule, however, a beginner should avoid coniferous trees, which supply wood for the construction trade. Species such as basswood, willow, poplar, Southern red gum, and alder are preferable. Their closer, more even grain and uniform texture make them easier to carve. As you progress and gain more experience, you can try other varieties of wood. In all cases, the wood should be clean and, if possible, without defects such as knots and cracks.

Because the choices available are likely to vary with the location of the lumberyard, it is best to consult with your supplier to determine which woods in his stock meet these requirements.

THE PROBLEMS OF THE GRAIN

The grain structure of wood is created by the annual growth of the tree from which the board has been taken. You will be faced continually with the problems presented by the direction of the grain. For my demonstration, the lines of the grain are shown in Plate 38, figs. 1 and 2 as coming from the lower left to the upper right of the board.

- ☐ Cutting from left to right is called cutting *with the grain*. The chips will probably curl up and splinter. The cut will come out clean and shiny (Plate 38, fig. 1).
- ☐ Cutting from right to left is *against the grain*. The tool will tend to follow the grain lines down the board, splitting the wood rather than cutting it. The chip will probably stay flat on the tool. The cut will be rough and splintery (Plate 38, fig. 2).
- ☐ Cutting *across the grain*, if the tool is sharp, will yield a cut which is clean but probably not shiny (Plate 38, fig. 3).
- ☐ Cutting *on the bias* will give a clean cut on the left side and a broken, splintered surface on the right (Plate 38, fig. 3). To handle the bias cut properly, you make a dividing cut with a V or U on the center line (Plate 39, fig. 1). You then cut the left side from left to right (Plate 39, fig. 2), and the right side from right to left (Plate 39, fig. 3).

When you are cutting inside or outside a circular figure, you must reverse the direction of your tool to accommodate the grain direction, as shown in Plate 40.

Grinding

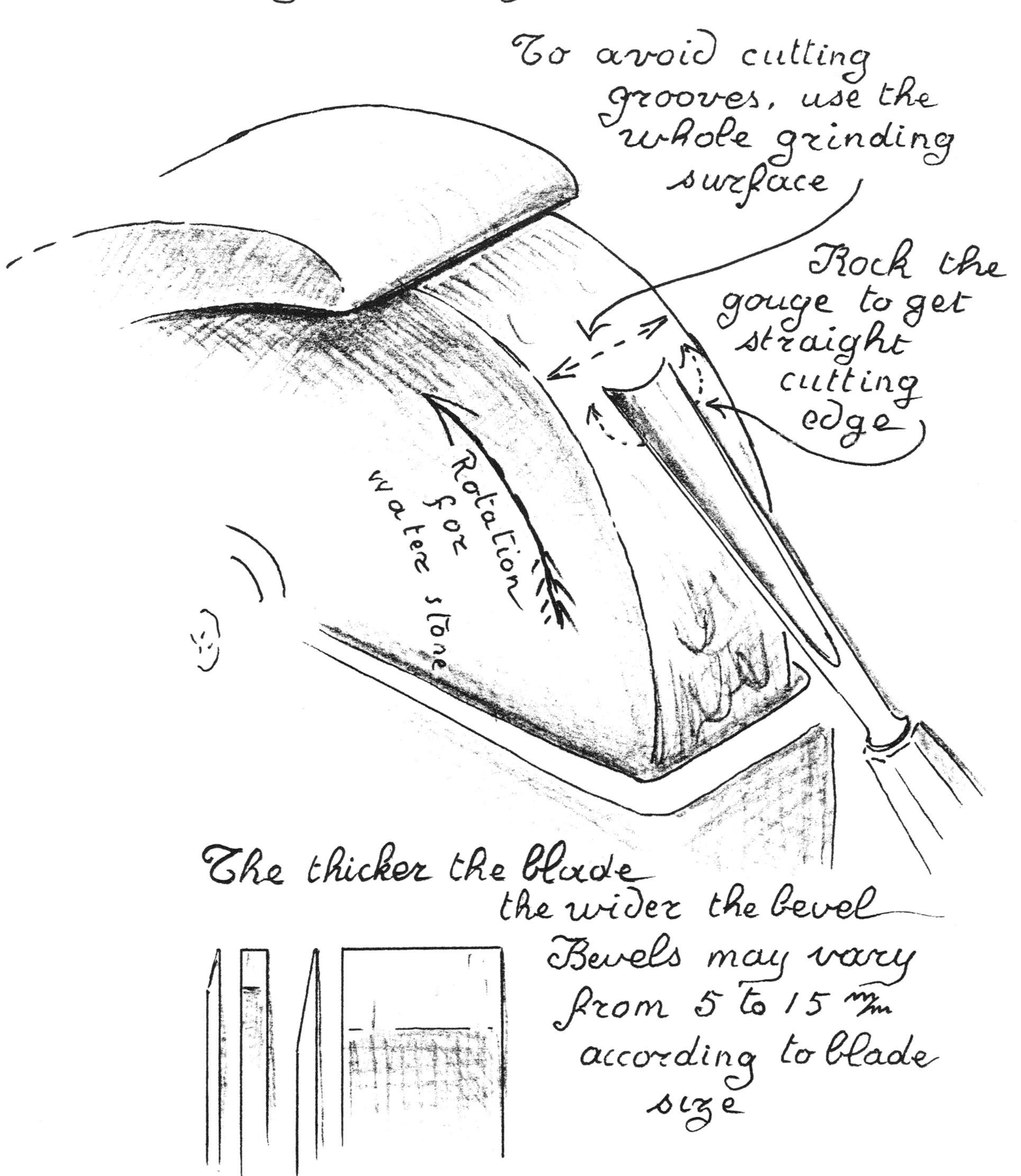
To avoid cutting grooves, use the whole grinding surface
Rock the gouge to get straight cutting edge
Rotation for water stone
The thicker the blade the wider the bevel
Bevels may vary from 5 to 15 m/m according to blade size

Plate 23

Grinding Tips

Forming the Bevel

Chisels are ground equally on both Sides.
When grinding on a flat Surface:

Wrong | Right

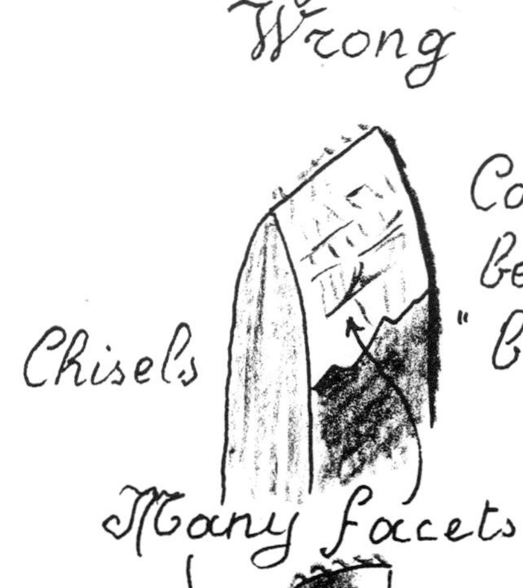

Gouges

When shaped on a Wheel, a slightly concave Surface is formed

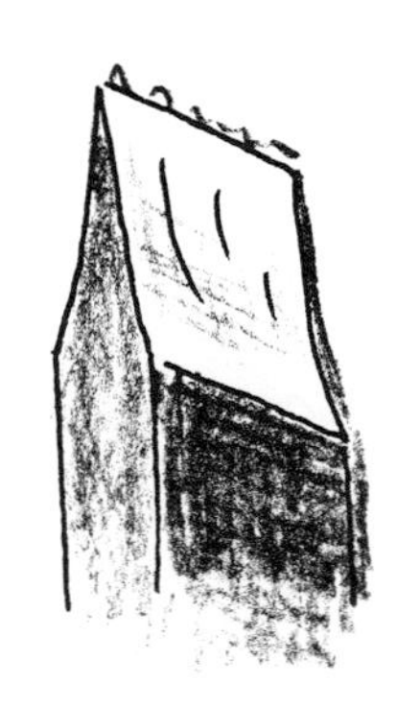

Even grinding
No facets

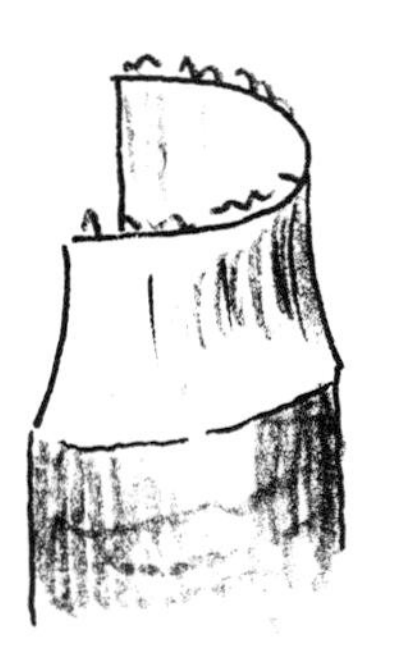

Plate 24

Grinding Tips

Shaping the Cutting Edges

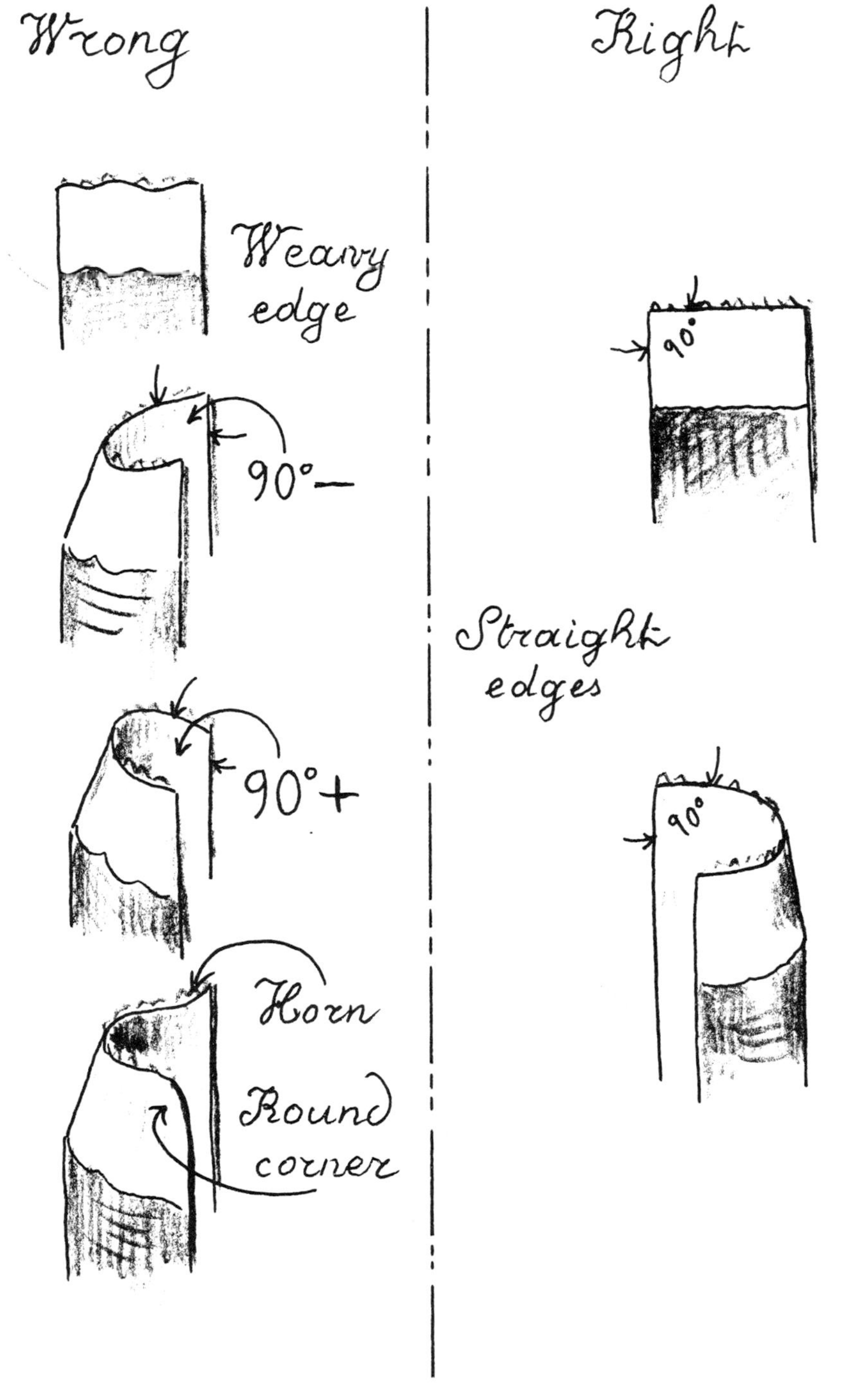

Wrong

Weavy edge

90°−

90°+

Horn

Round corner

Right

90°

Straight edges

90°

Plate 25

Grinding Exceptions

A firmer is ground on one side only

The Skew is a pointed chisel sharpened to cut in tight corners.

If sharpened on one face only it may be advisable to have a set of R and L skews

The V may be ground straight across at a 90° or slightly smaller angle. The grinding will leave a spur at the apex of the V

Note that al grinding should leave a "Feather Edge" on the cutting edge, showing that the tool is ready for whetting, honing and stropping

Plate 26

Whetting, Honing, Stropping

Proper Slips for:

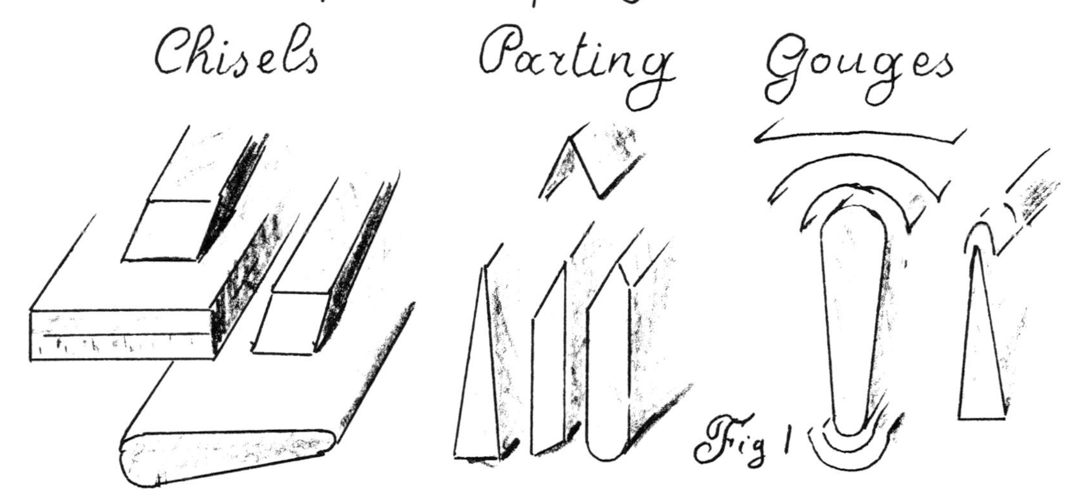

The slips are not to be held between thumb and fingers or in the palm of the hand. Hold with thumb and index finger below cutting edge.

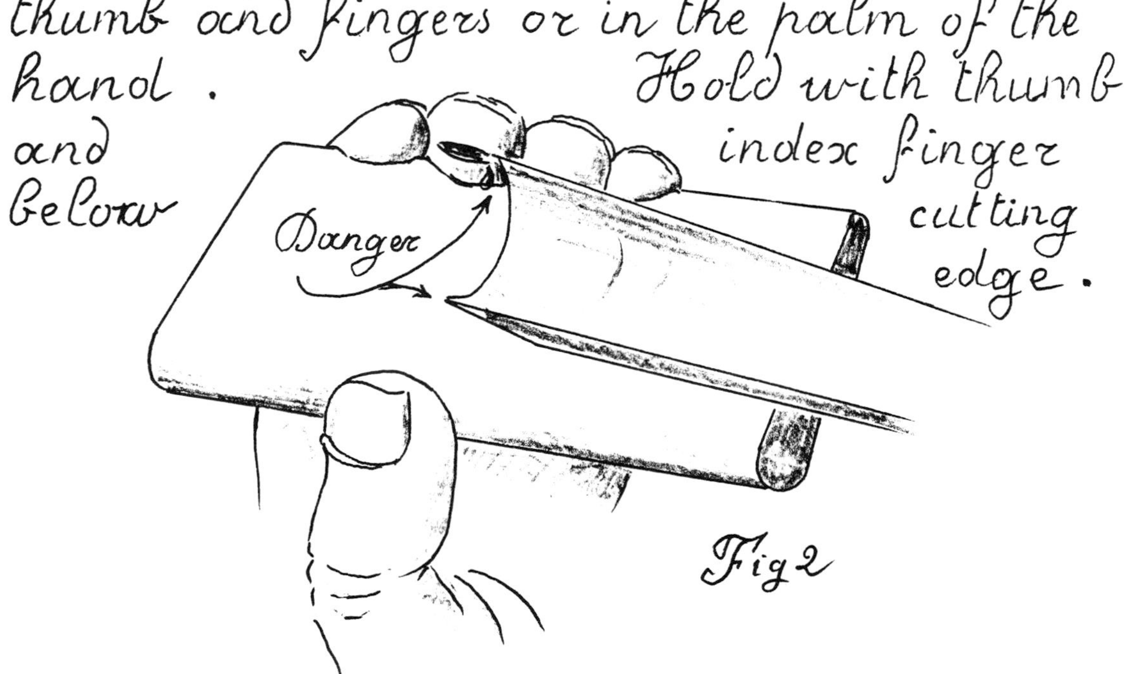

Plate 27

Honing Technique

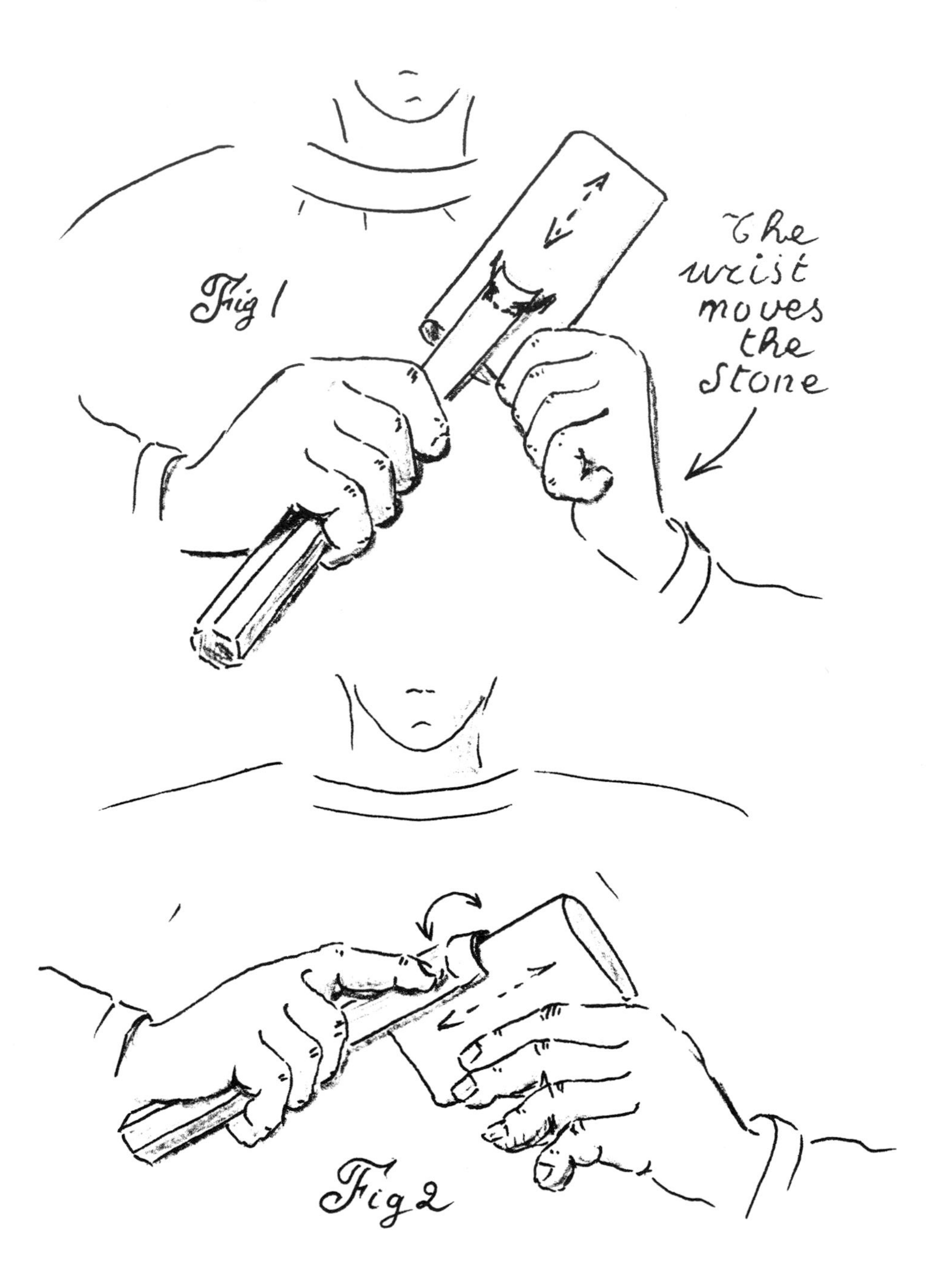
Fig 1
The wrist moves the stone
Fig 2

Plate 28

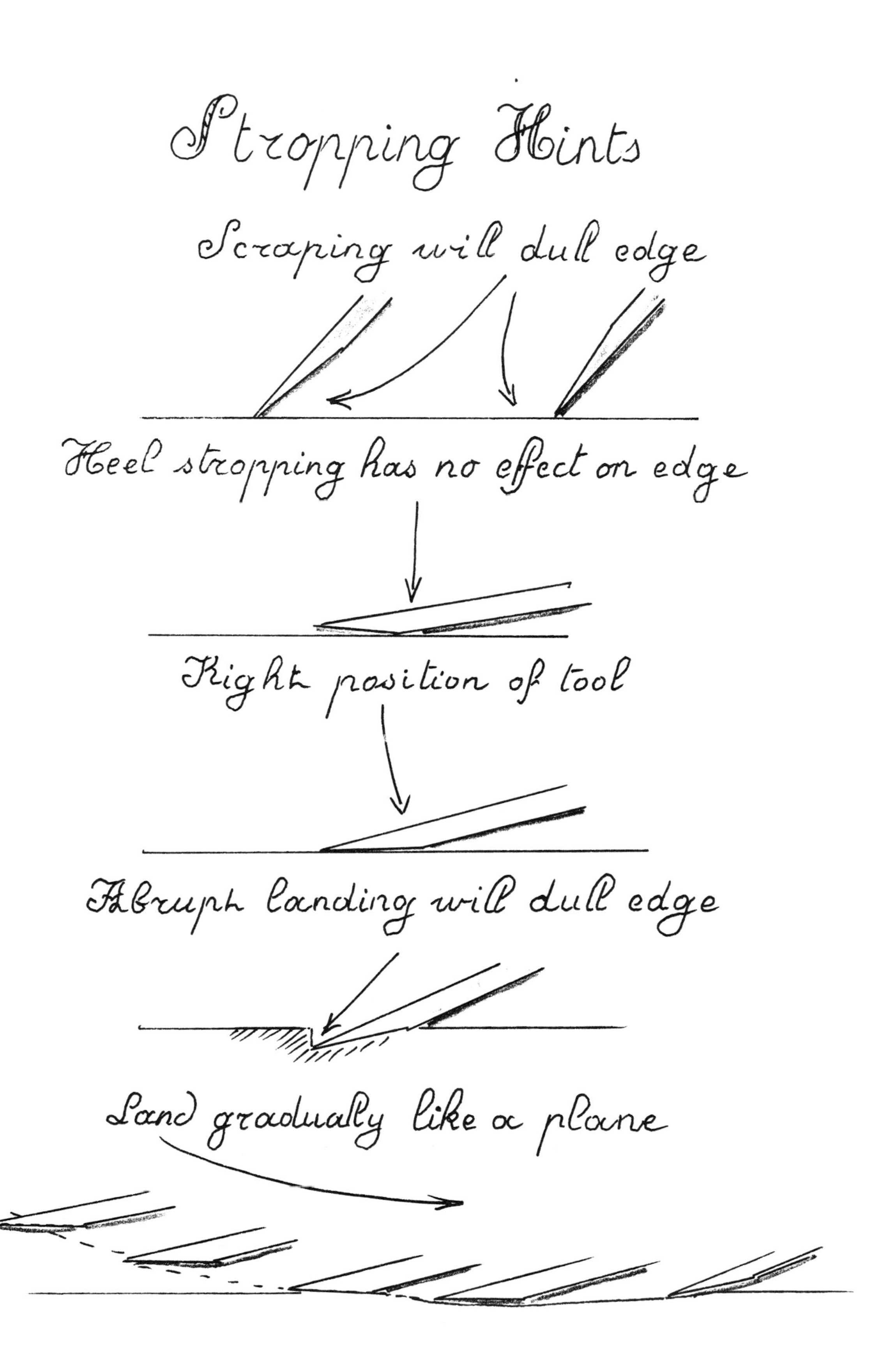
Stropping Hints
Scraping will dull edge
Heel stropping has no effect on edge
Right position of tool
Abrupt landing will dull edge
Land gradually like a plane

Plate 29

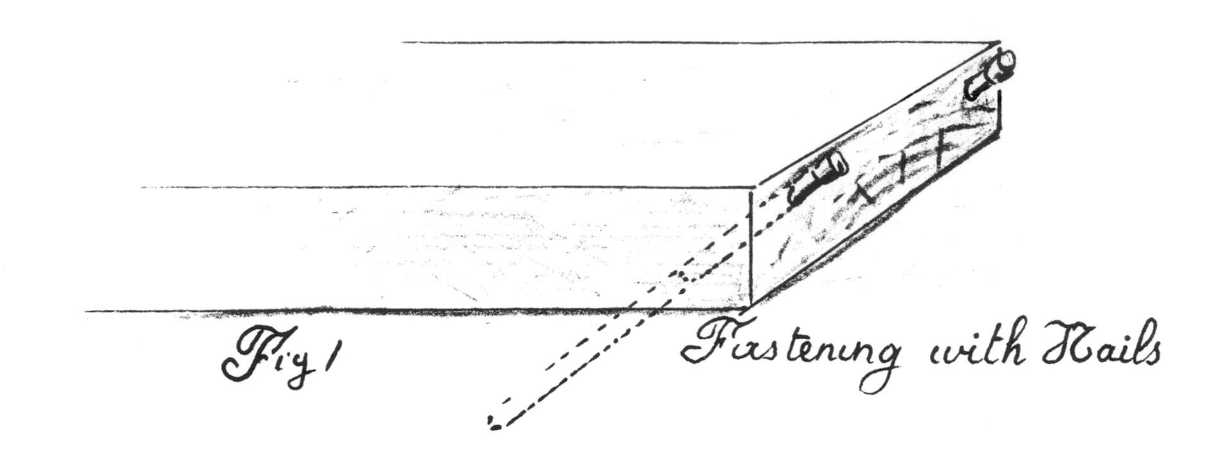
Fig 1
Fastening with Nails

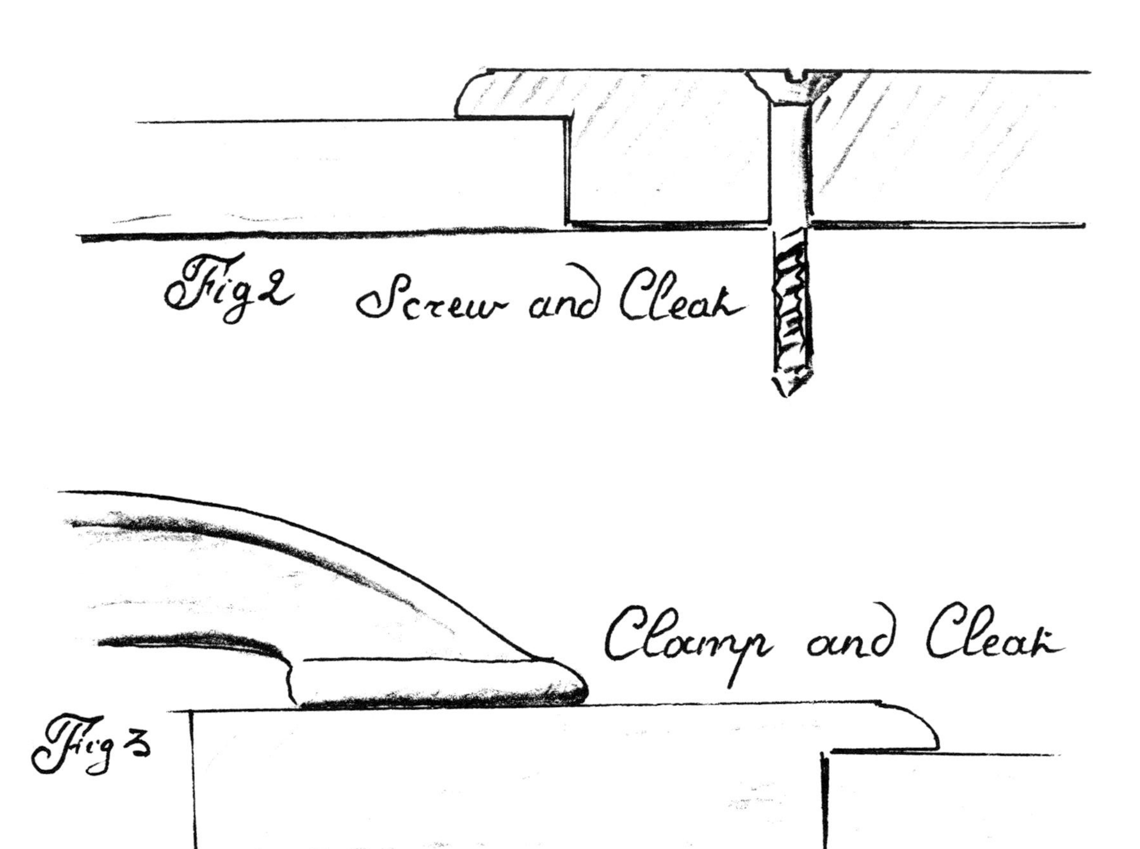
Fig 2 Screw and Cleat
Clamp and Cleat
Fig 3

Plate 30

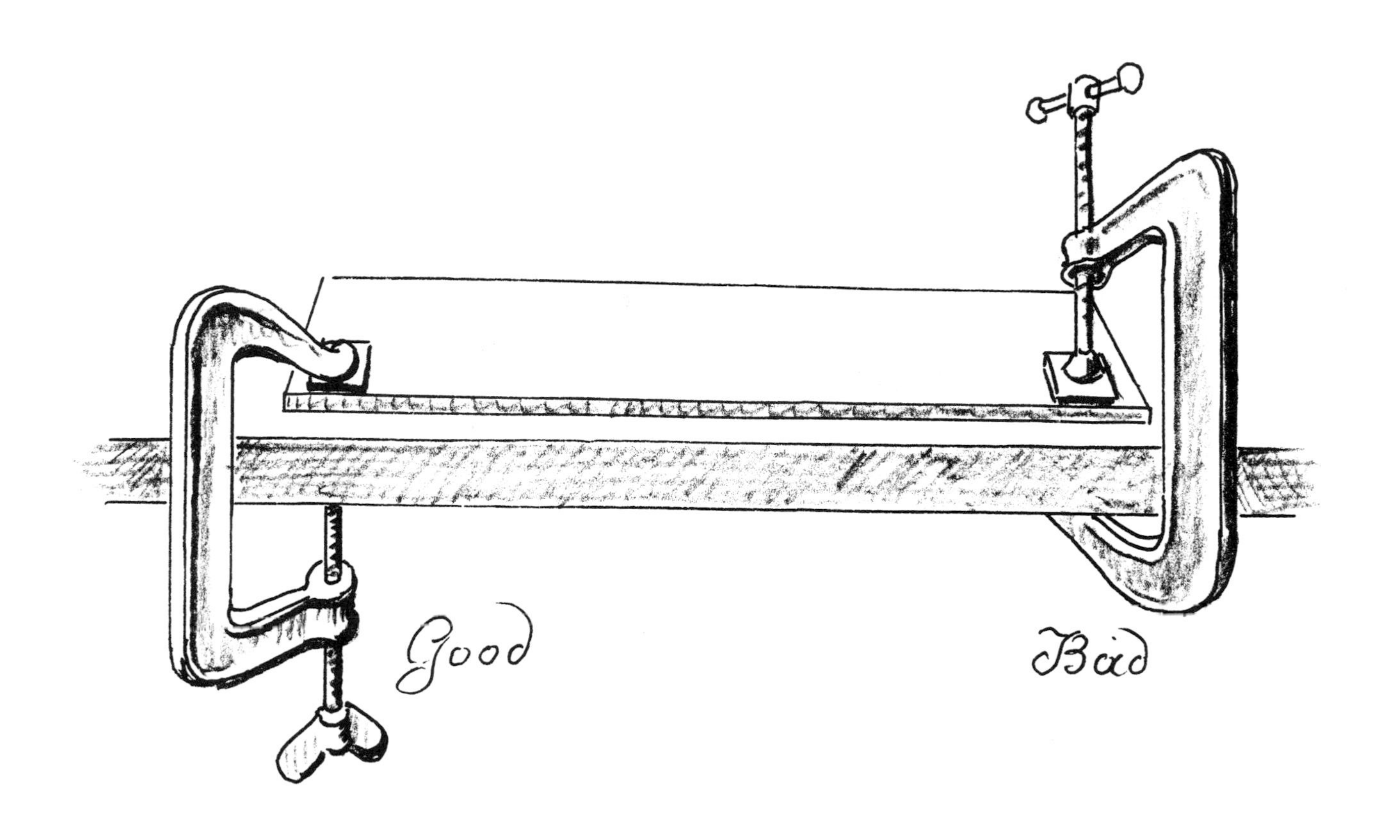

Proper clamping permits Freedom of Movement

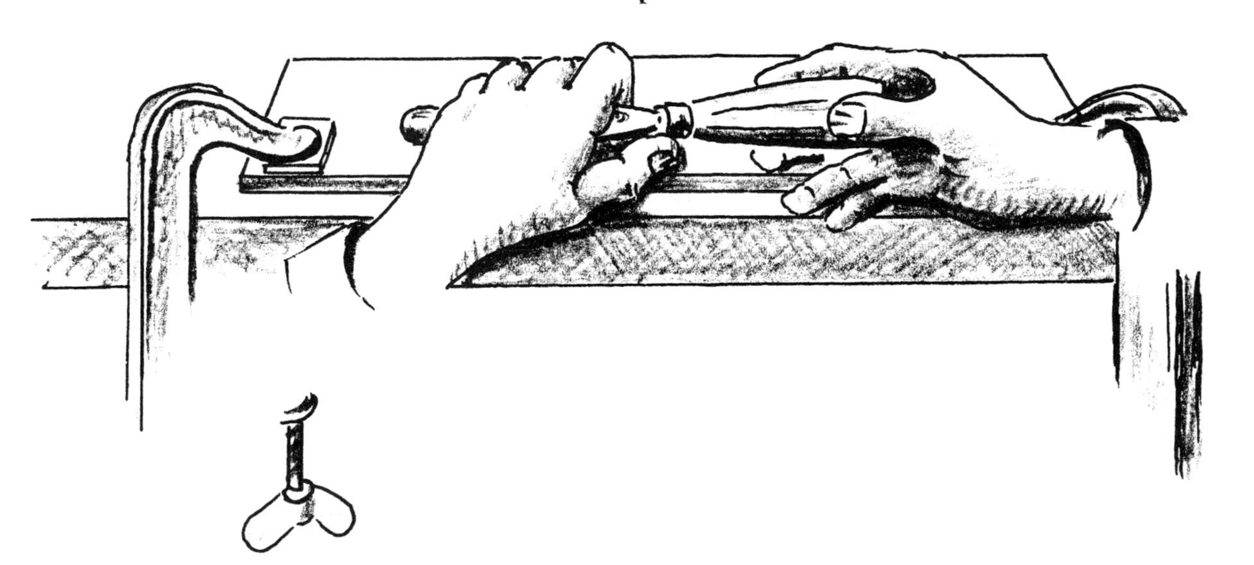

Plate 31

How to use the most practical Carver's Anchor Screw

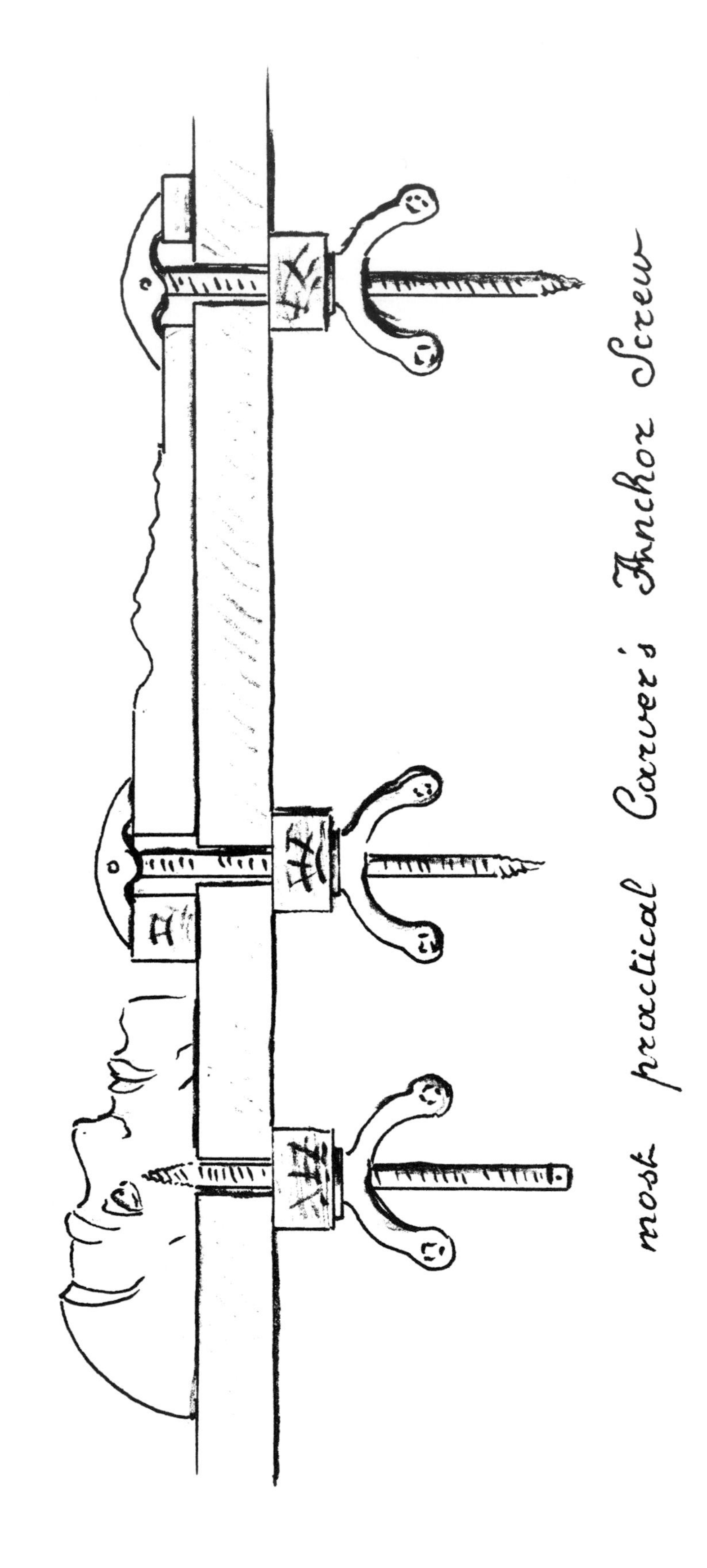

Plate 32

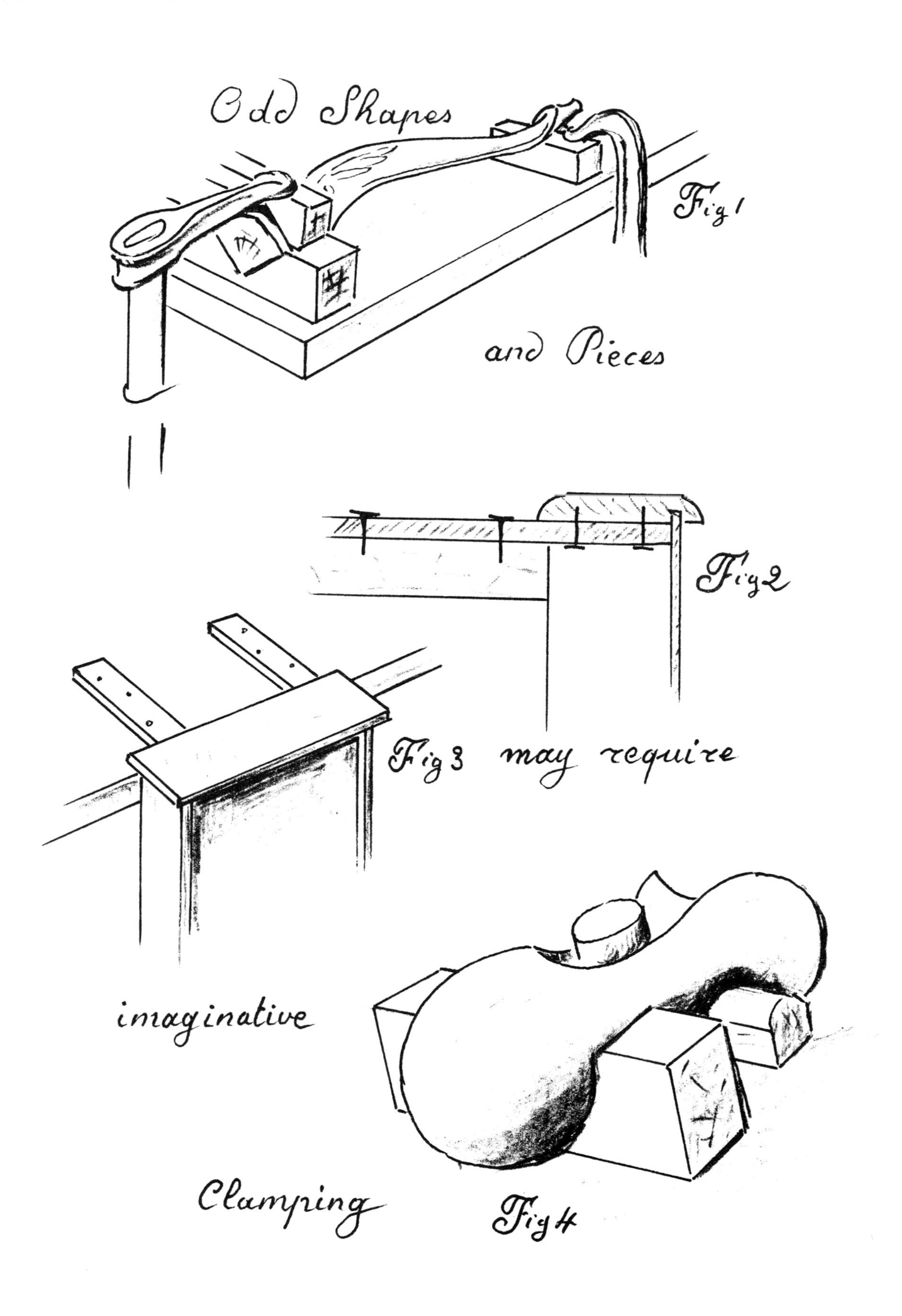
Odd Shapes
Fig 1
and Pieces
Fig 2
Fig 3 may require
imaginative
Clamping
Fig 4

Plate 33

The carving Position

The Carver leans on the Forearm which rests flat on the Bench

Plate 34

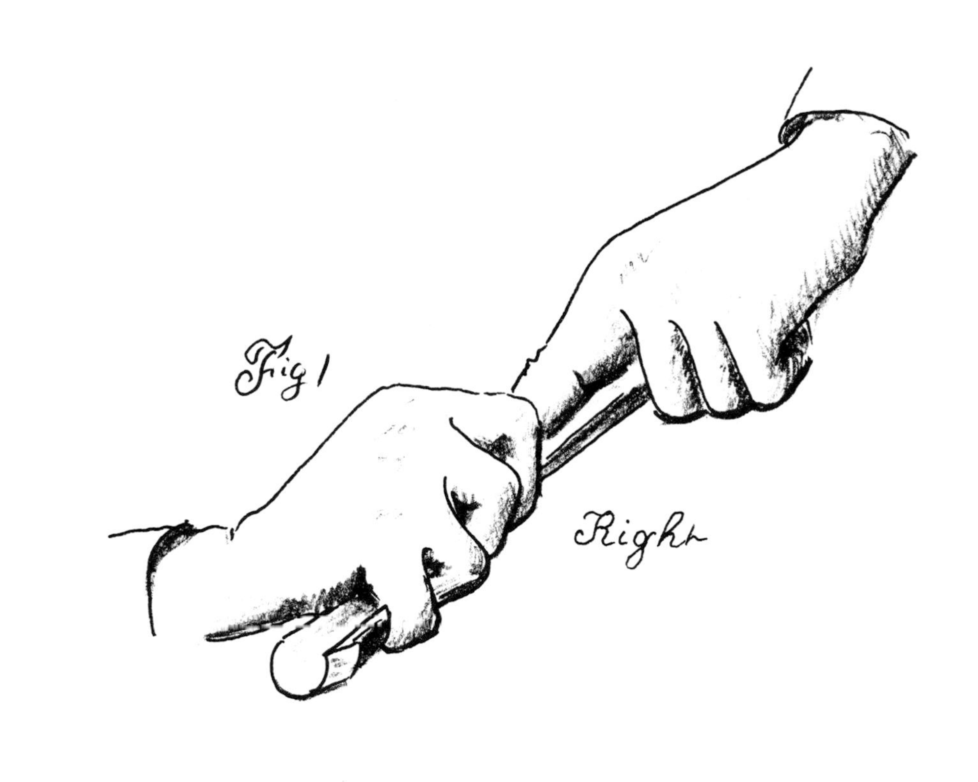

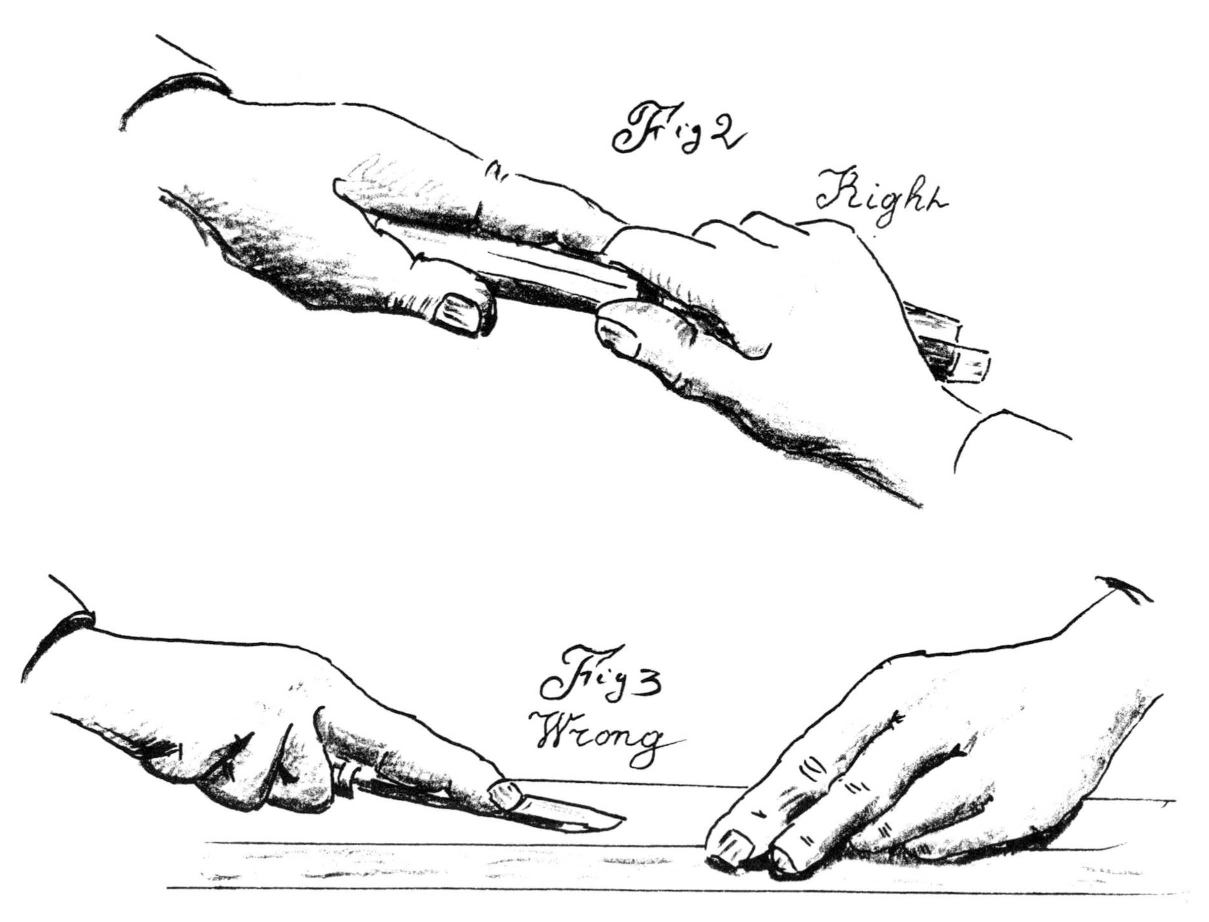

Plate 35

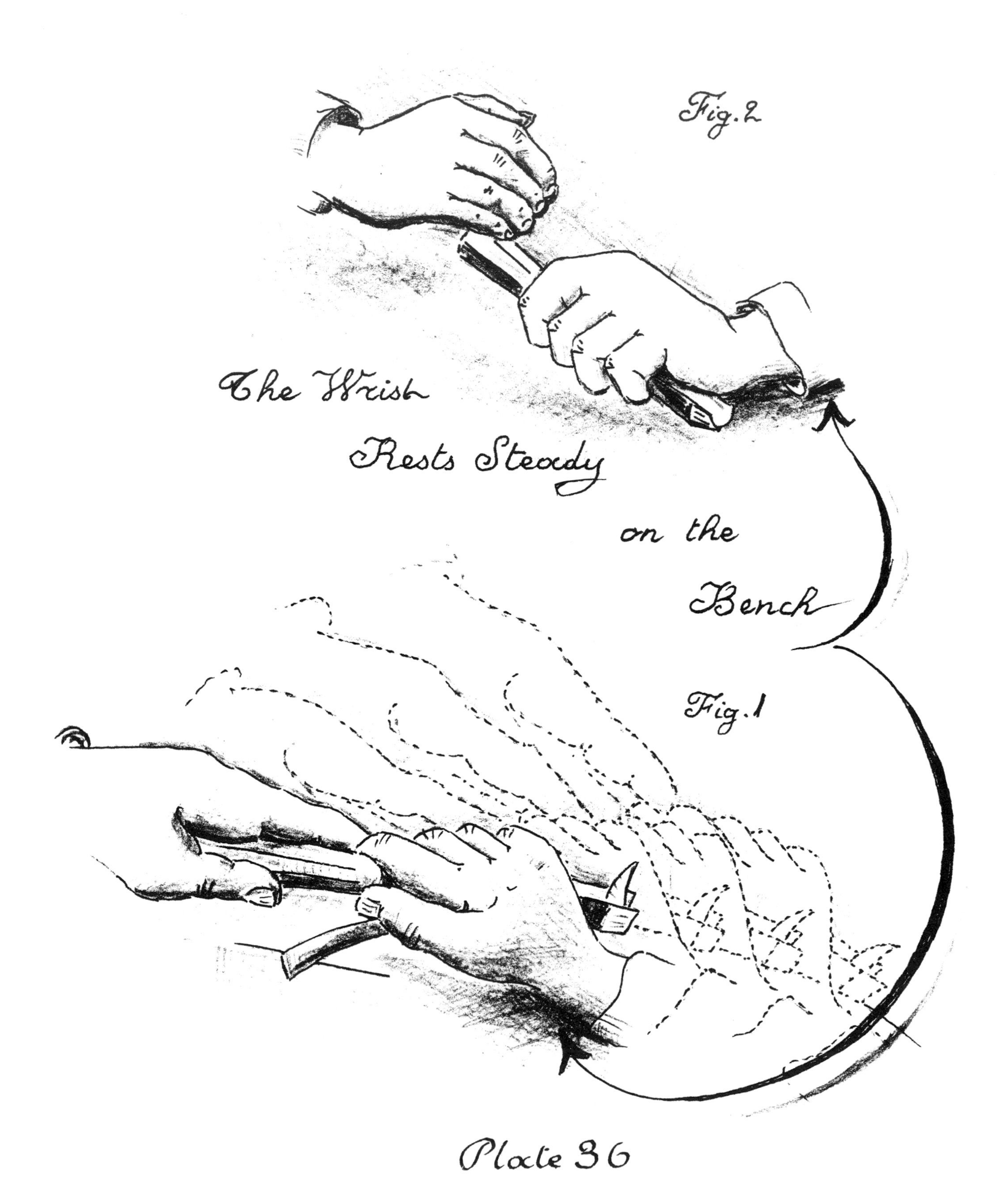
Fig. 2
The Wrist Rests Steady on the Bench
Fig. 1

Plate 36

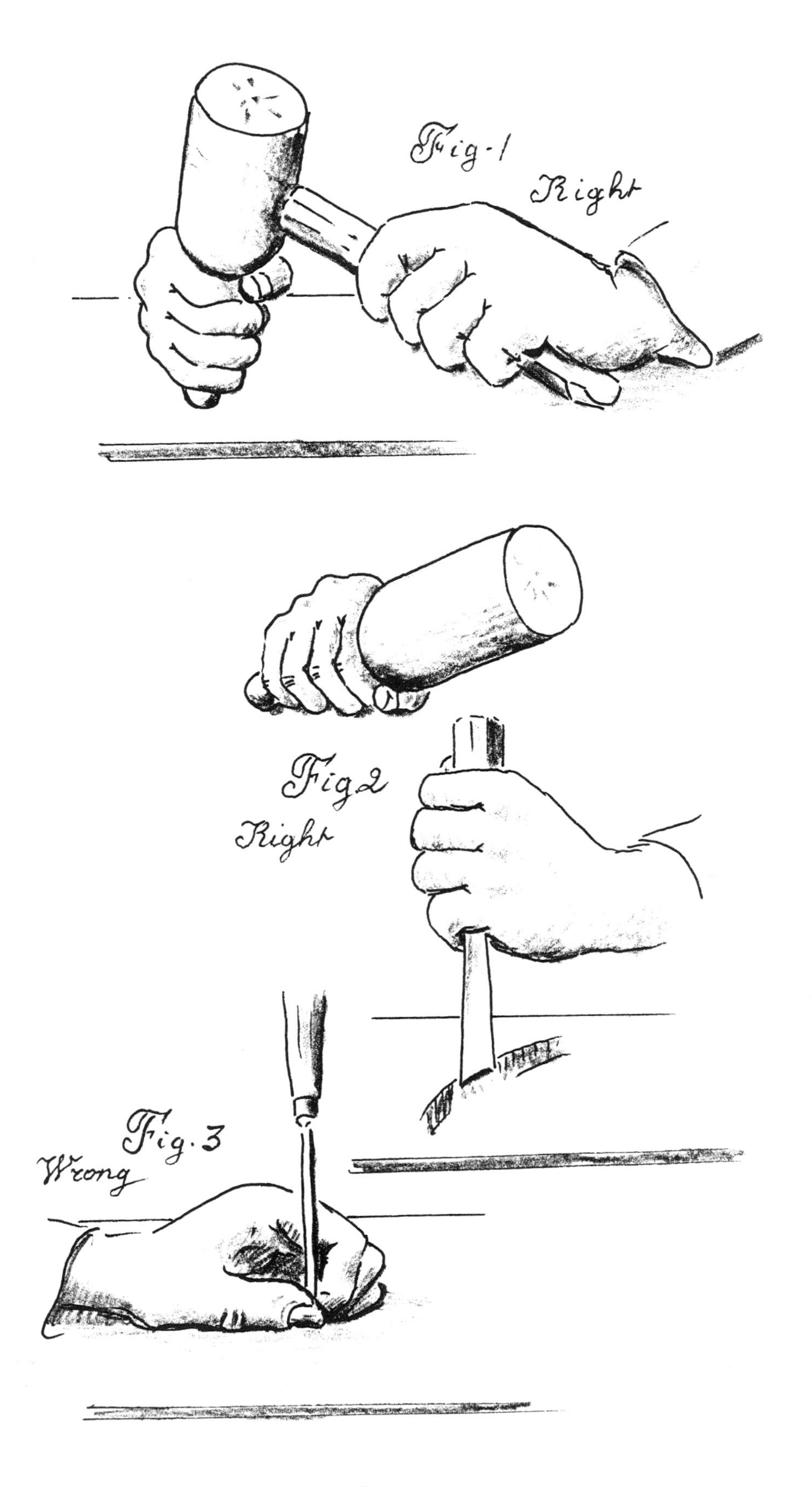
Fig. 1
Right
Fig 2
Right
Fig. 3
Wrong

Plate 37

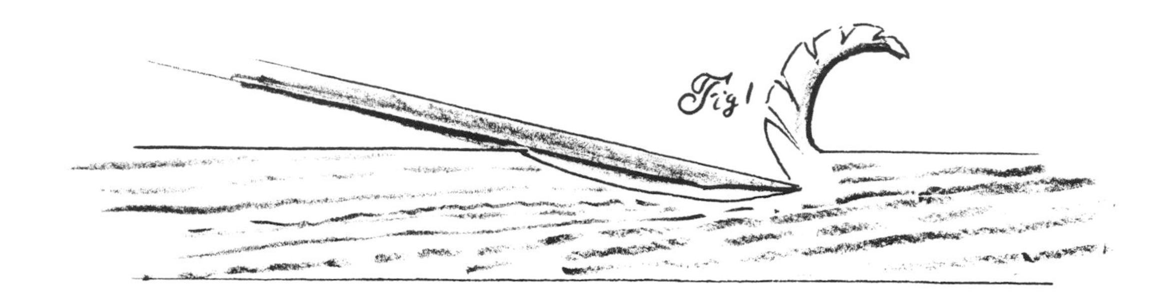

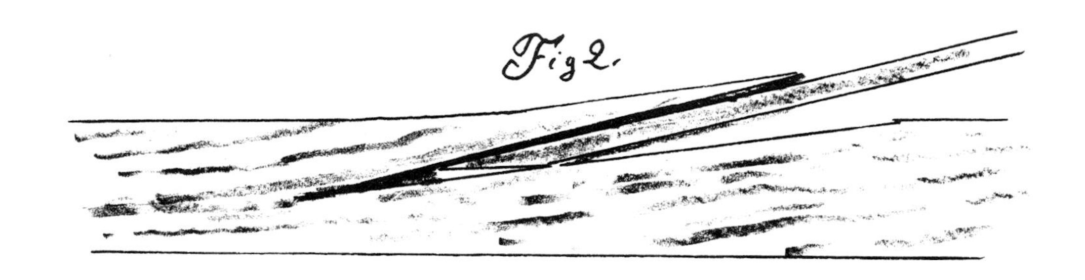

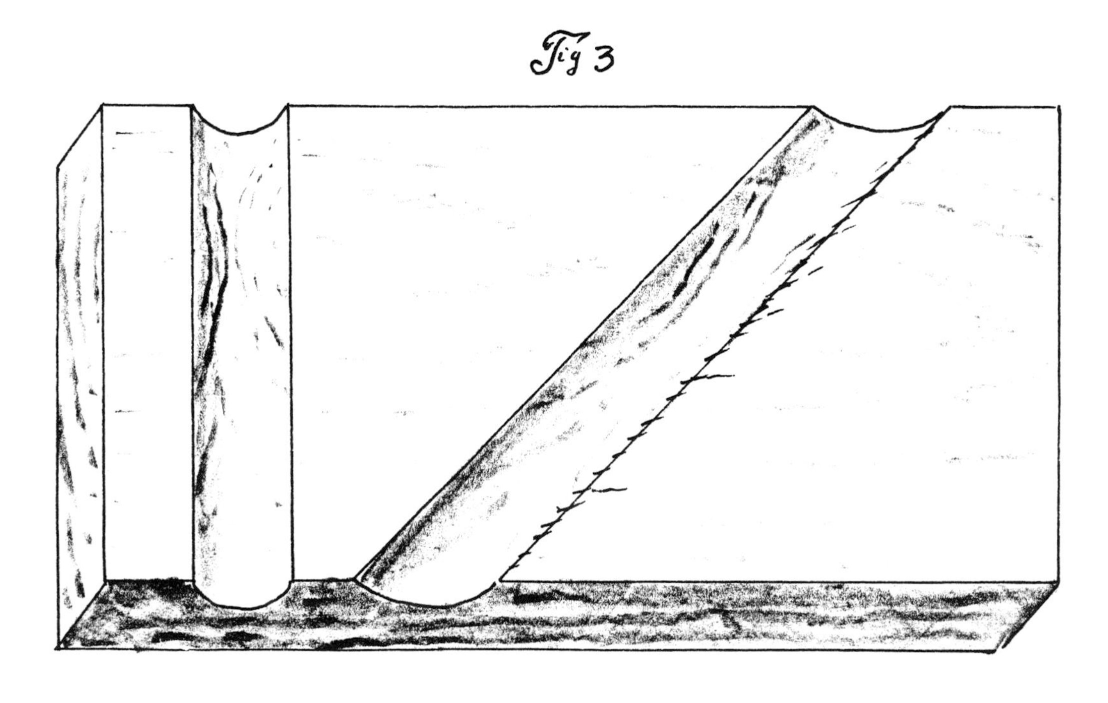

Plate 38

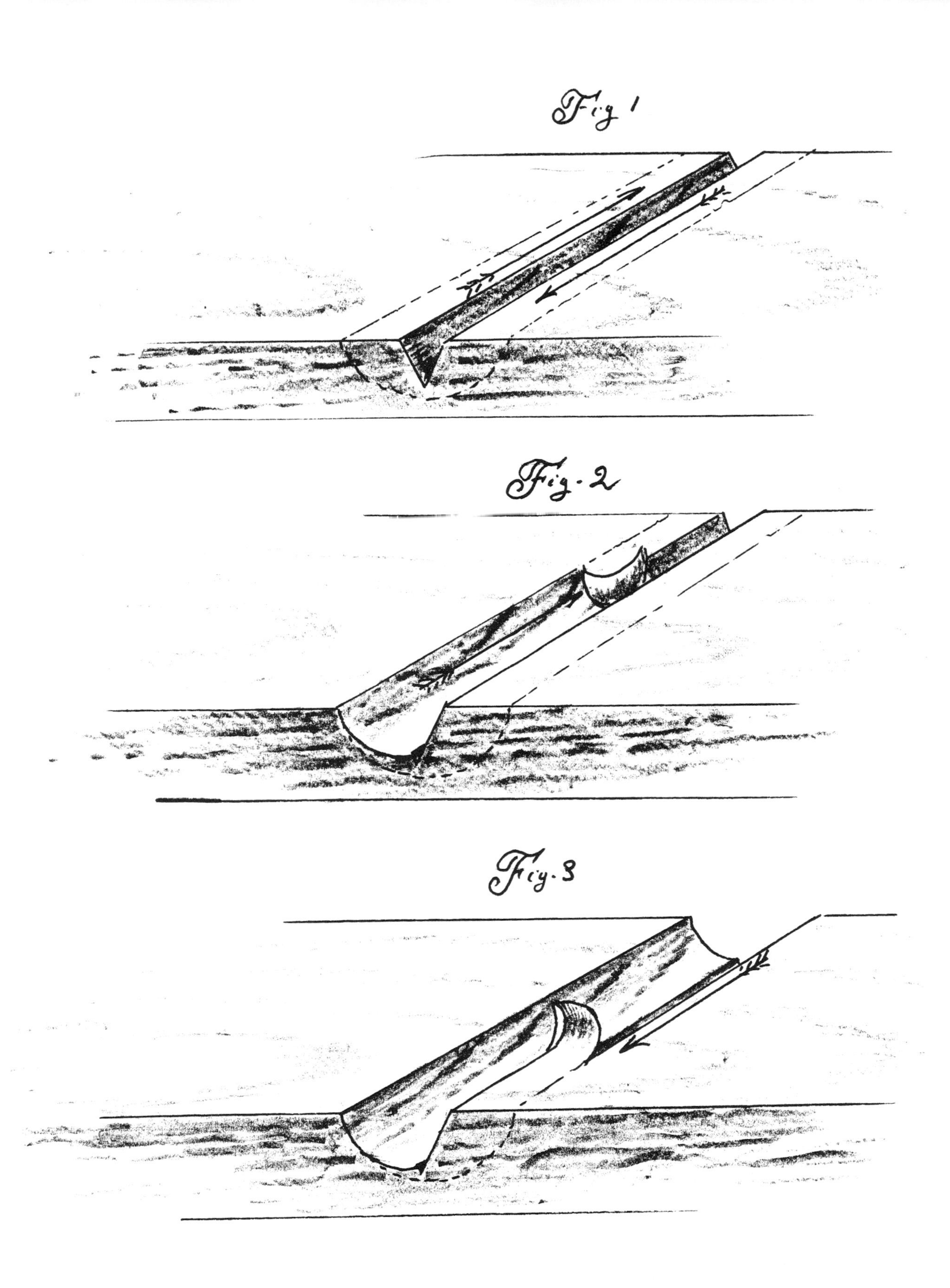

Plate 39

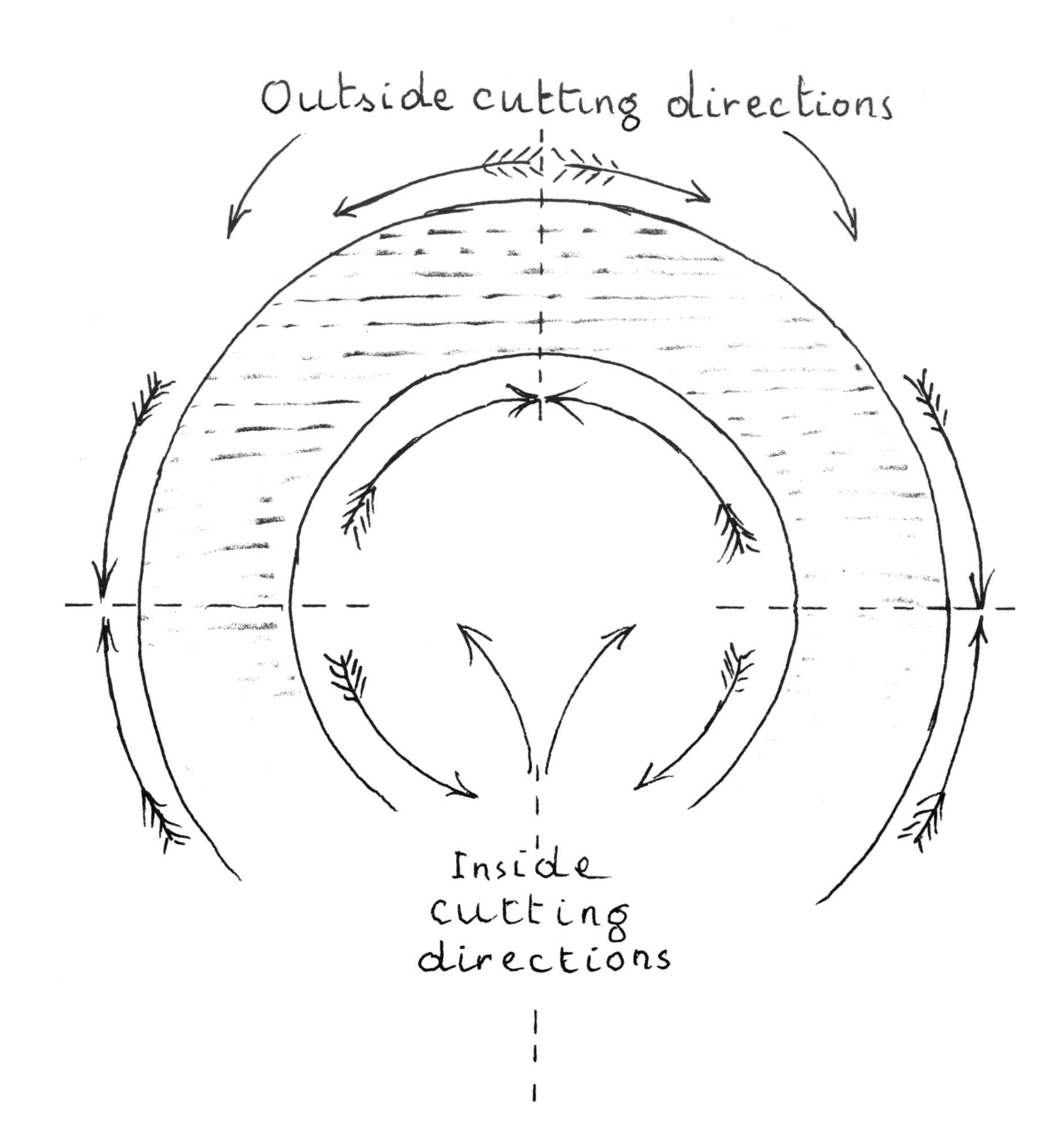

Plate 40

Part III

Seven Carving Problems

Before starting any one of these problems, you must first take time to become familiar with the whole procedure. Make a careful study of the text and sketches. The exercises should be executed in the order given; the success of each is dependent upon the preceding experience. Skipping a problem because it seems too elementary at first glance is likely to be a source of embarrassment and frustration later.

Although all the tools suggested in Plate 10 are not necessary to start working, an effort should be made to acquire them soon. Otherwise you will be hampered in your progress.

PROBLEM I: CUTTING A SIMPLE TRAY

This first exercise is a study in cutting the grain and selecting the proper tools. You are to choose the shape of the tray as well as the treatment of its sides (Plate 41) in relation to the tools you have available to you.

Procedure

- ☐ Trace the design on the wood (Plate 42, fig. 1).
- ☐ Make the board fast on the bench.
- ☐ You can construct a depth gauge from a small wooden ruler and a nail, to ensure even depth of cut and to avoid going through the bottom (Plate 42, figs. 1 and 2).
- ☐ Select a tool to excavate most of the inside. A flatter gouge, such as the #3, will even out the rough surfaces; a sharper bent will cut around the curling edges if necessary.
- ☐ After the tray has been dug, cut the outside tracing with chisel, jigsaw, band saw, coping saw, or whatever appropriate equipment is available. A coping saw setup is suggested in Plate 43.
- ☐ Work the border with the help of a piece of scrap wood cut to fit the depth of the tray (Plate 44). Rounding the ridge on one face will keep you from damaging the bottom of the tray.

PROBLEM II: BASIC CHIP CARVING

This problem introduces you to basic chip carving, and provides experience in precision tracing and cutting. See Plate 45.

Procedure

- ☐ **Tracing.** After selecting a clean board approximately 14 cm. wide, dress one edge to serve as the base for all measuring and tracing. The vertical center line is traced with the square. Be very careful that the square's heel stays in full contact with the dressed edge (Plate 46) to prevent crooked lines. The other vertical lines can be evenly spaced with the help of a compass or graduated ruler (Plate 47). The measurements given in Plate 48 are only suggested and can be adjusted to fit the size of the board. You can readily trace a parallel line close to a dressed edge free of possible slivers by using the middle finger as a guiding gauge (Plate 49, figs. 1 and 2). With the four rectangles properly established, run diagonals from the opposite corners (Plate 50, fig. 1) to form eight triangles. Taking one triangle at a time, divide each angle in two equal parts. This is generally done free hand with only the help of a pencil (Plate 50, fig. 2). The three dividing lines should meet at the exact center. When the tracing is completed, make the board fast to the bench in preparation for cutting.
- ☐ **Cutting.** With mallet and chisel (the flat of the chisel held in a vertical plane but leaning toward the center), take cuts from zero depth at points a, b, and c, in Plate 51, going deeper toward the center. Instead, you can use the V and take a cut from zero depth, again at the apex, again going deeper toward the center (Plate 52, fig. 1). Next, with the chisel or a #3 wide gouge, remove excess wood (Plate 52, fig. 2), working with the grain. It does not pay to go too deep, since the cleaning difficulties increase with depth. Plate 53 shows variations in cutting.

PROBLEM III: THE BASIC ROSE, OR ROSETTE

This problem introduces the basic rose, or rosette, providing experience in curved V tooling, grain handling, tool selecting, and center button rounding. See Plate 54.

Procedure

- ☐ Plate 55, fig. 1 is the only design necessary at this time. Cut the exterior line with the V (Plate 55, fig. 2).
- ☐ Cut a groove close to the center button line (Plate 56, fig. 1). The button line is cut down (Plate 56, fig. 2). The gouge handle leans slightly toward the center. The button is then cut free (Plate 56, fig. 3).
- ☐ Excavate to form the saucer shape (Plate 57, fig. 1). Plate 57, fig. 2 shows the directions of the grain when you are forming the saucer.
- ☐ Plate 58, fig. 1 shows the saucer shape. Next, the petals are traced, then separated with a V, starting on the outside to end lightly at the button (Plate 58, fig. 2). The petals' curves are then traced free hand.
- ☐ The gouge is held at a low angle and the curves are cut (Plate 59, fig. 1). Next, remove the chips (Plate 59, fig. 2).
- ☐ Plate 60, fig. 1 shows the finished petals. If fluter decorations are desired, they should be cut, starting deep from the exterior to ease out close to the

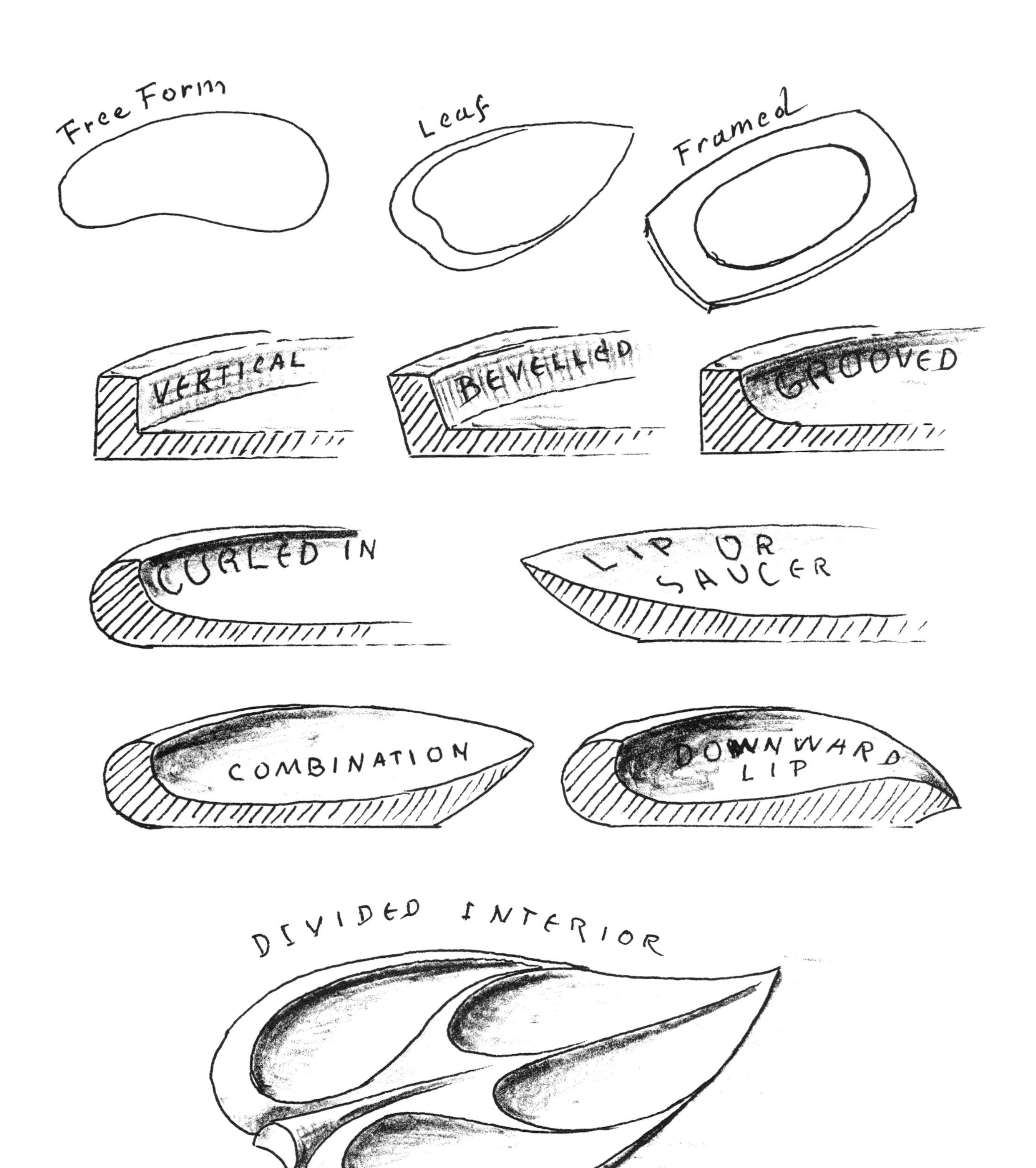
Free Form
Leaf
Framed
VERTICAL
BEVELLED
GROOVED
CURLED IN
LIP OR
SAUCER
COMBINATION
DOWNWARD
LIP
DIVIDED INTERIOR

Plate 41

button. Next, round the button. The movements of the gouge are indicated by the arrows in Plate 60, fig. 2.

PROBLEM IV: THE CUTTING OF TWININGS

This exercise teaches cutting of twining and suggests uses for twining (Plate 71). Instructions are found in Plates 62 through 67.

PROBLEM V: CARVING A WILD ROSE TWIG

This problem in carving a wild rose twig is an exercise in surface incised carving, permitting a freer and individualized interpretation of treatment. Leaves or flowers may be added or modified at will.

The outlines, once drawn, may be taken as is on the tracing paper (Plate 68) and transferred onto the clean wood (Plate 69). Only the outline is rather deeply V tooled (Plate 69). The suggested modeling of the details can vary from leaf to leaf to break a monotonous rendering. For instance, "a,c," shown concave in Plate 70, may become convex on the next leaf, while "b,d," shown convex, can be cut concave. Light fluter cuts and irregularities on the stem and petals' edges enhance realism.

PROBLEM VI: A CLASSIC ACANTHUS LEAF

This classic acanthus leaf in *champleve*, or carved in relief (Plate 72), is an exercise in cutting sharp outlines and a clean, even background, the handling of frame corners, and the use of the stippling tool for background treatment. Plate 80 shows suggestions for using this design.

Procedure

- ☐ After the design has been transferred to the wood, V-tool the frame outline (Plate 73, Step 1).
- ☐ Next, cut a groove, cutting all around close to the outlines of the leaf and inside the frame (Plate 73, Step 2).
- ☐ Clear off the excess wood (Plate 73, Step 3).
- ☐ V tool the corners (Plate 73, Step 4).
- ☐ Groove the inside of the frame along the V tool line (Plate 74).
- ☐ Cut down the outline of the leaf to the bottom level and clean the background (Plate 75).
- ☐ Shape the leaf surface (Plates 76 and 77).
- ☐ Plate 78 shows the treatment of the volute and hooks.
- ☐ Use the compass to trace the inside of the frame (Plate 79).
- ☐ Stipple the background from the leaf to the inside frame tracing, and then V tool the inside frame.

PROBLEM VII: THE SIMPLE CARVING IN THE ROUND

This simple carving in the round (Plate 81) is an exercise in clamping, shaping the main form (Plate 82) and working in details. The suggested procedure will accommodate a variety of simple shapes; so you may wish to treat a different subject than the one presented.

Whatever design you select, remember to keep the main shape simple. In this exercise a base has been included for clamping purposes (Plate 83). It can be eliminated later if so desired.

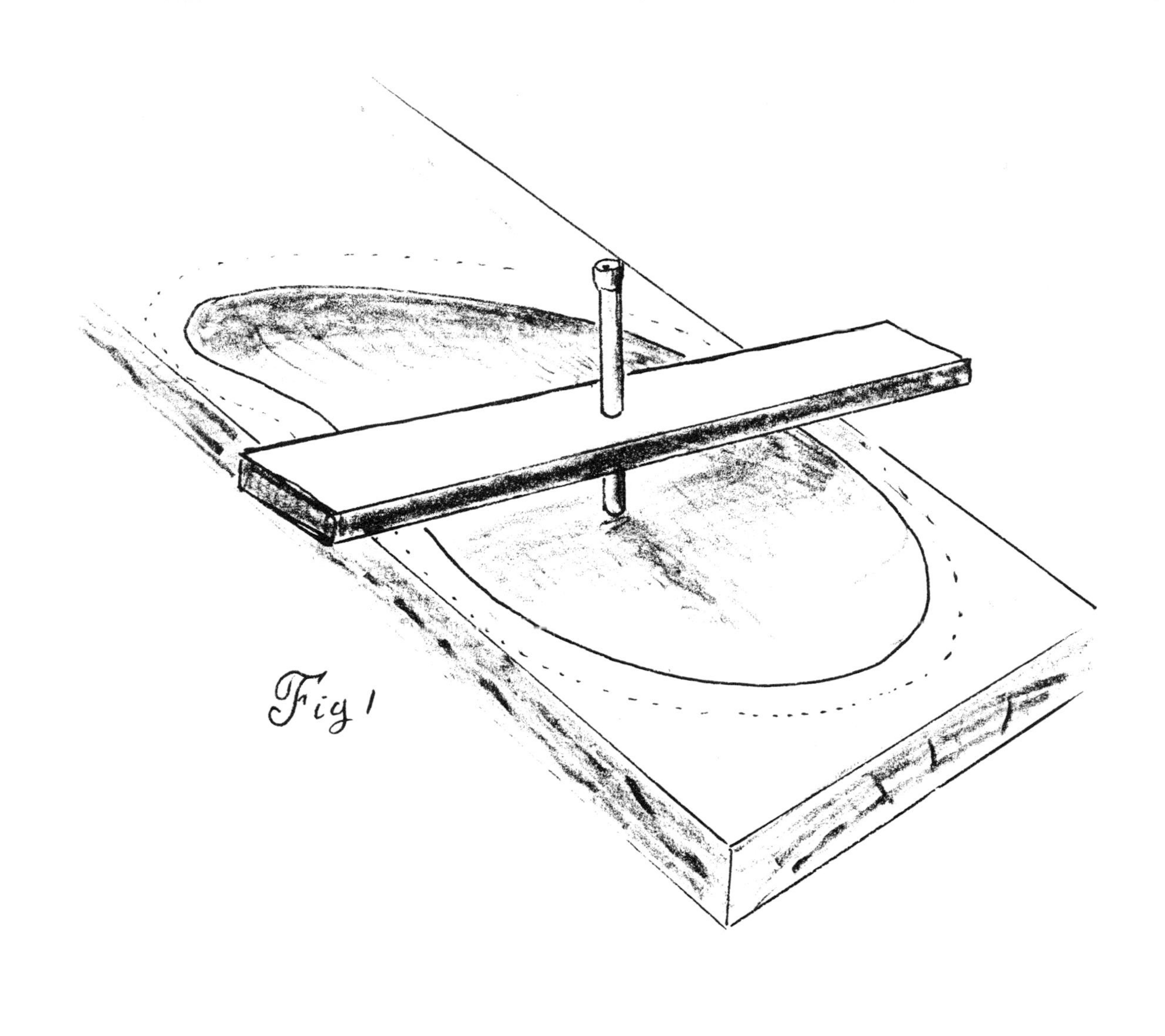

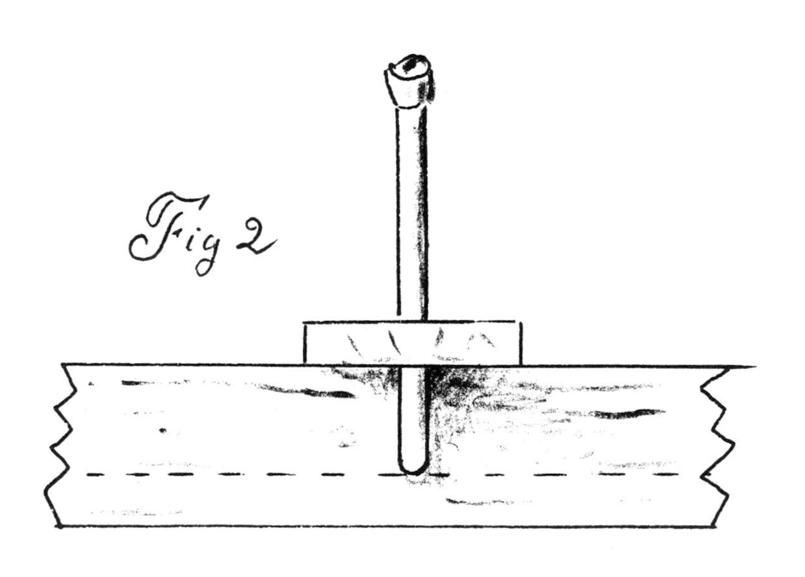

Plate 42

Sketching a project in all directions can be of great help, because the direct tracing on the piece is continually being cut out. The use of hand saws or band saws often will help in roughing out the work. Rasps and files will help in shaping and making the surface clean to receive the tracing of details (Plate 84).

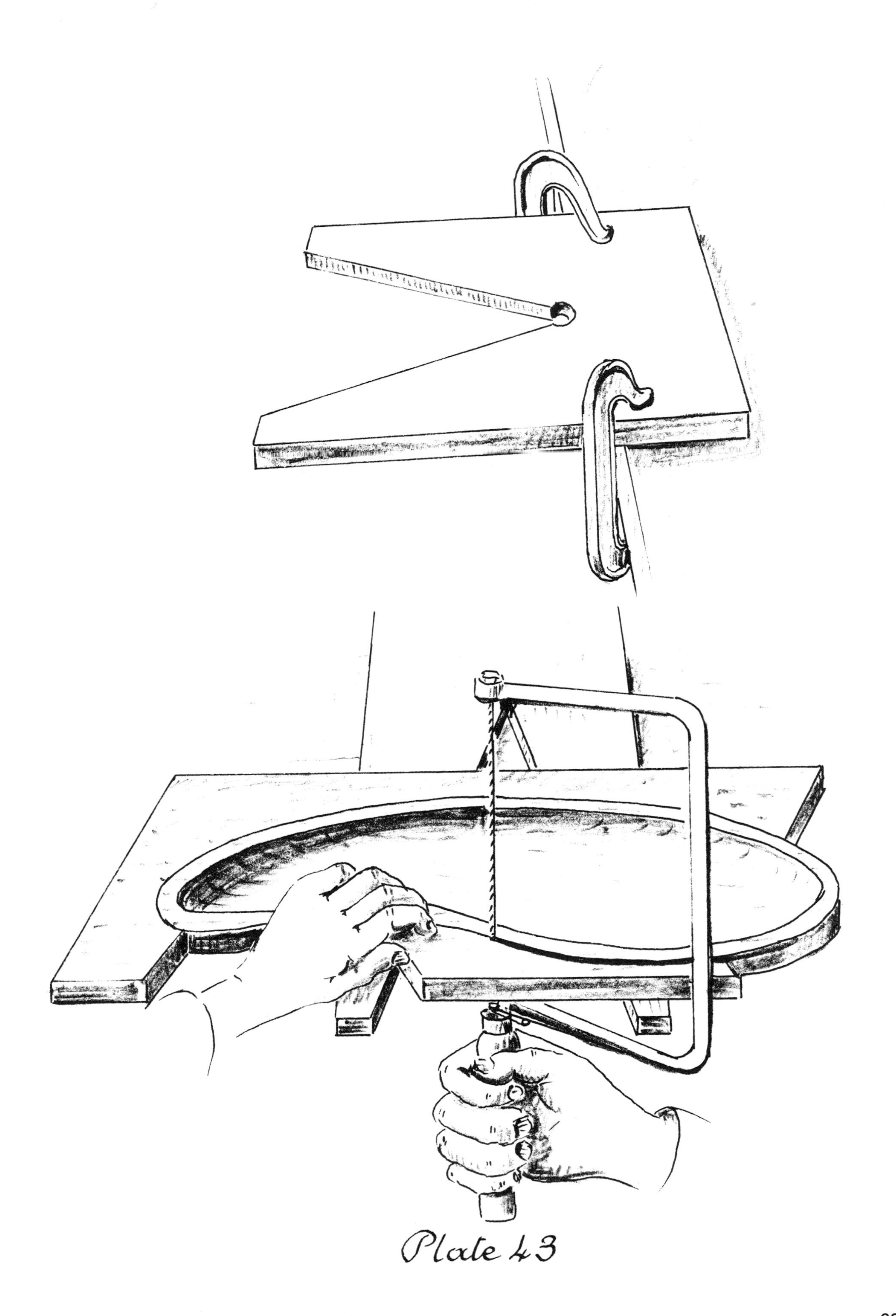

Plate 43

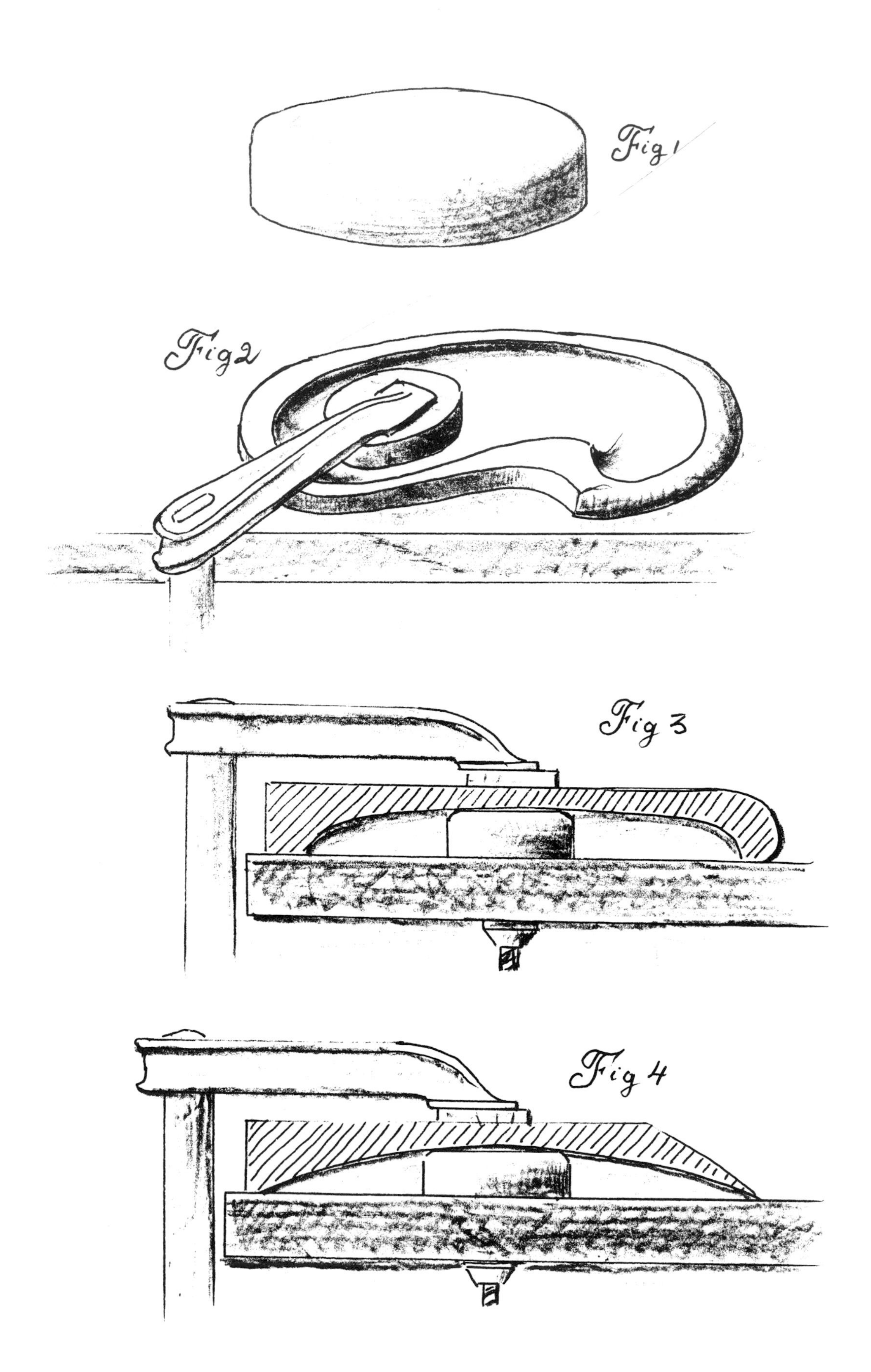

Plate 44

Plate 45

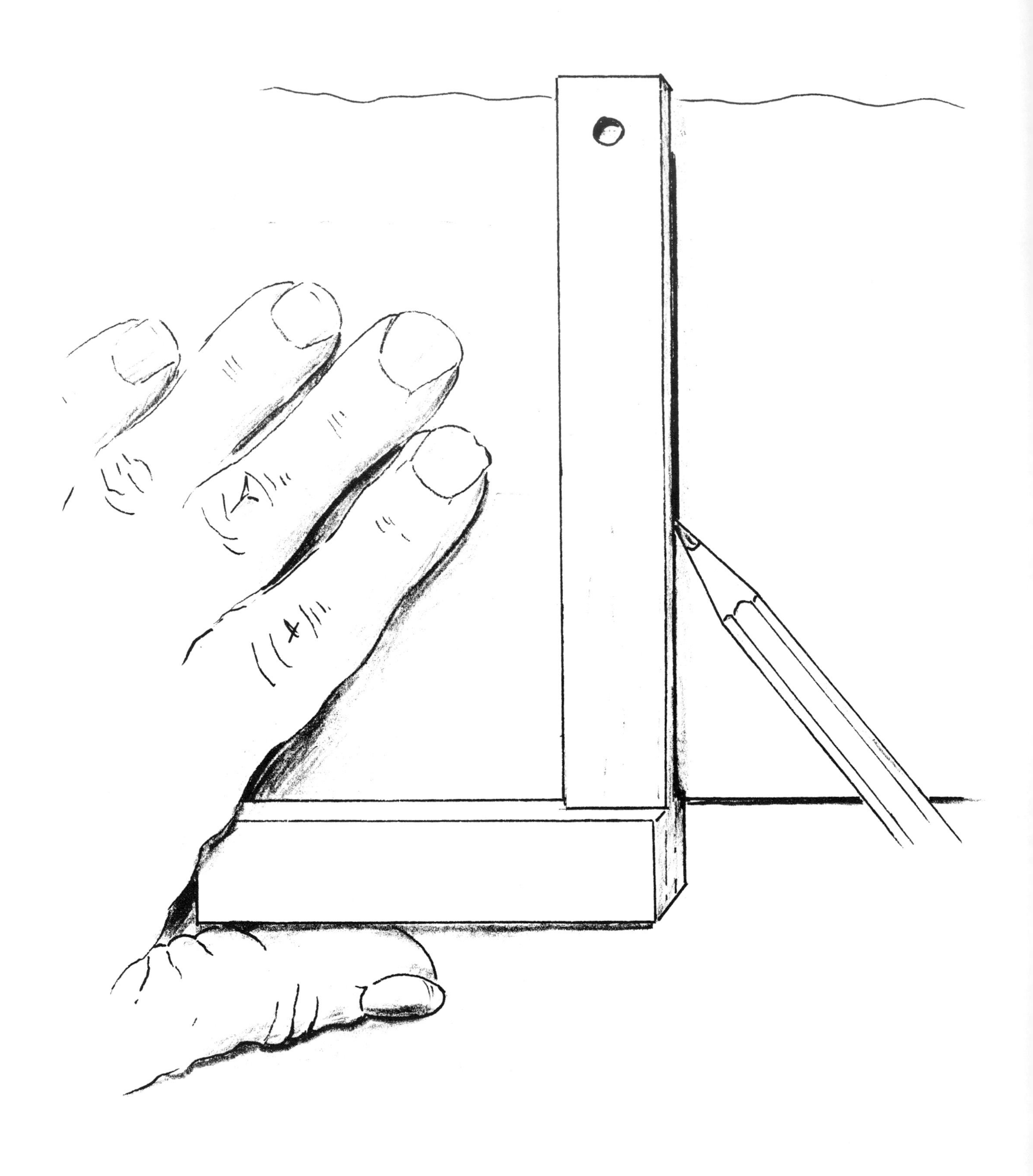

Plate 46

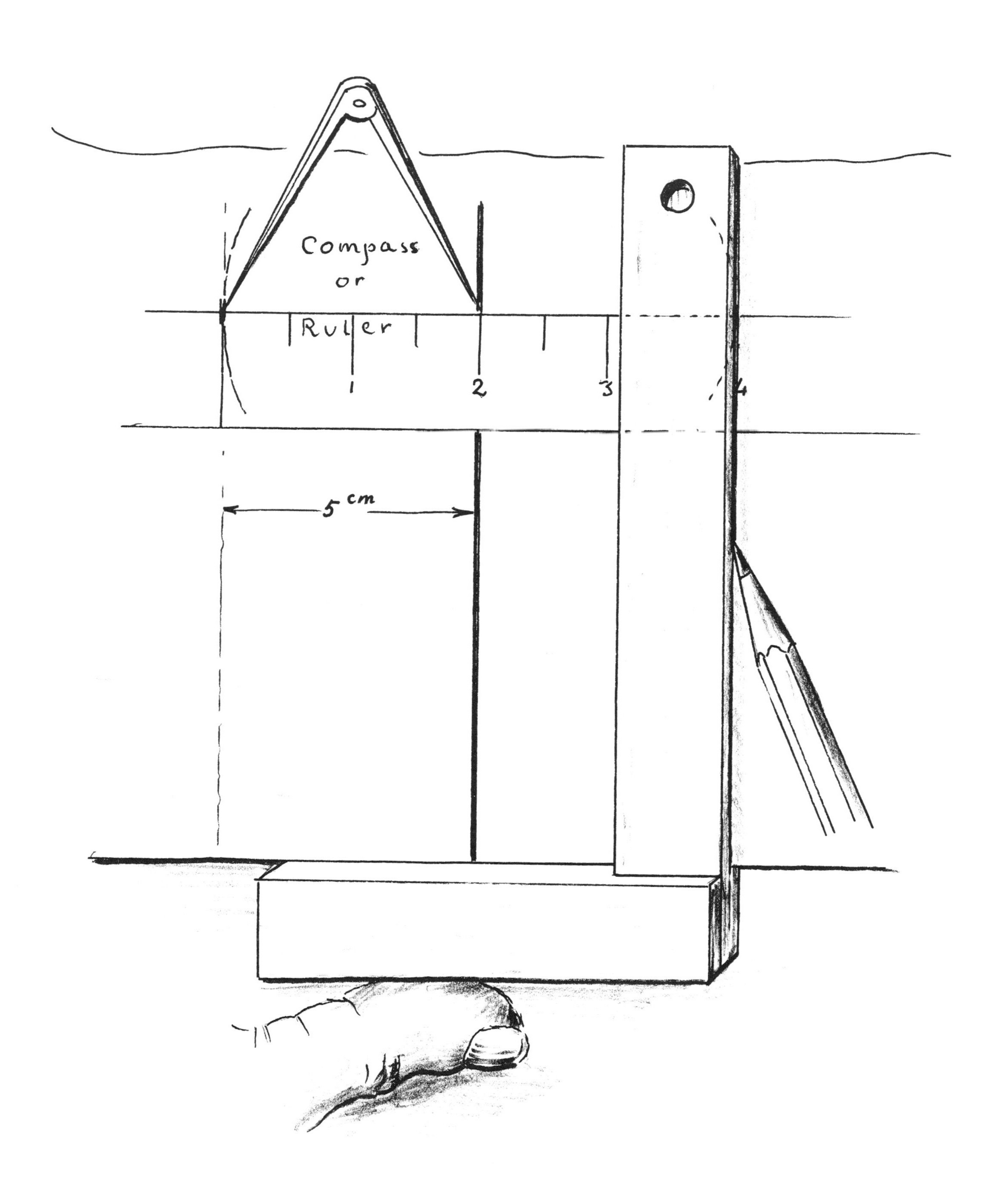
Compass
or
Ruler
1
2
3
4
5 cm

Plate 47

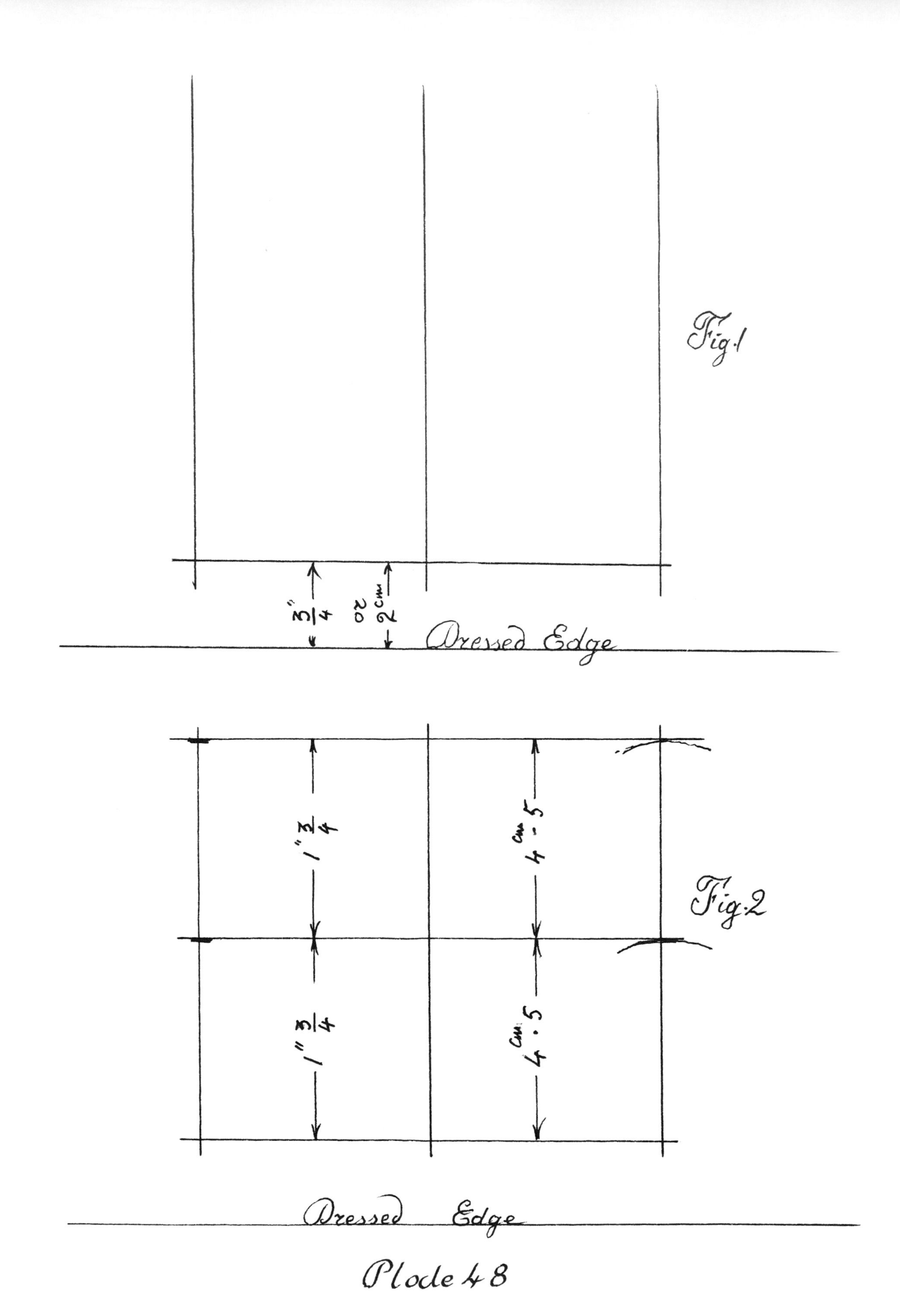
Fig. 1
3/4"
or
2 cm
Dressed Edge
1" 3/4
4 cm · 5
Fig. 2
1" 3/4
4 cm · 5
Dressed Edge

Plode 48

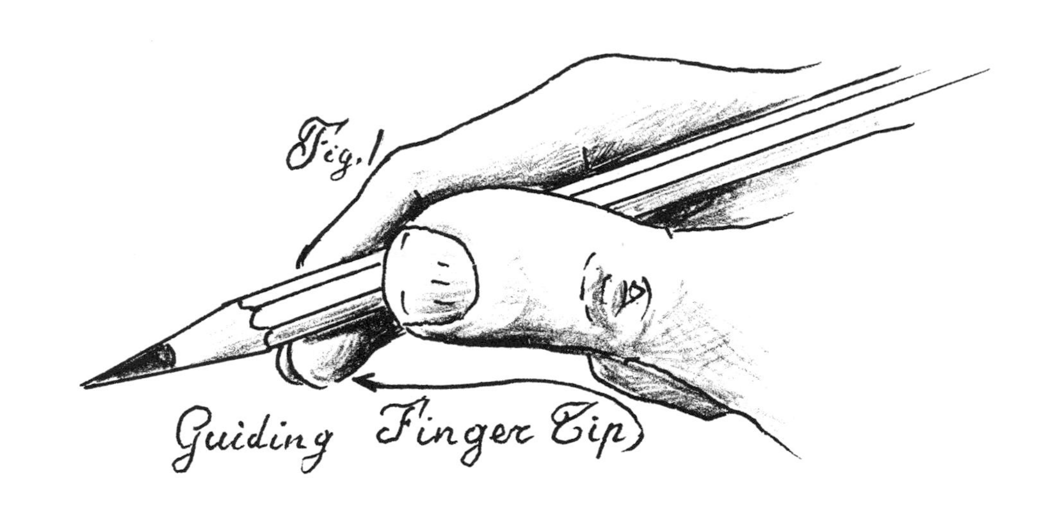

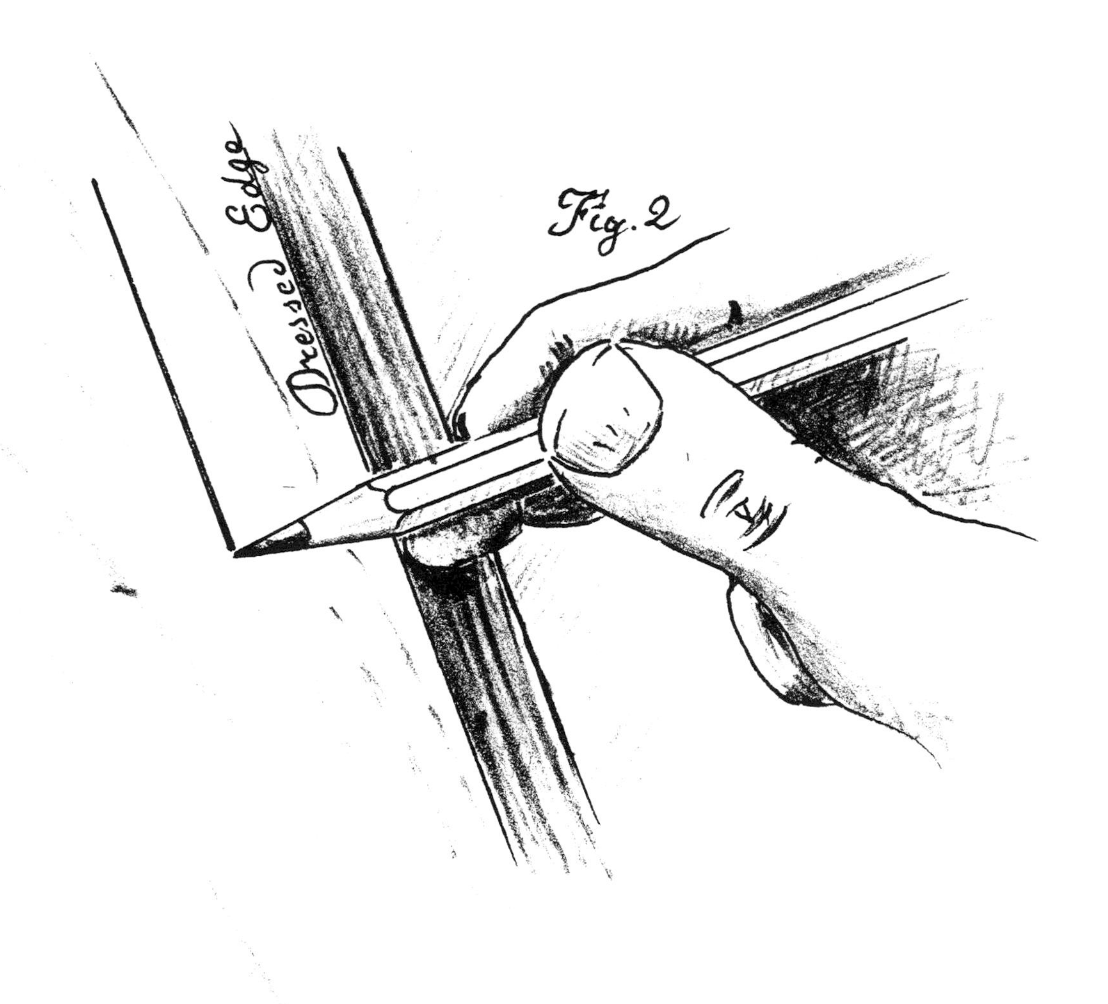

Plate 49

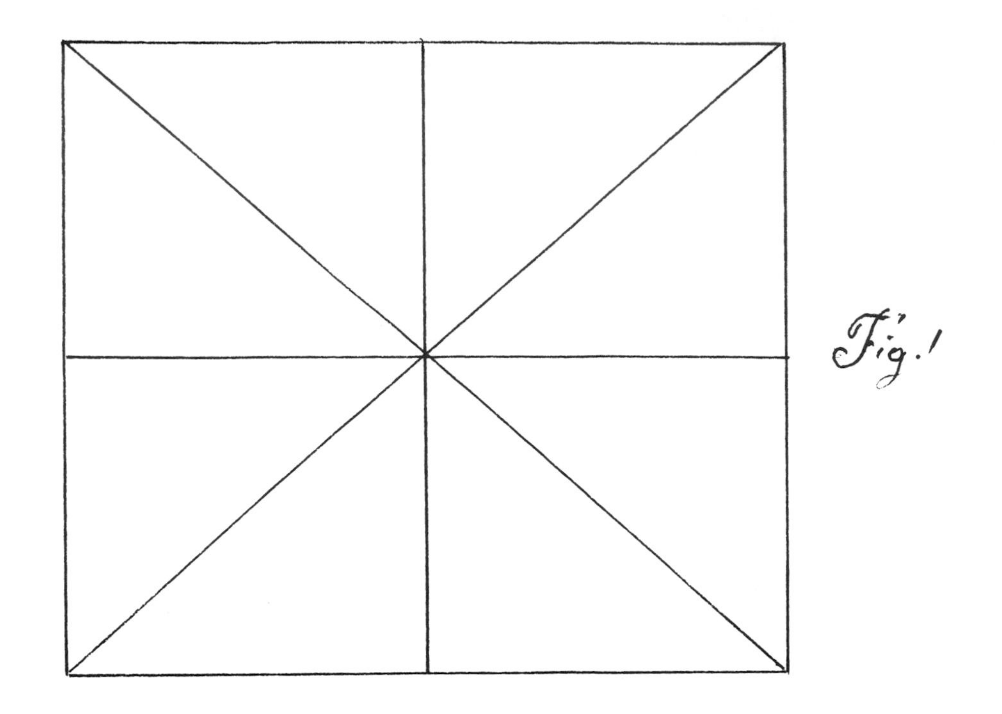

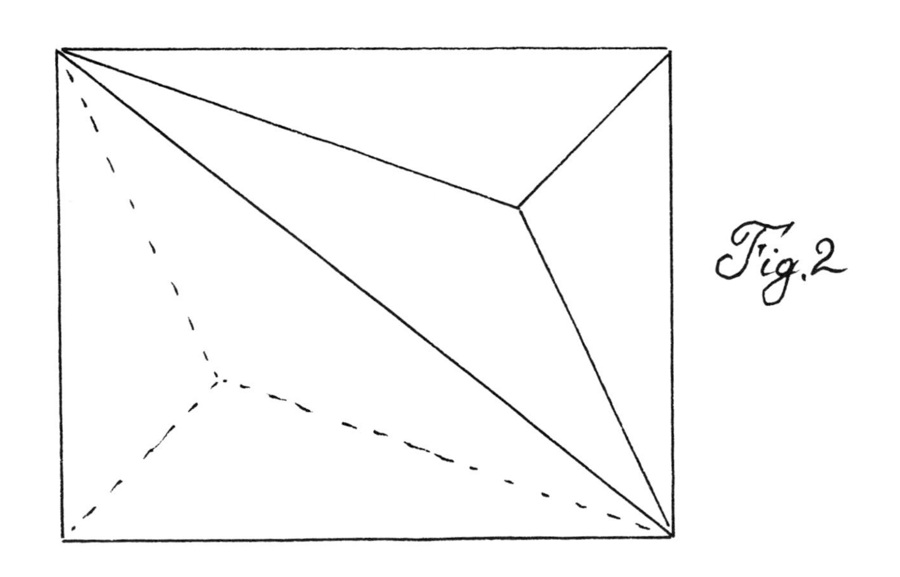

Plate 50

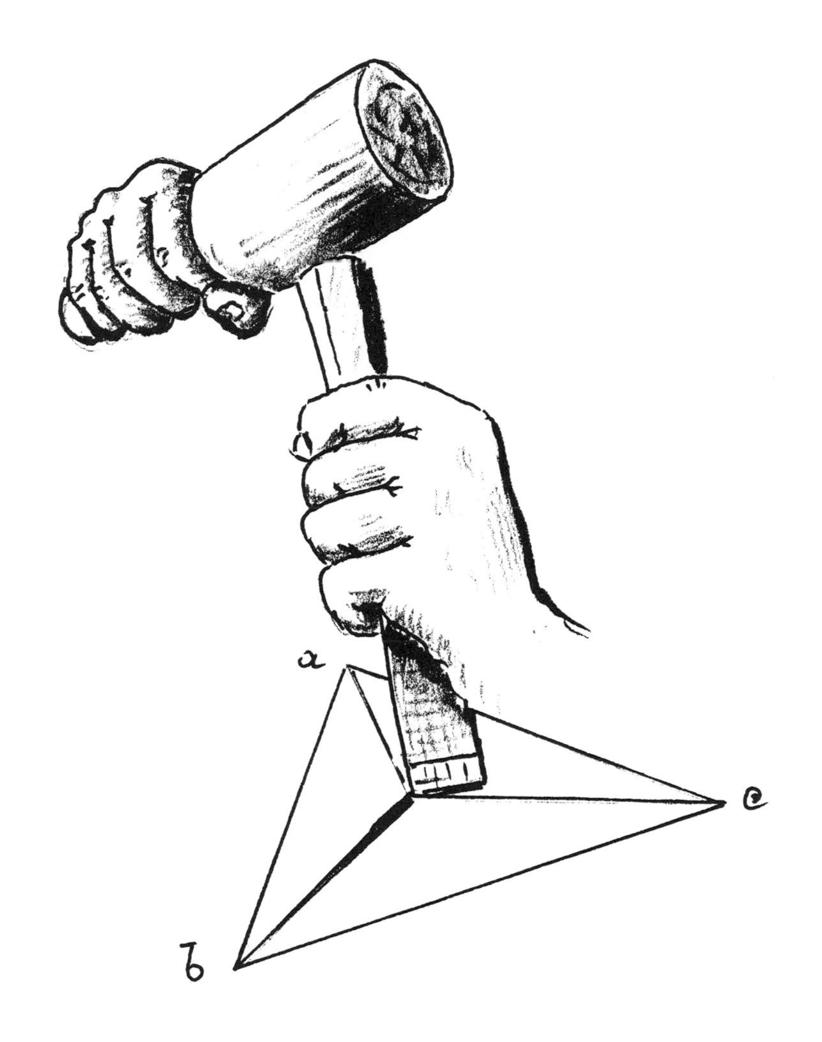

Plate 51

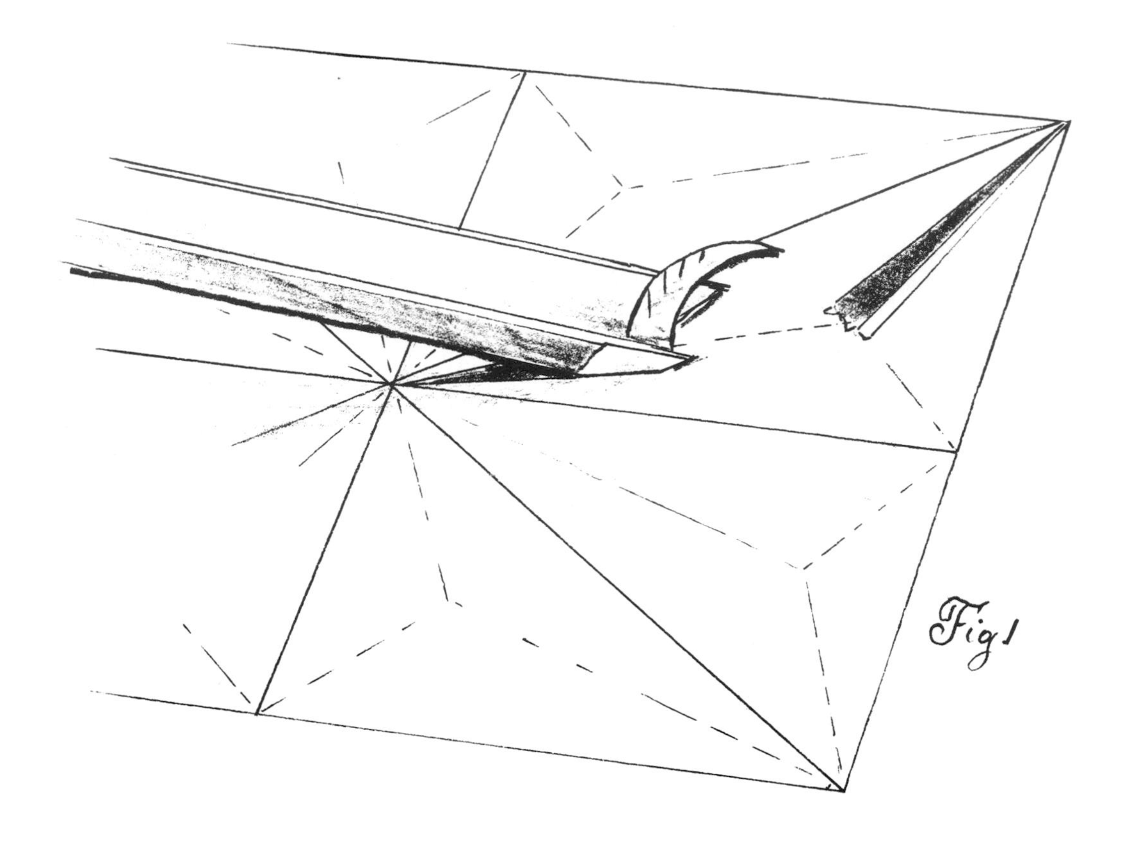

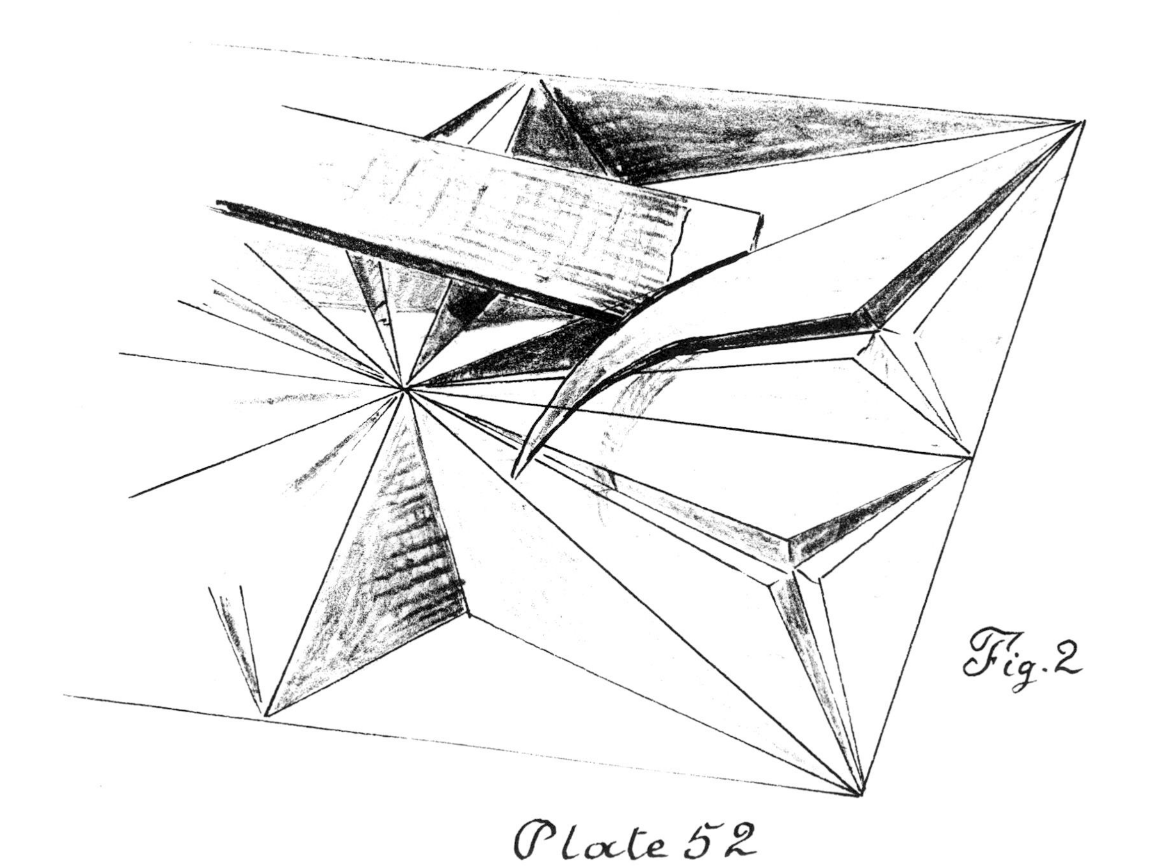

Plate 52

Variations

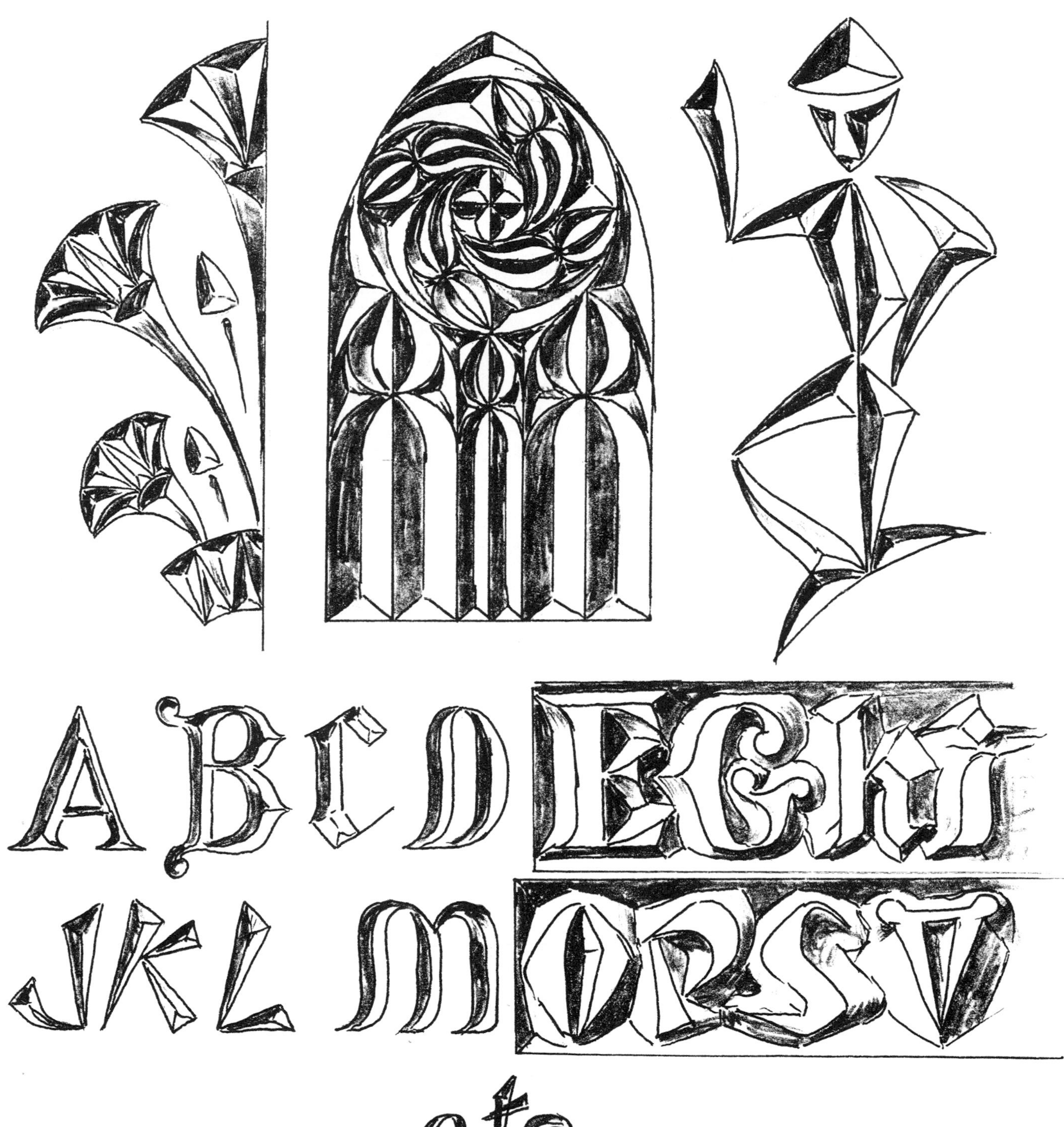

Plate 53

THE BASIC ROSE

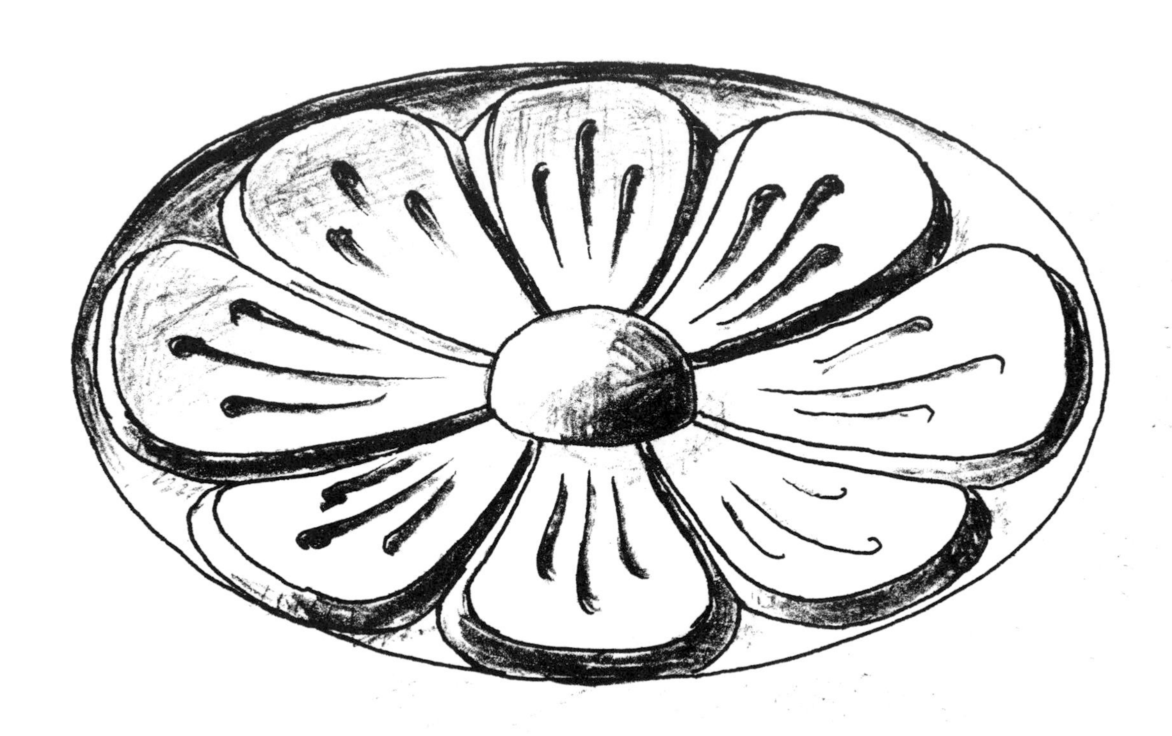

Plate 54

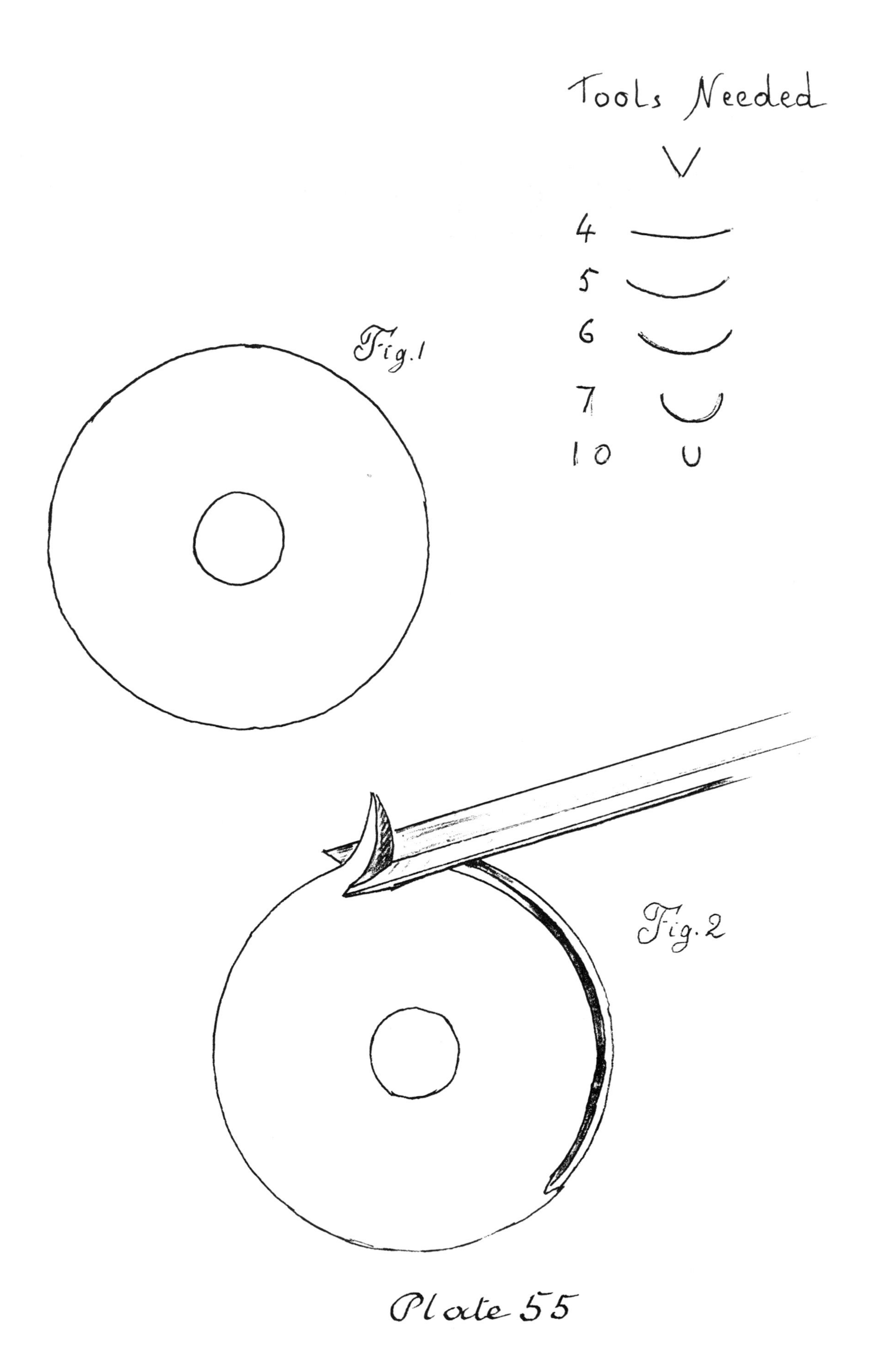

Plate 55

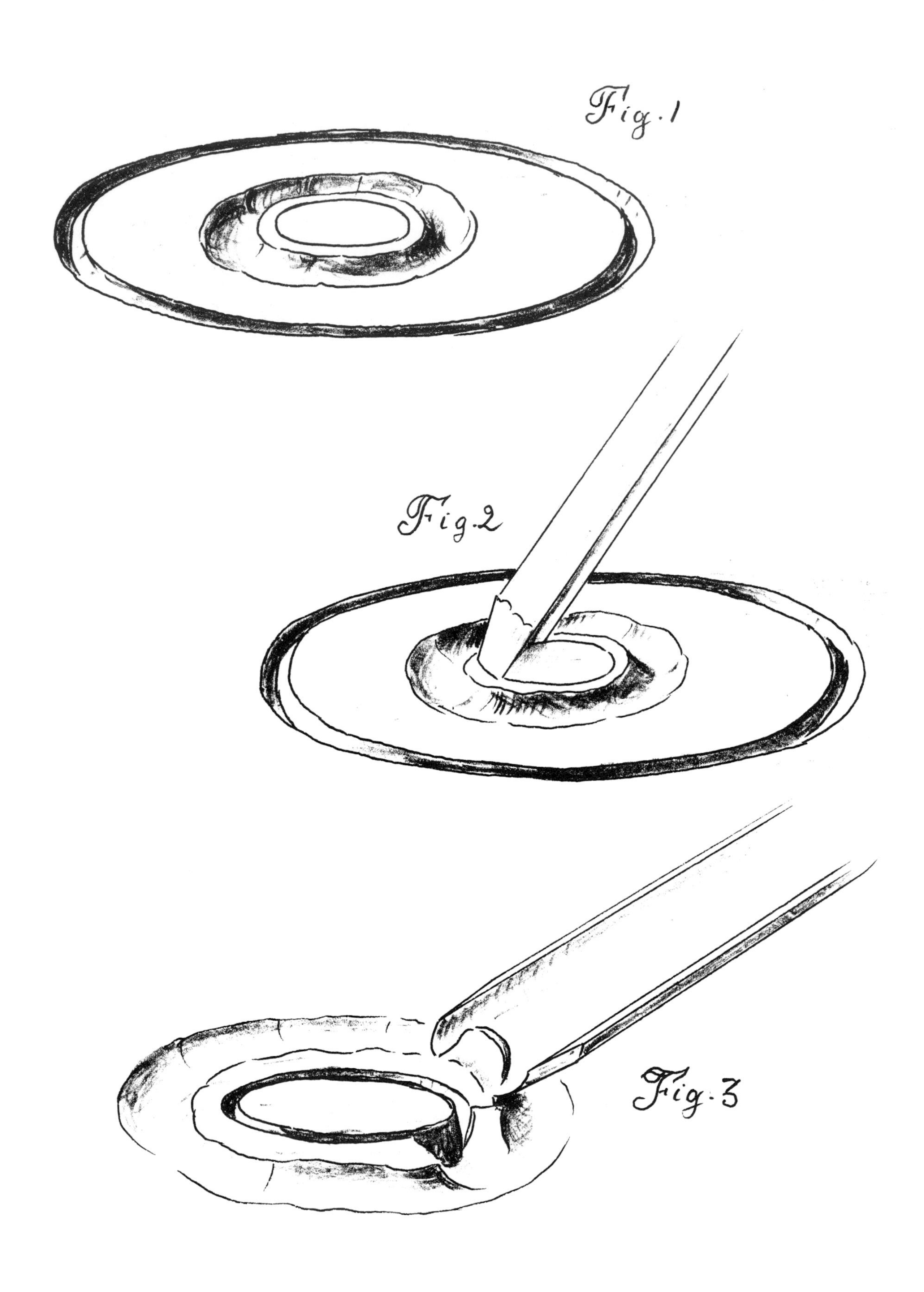

Plate 56

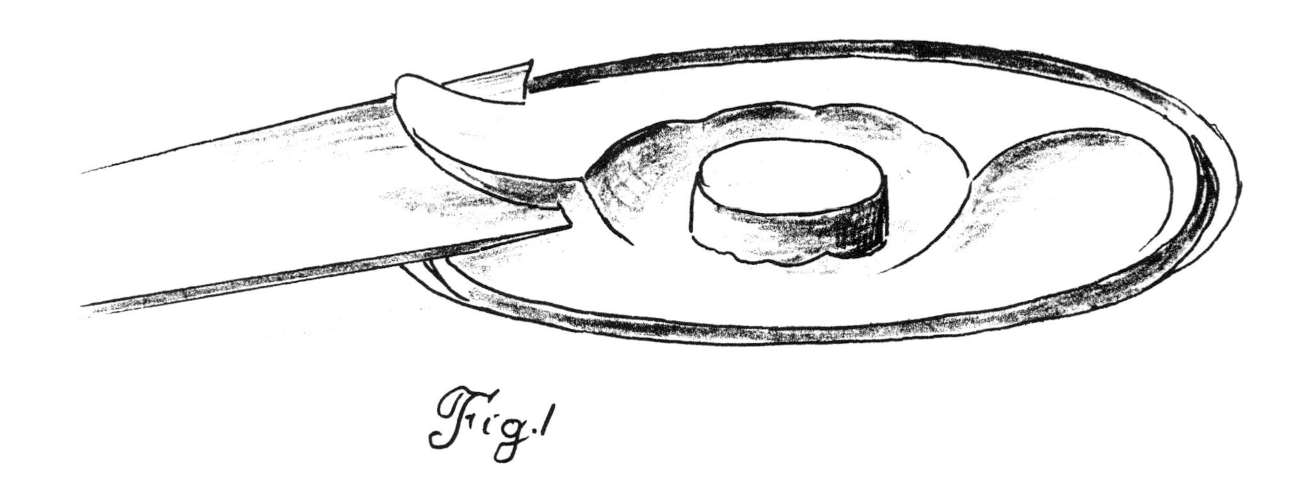

Fig. 1

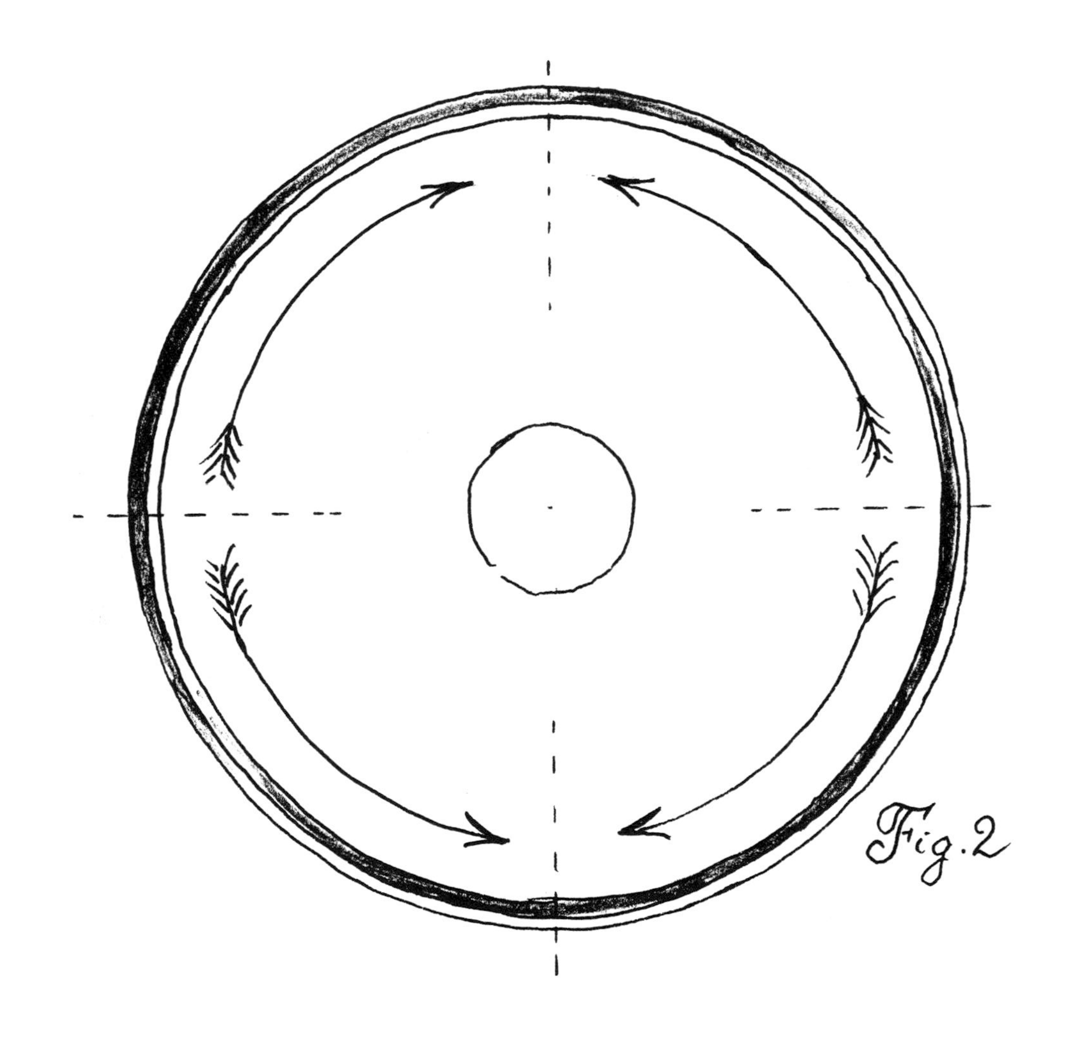

Fig. 2

Plate 57

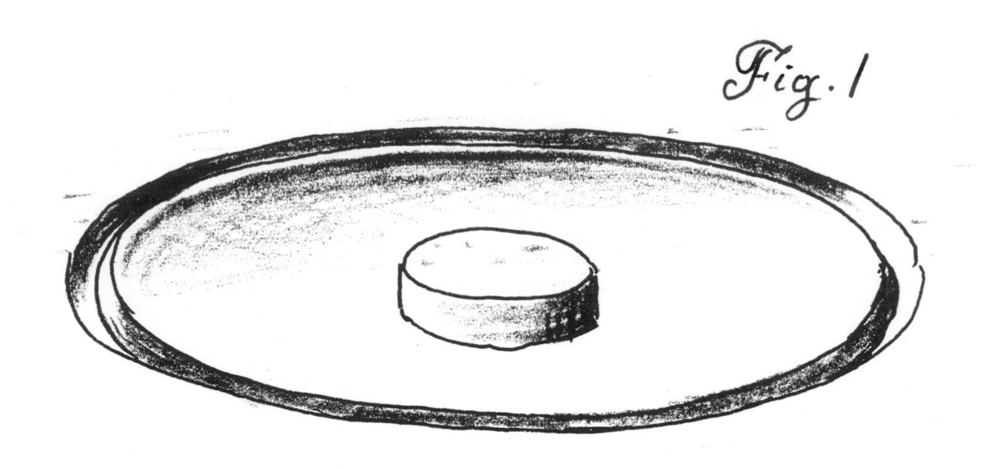

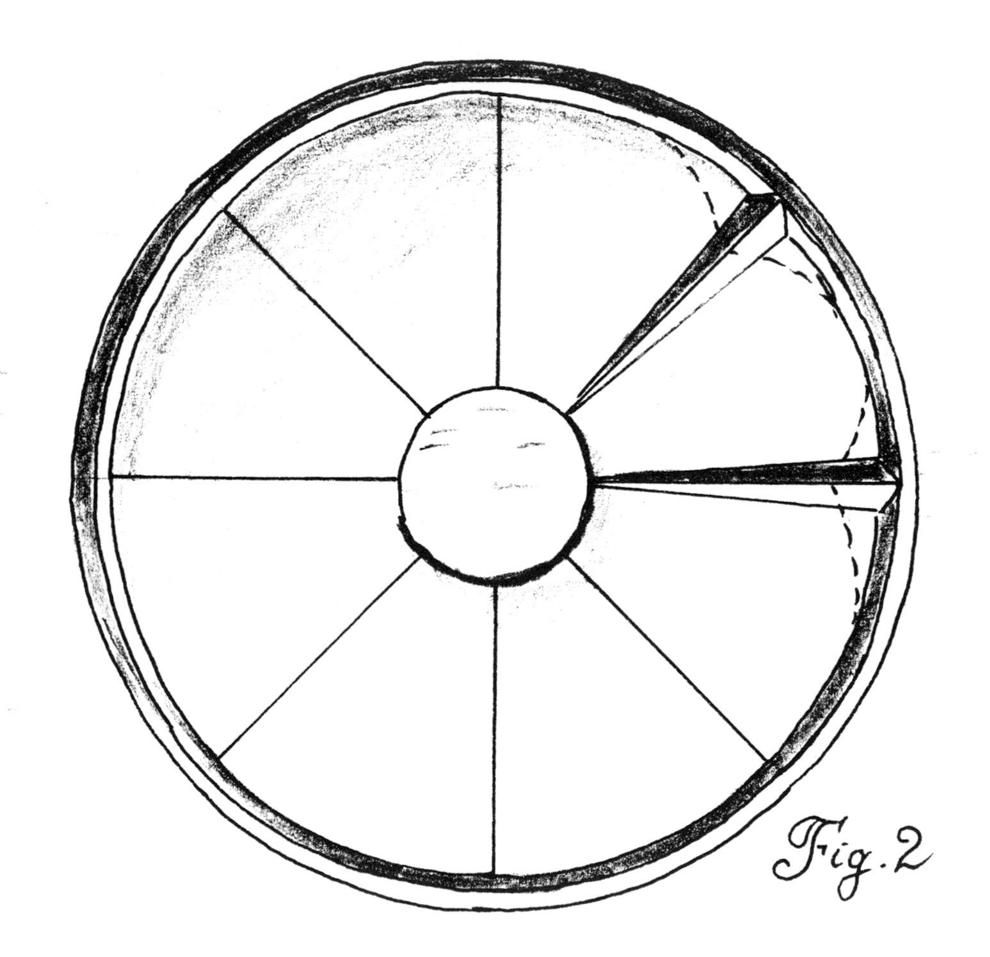

Plate 58

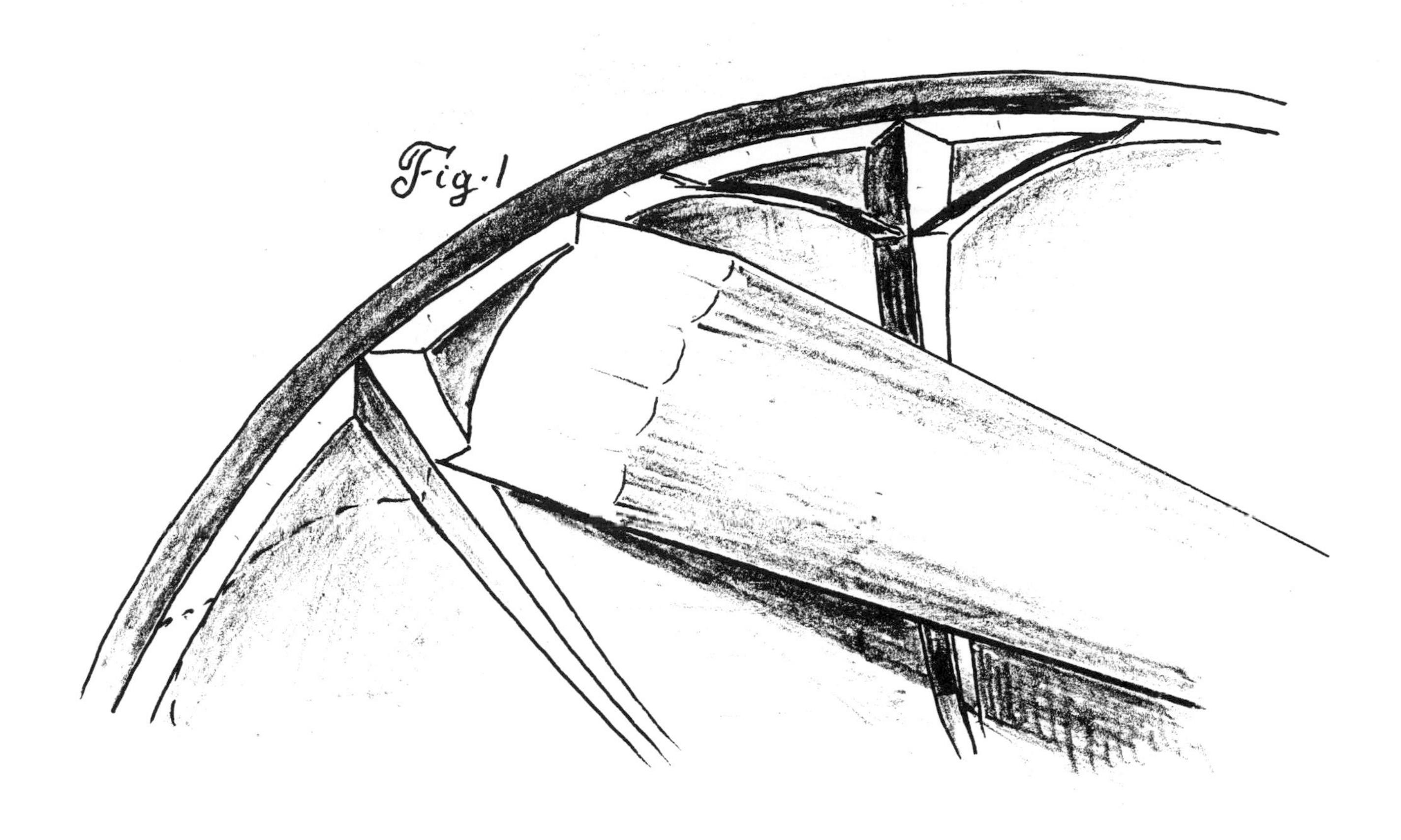

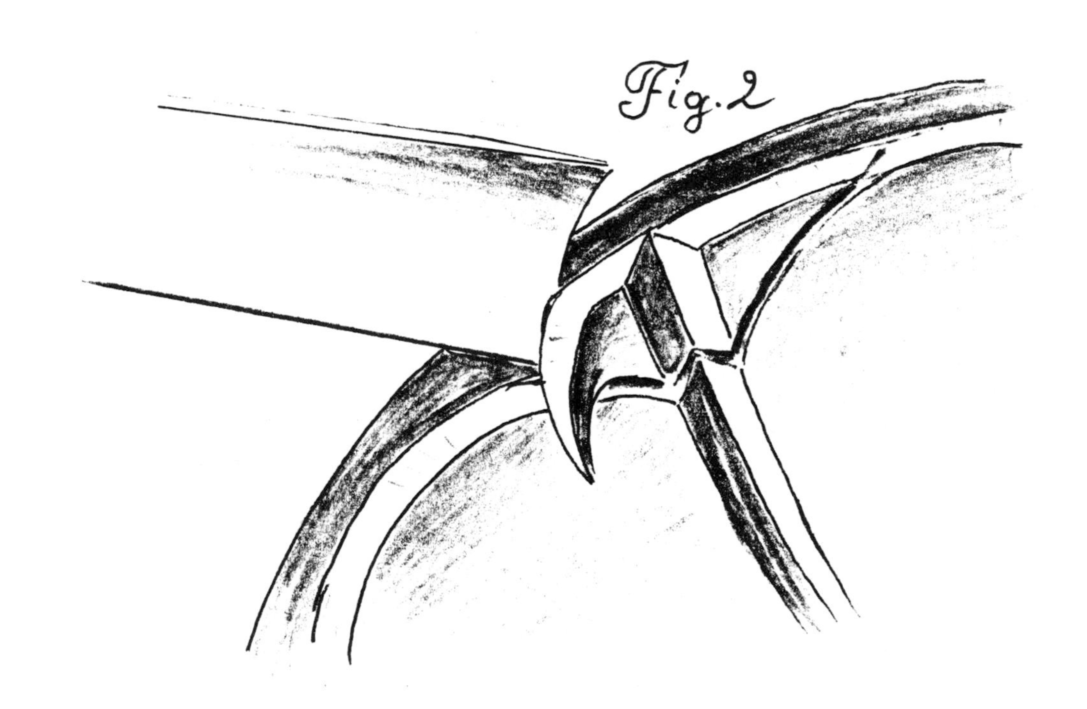

Plate 59

Fig. 1
Fig. 2
Plate 60

Variations on the Rose

Plate 61

Twinings

Plate 62

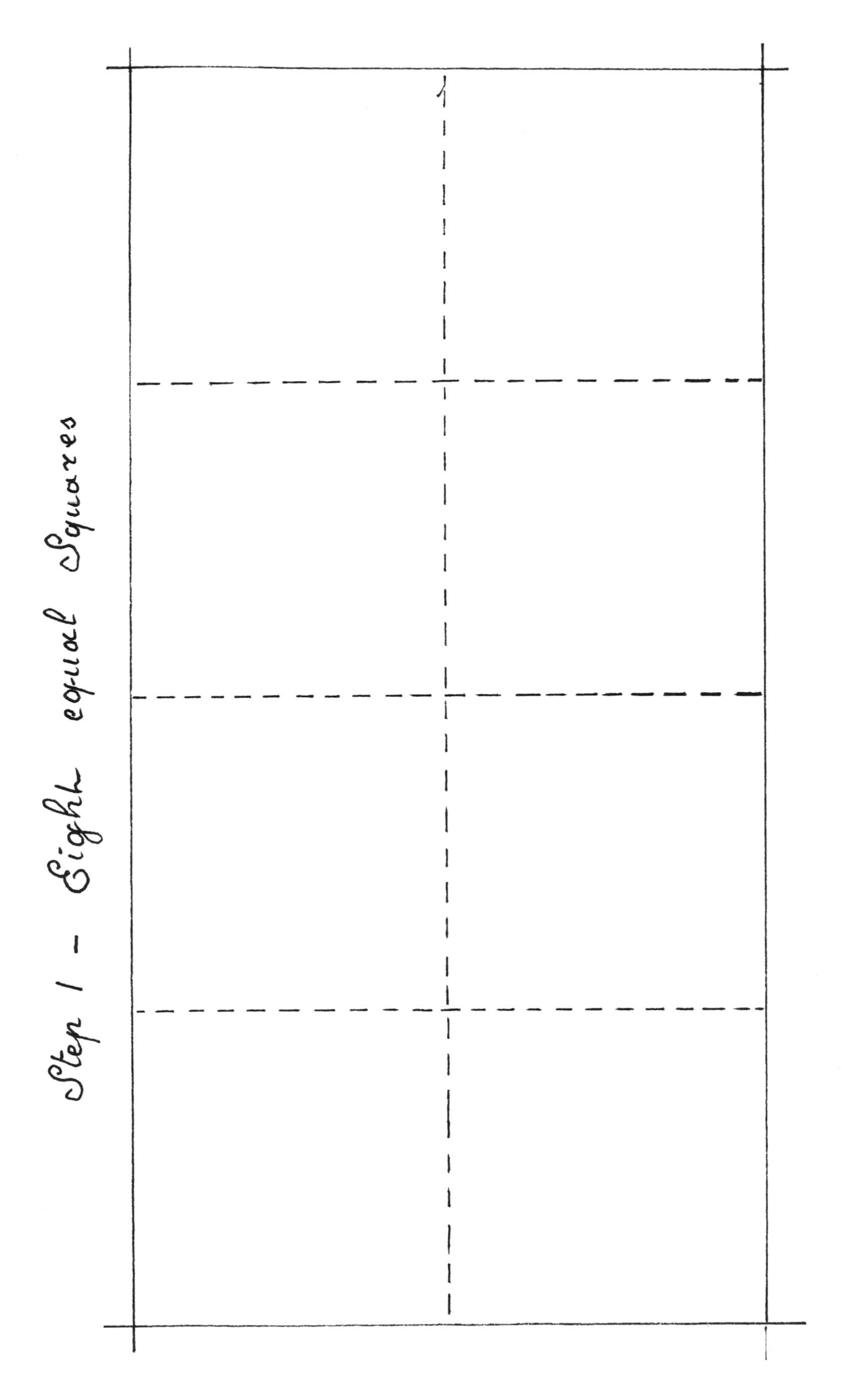

Plate 63

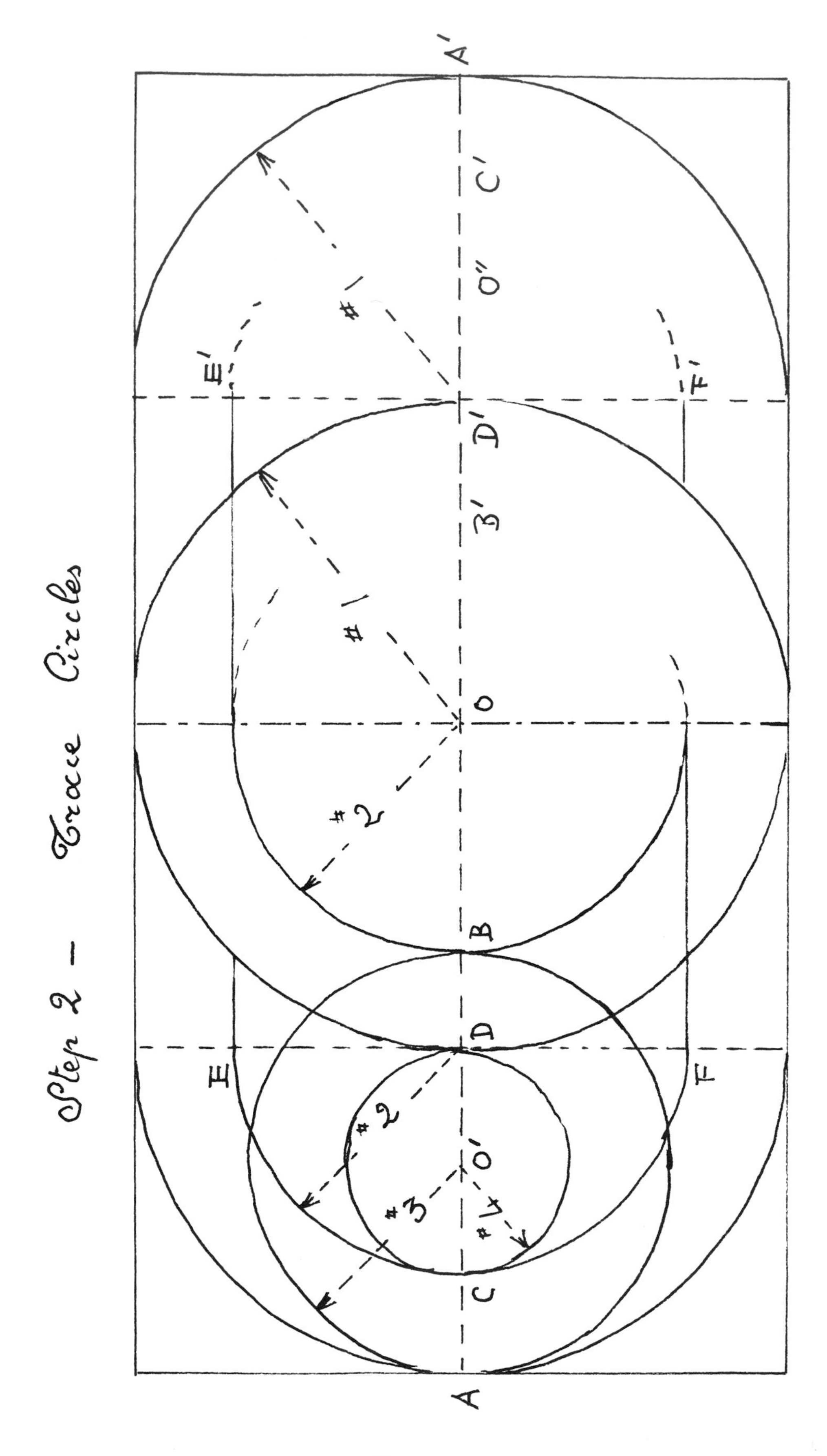

Plate 64

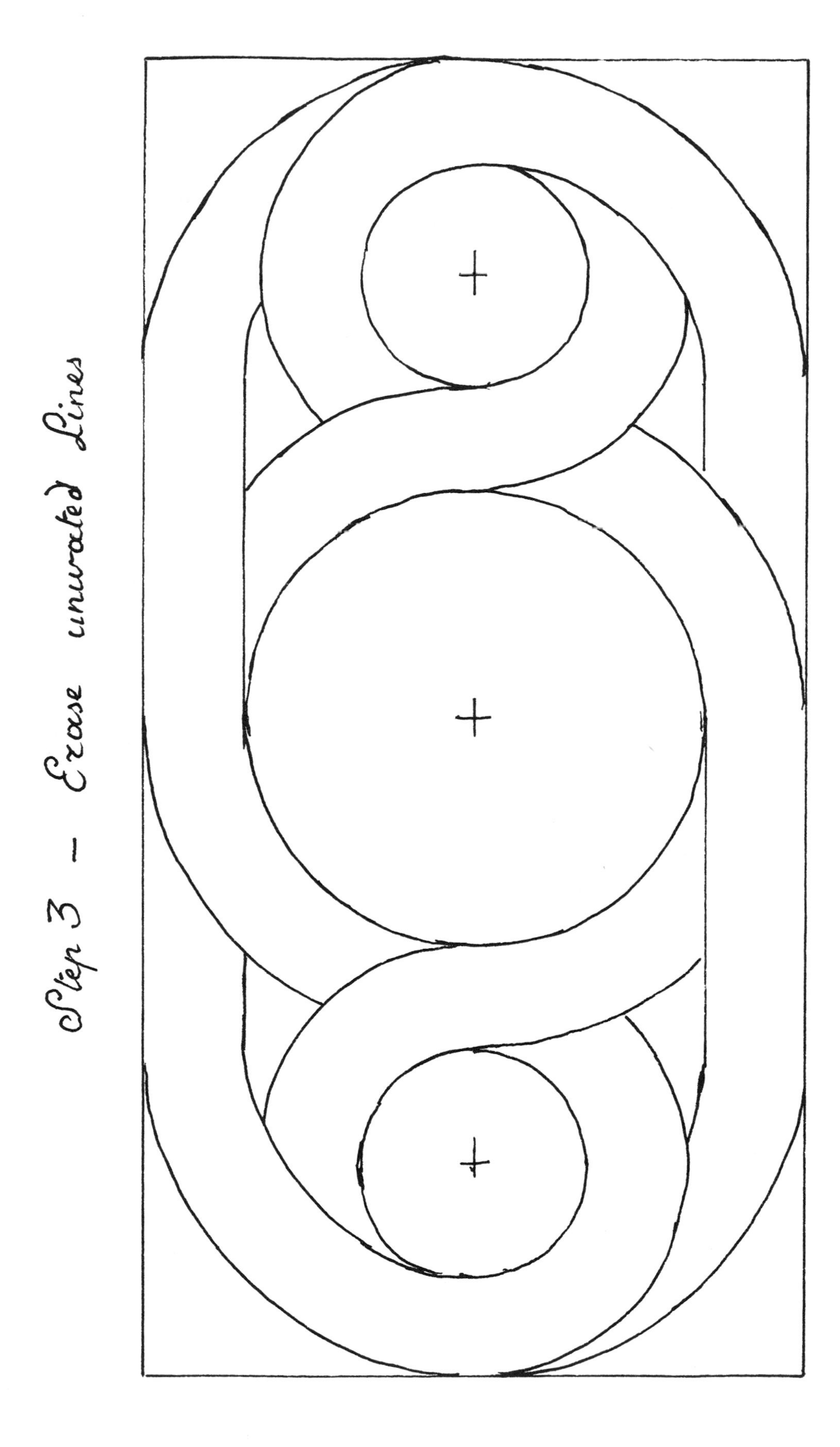
Step 3 – Erase unwanted Lines

Plate 65

Step 4 - Groove out Twinings

The Arrows indicate the Direction of cutting on each Side of Center Cut

Plate 66

Twinings Suggestions

Plate 67

Plate 68

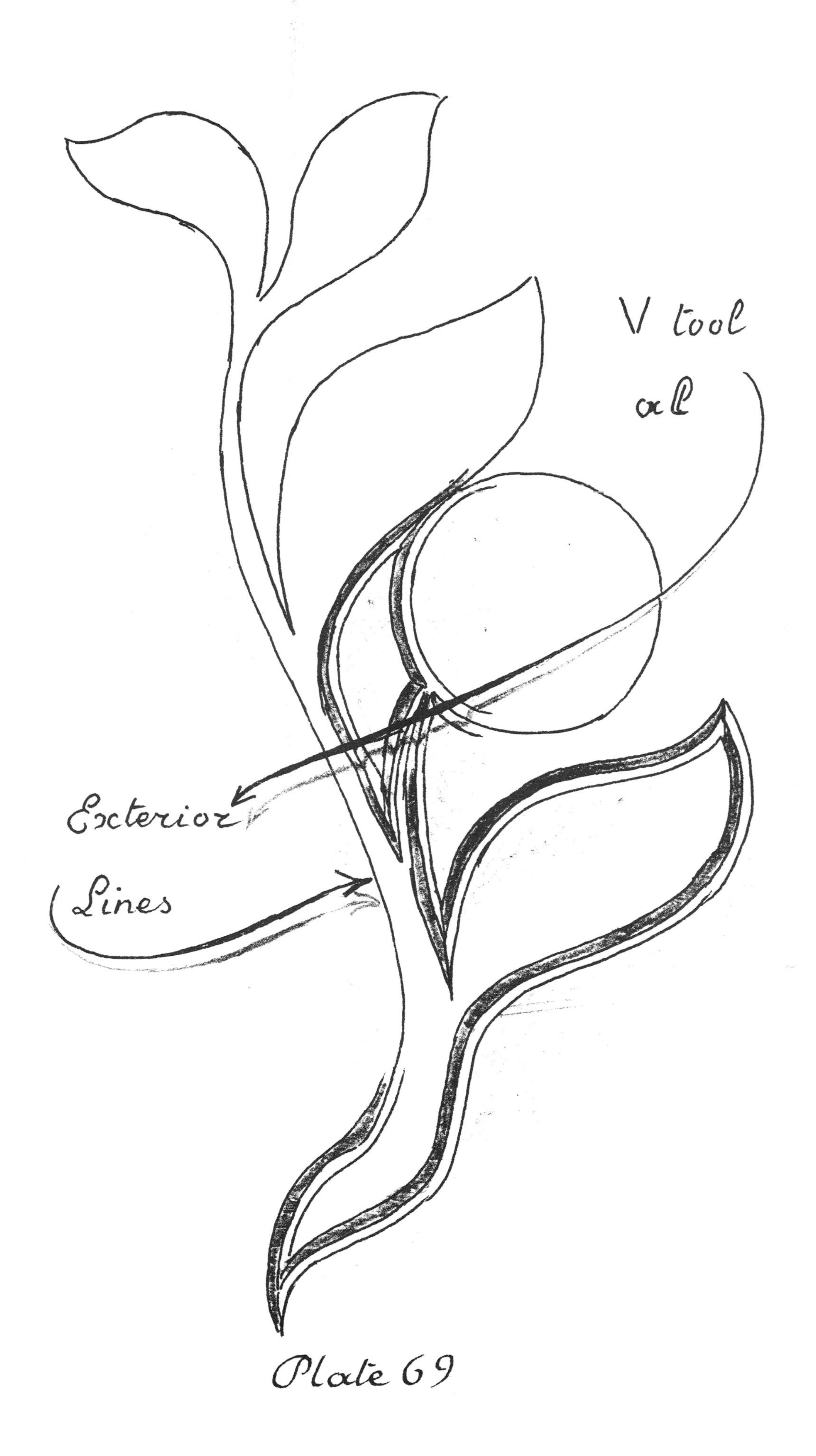
V tool
all
Exterior
Lines

Plate 69

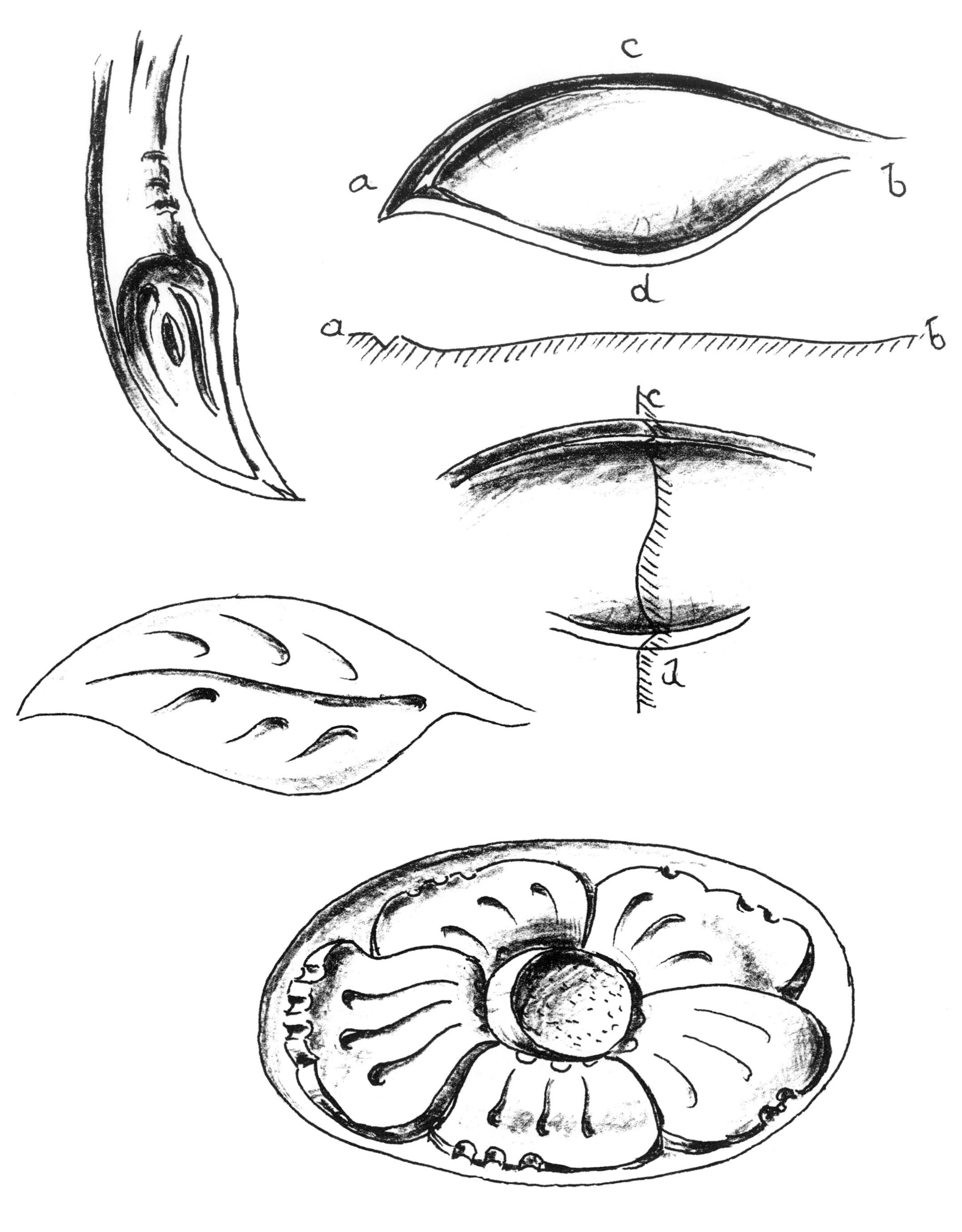

Plate 70

Plate 71

Plate 72

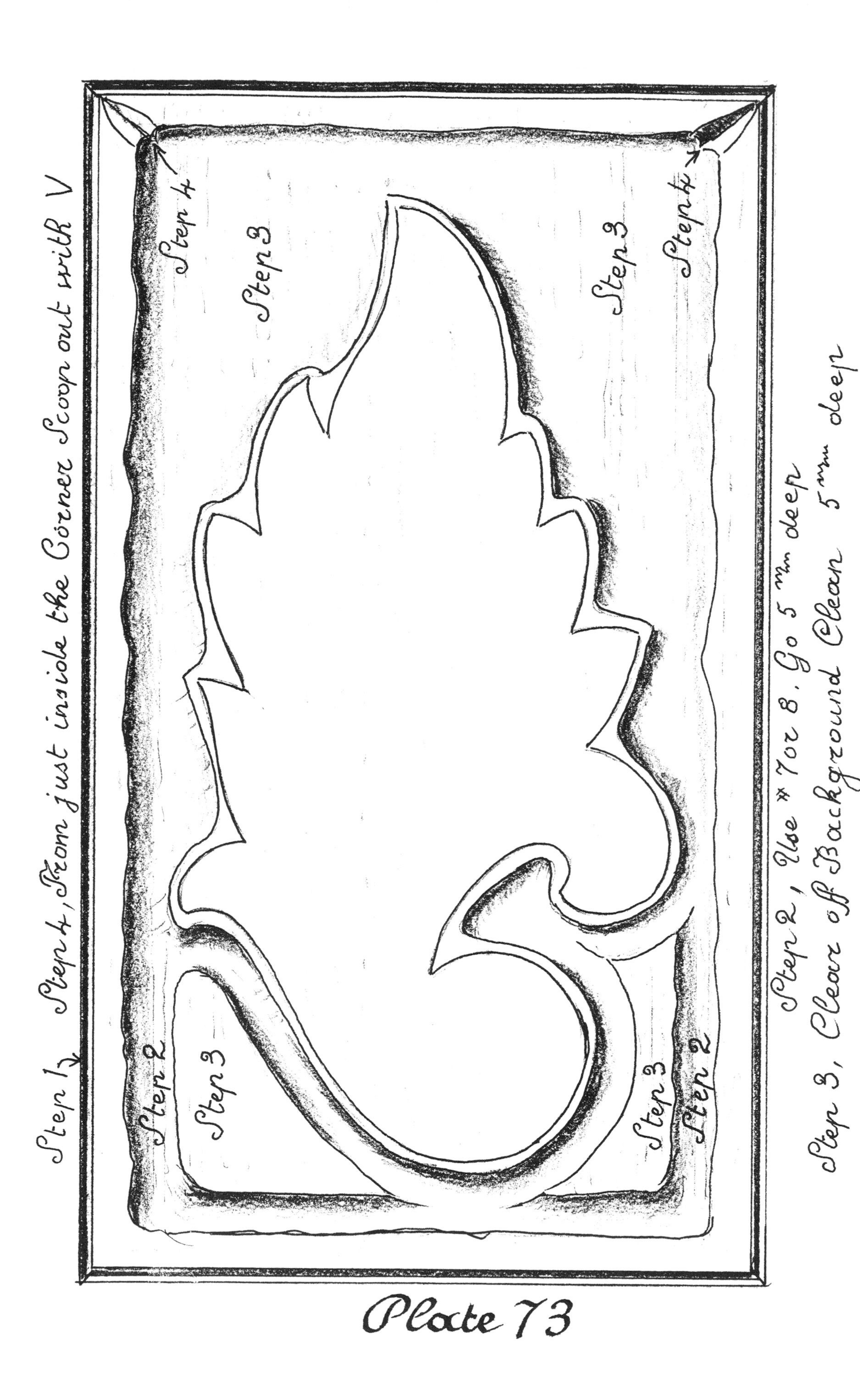

Step 1
Step 4, From just inside the Corner Scoop out with V
Step 4
Step 3
Step 3
Step 4
Step 2
Step 3
Step 3
Step 2
Step 2, Use # 7 or 8, Go 5 mm deep
Step 3, Clear off Background Clean 5 mm deep

Plate 73

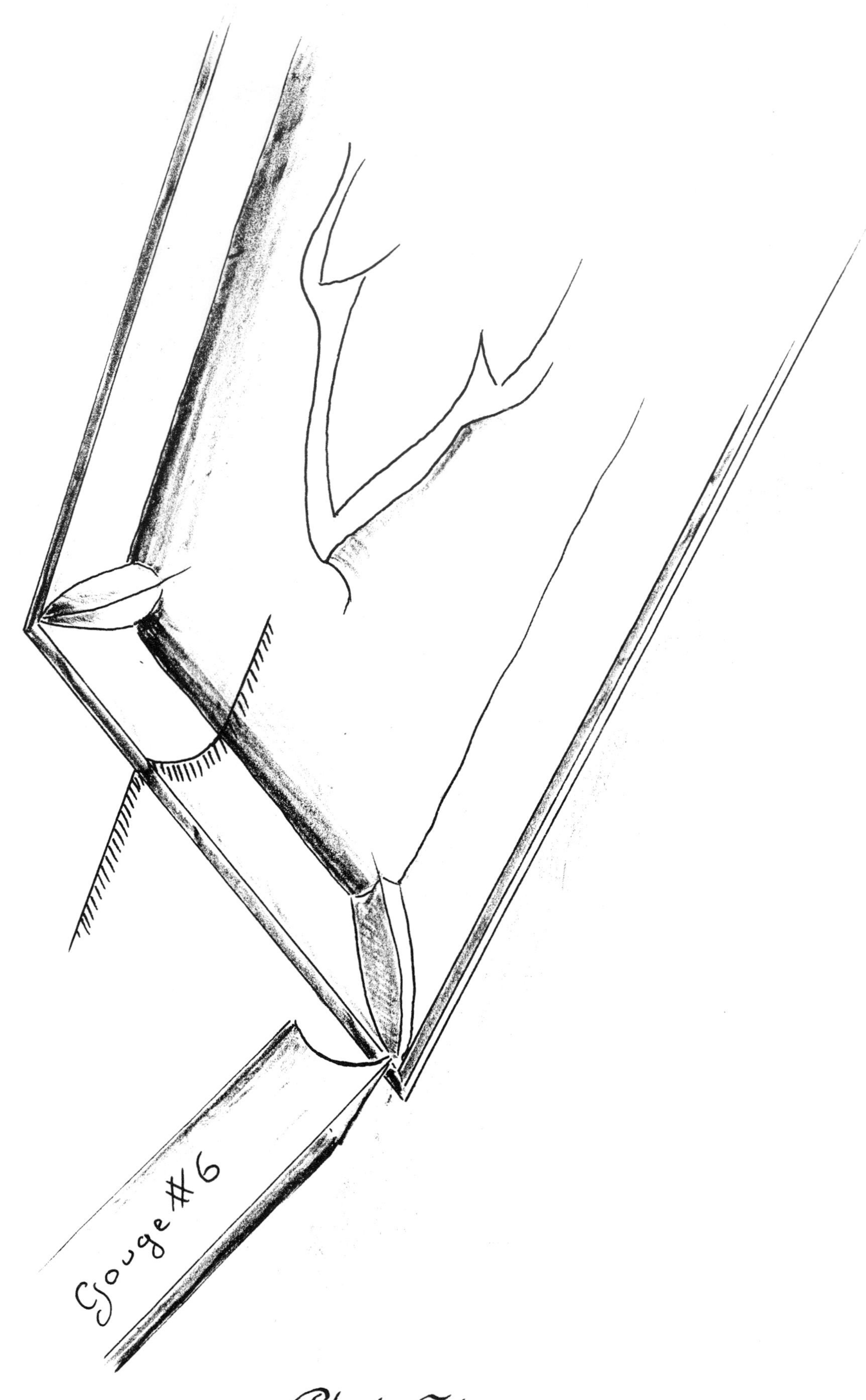

Plate 74

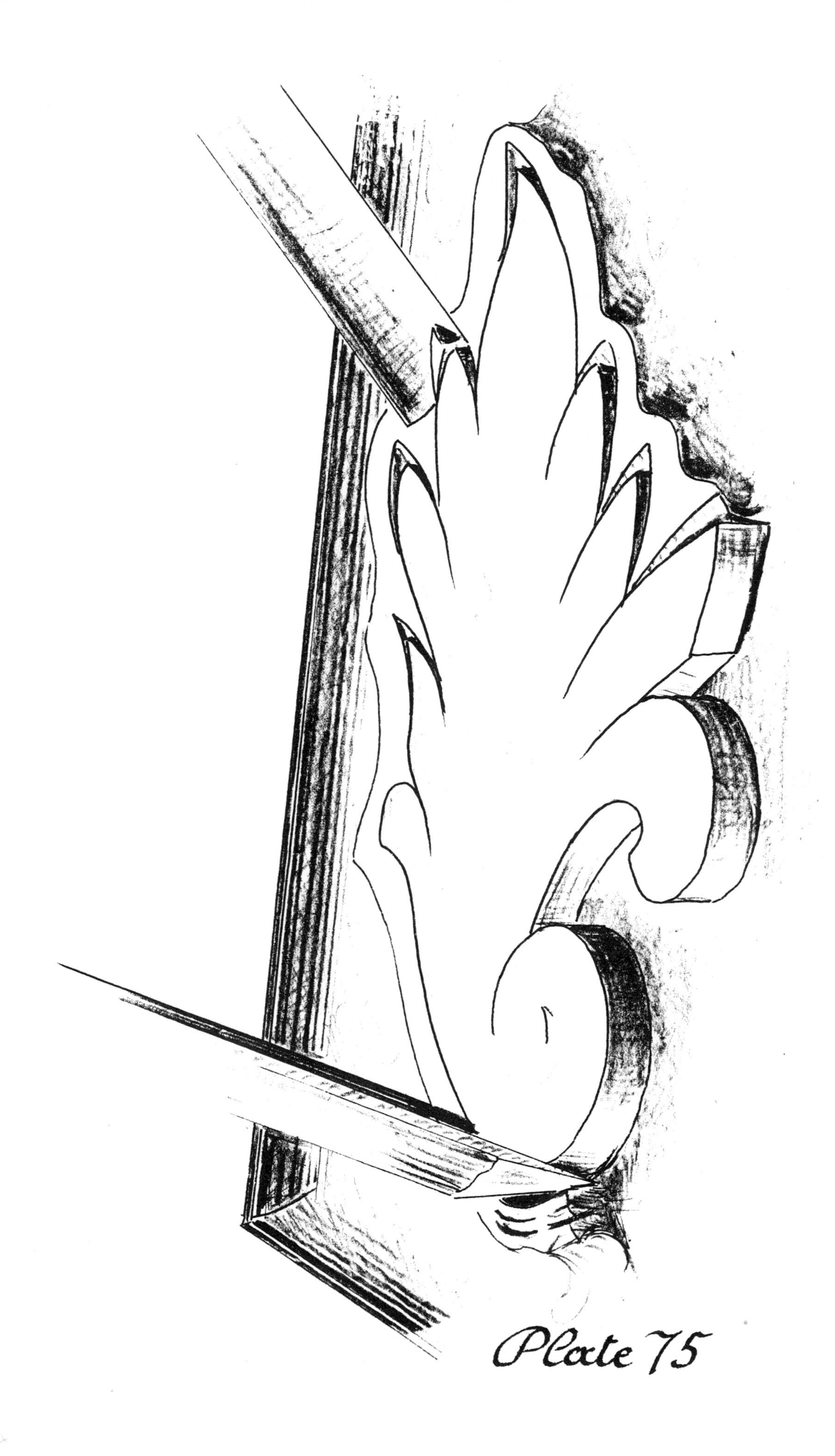

Plate 75

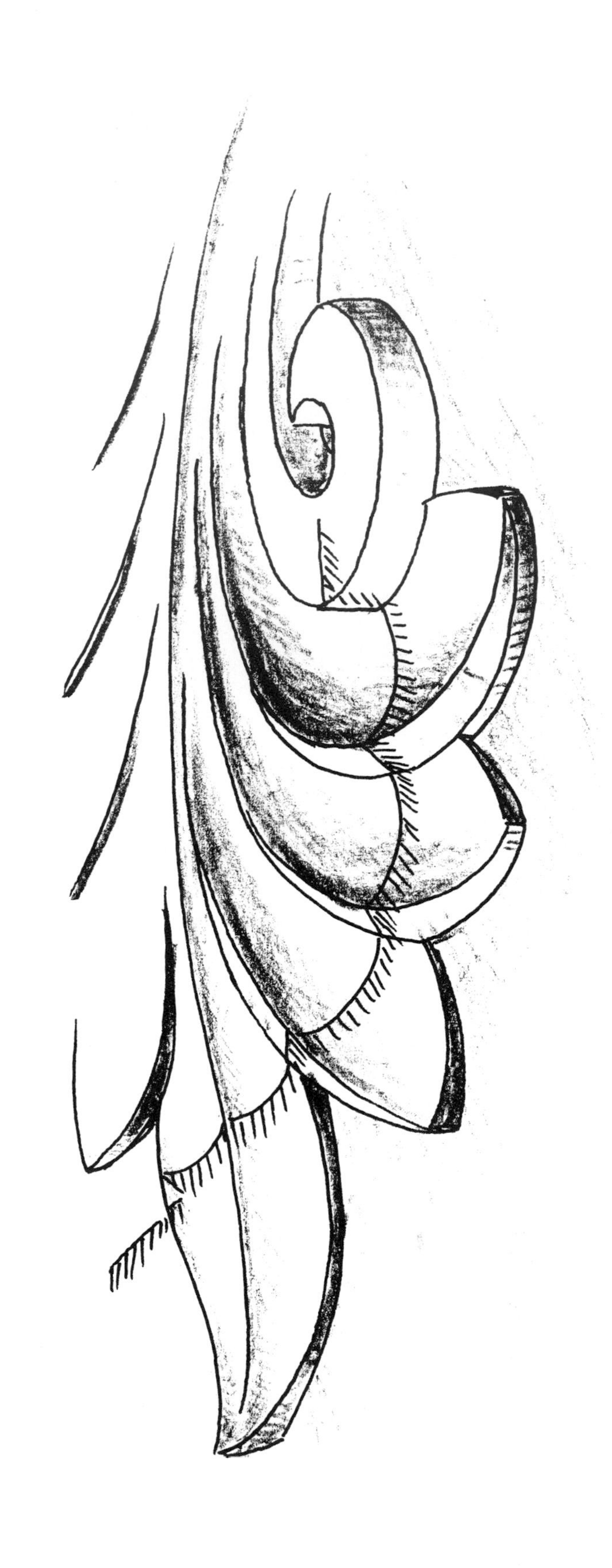

Plate 76

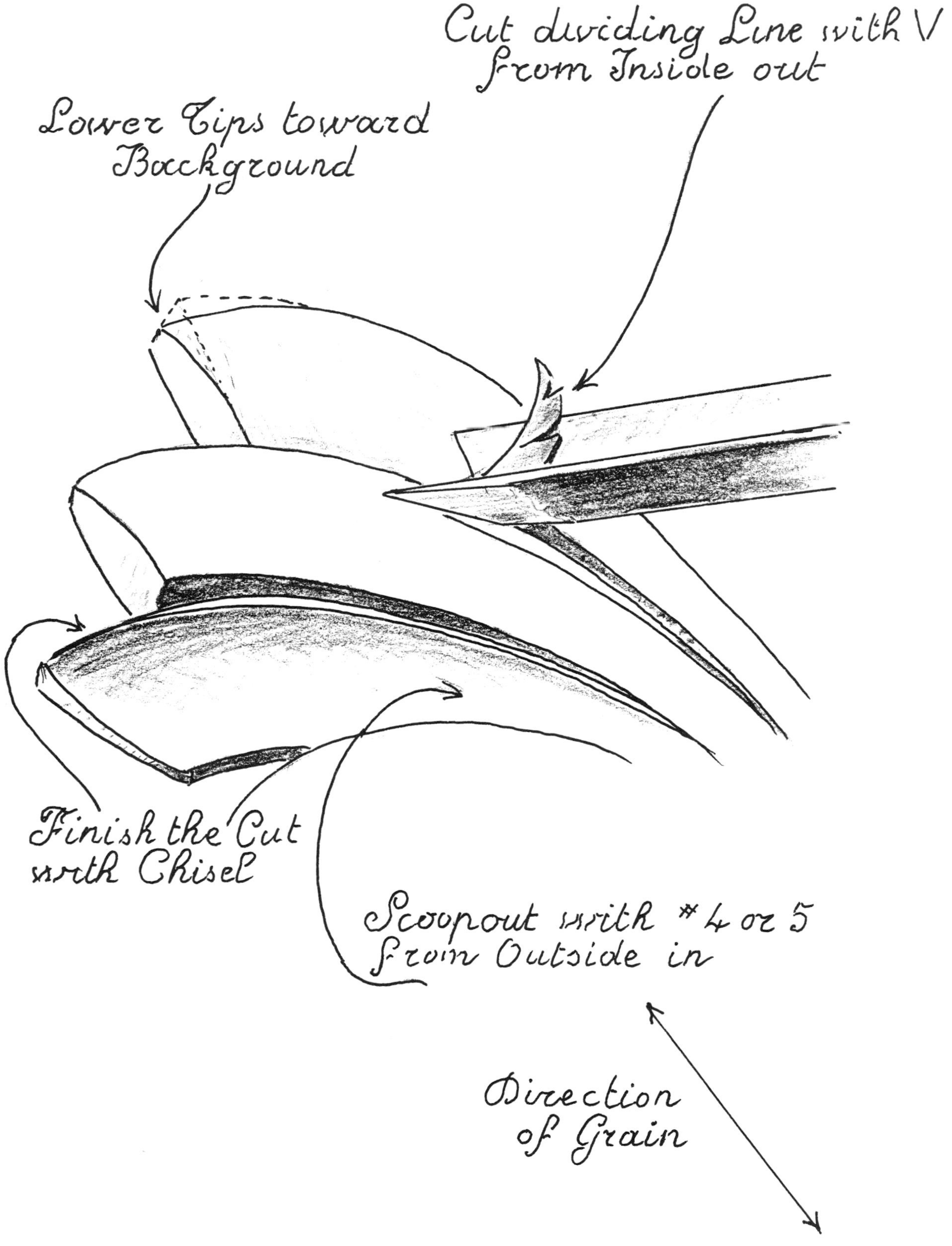

Cut dividing Line with V
from Inside out

Lower Tips toward
Background

Finish the Cut
with Chisel

Scoopout with #4 or 5
from Outside in

Direction
of Grain

Plate 77

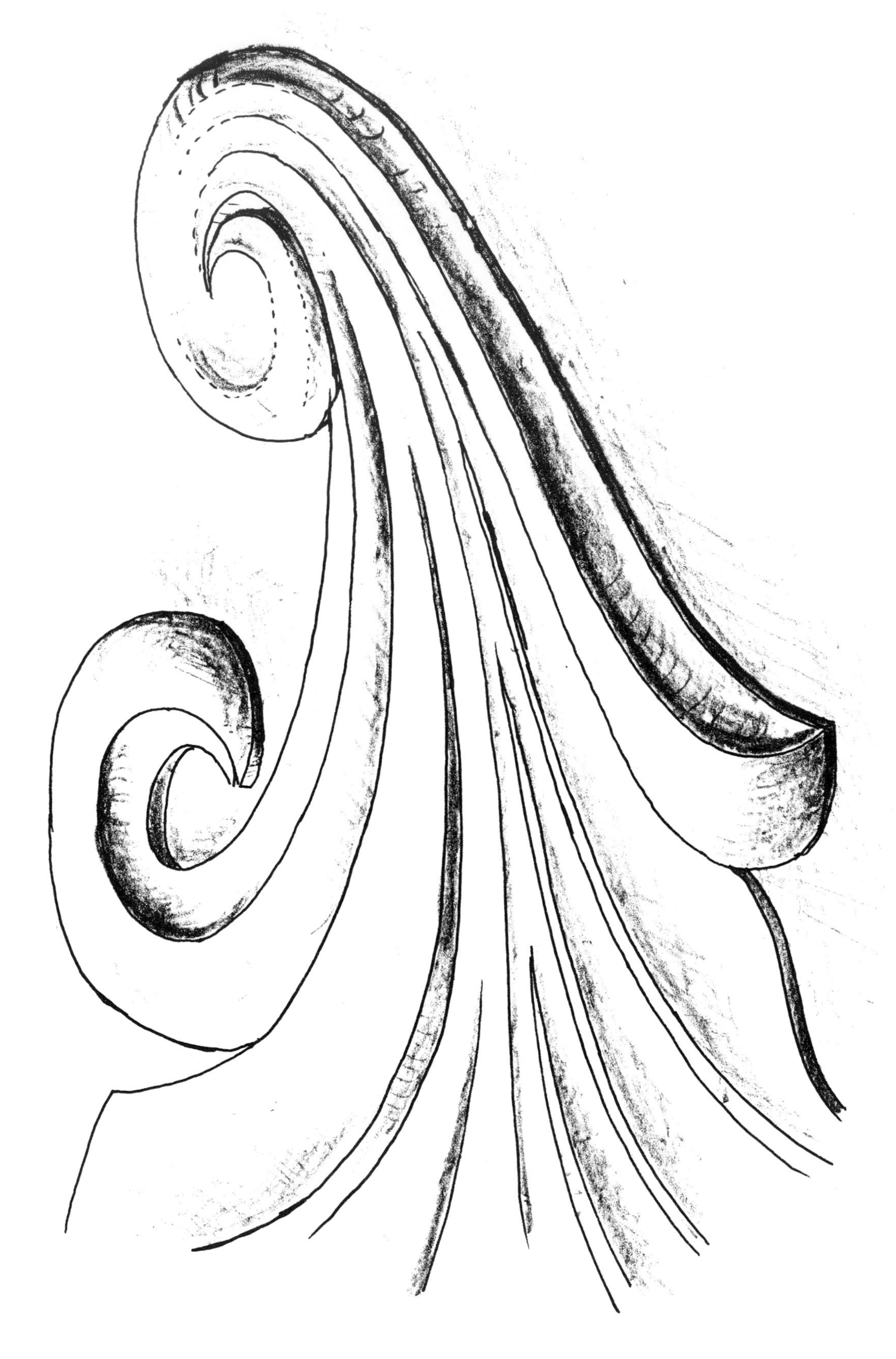

Plate 78

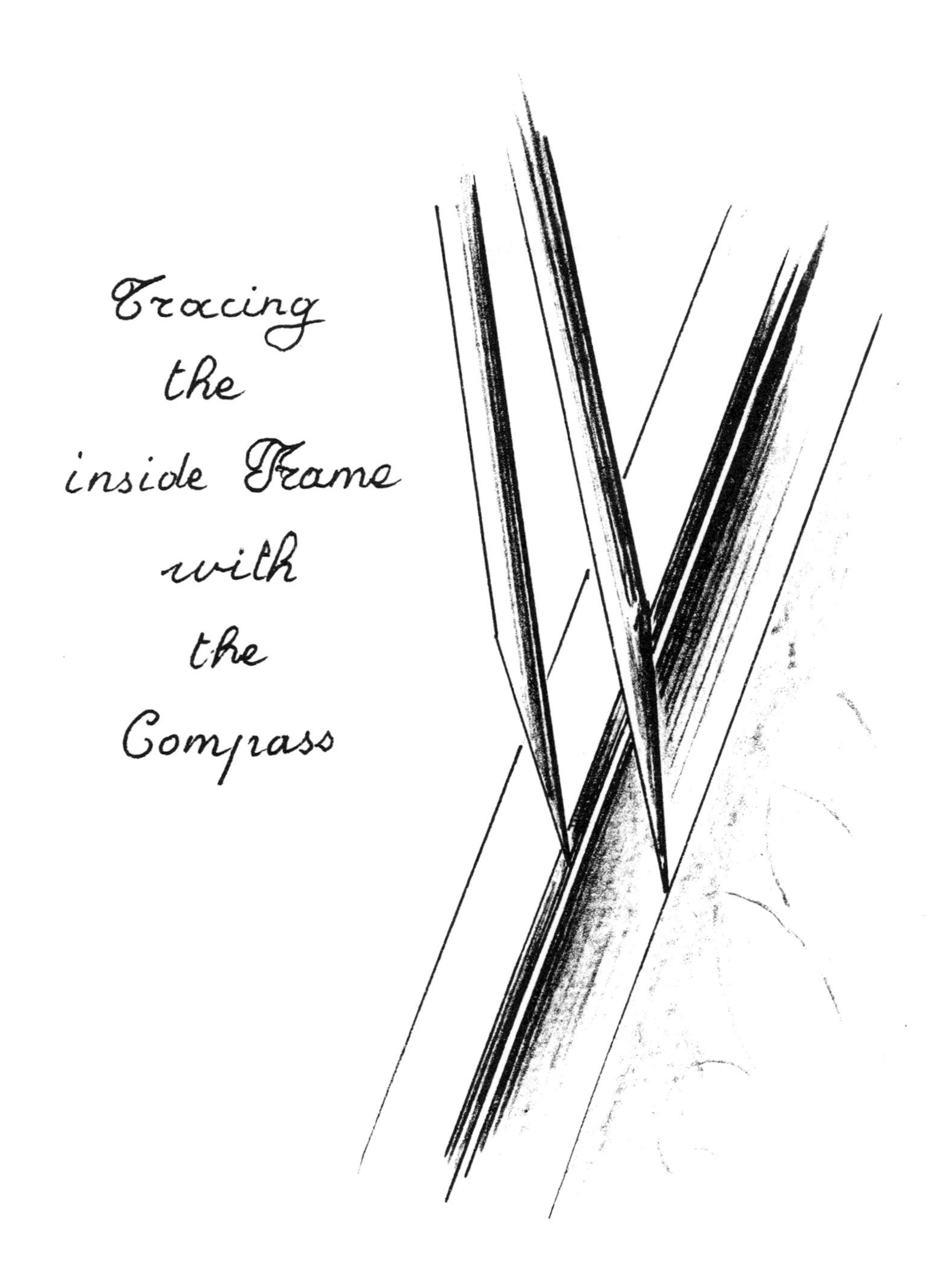

Plate 79

Suggestions

Plate 80

Plate 81

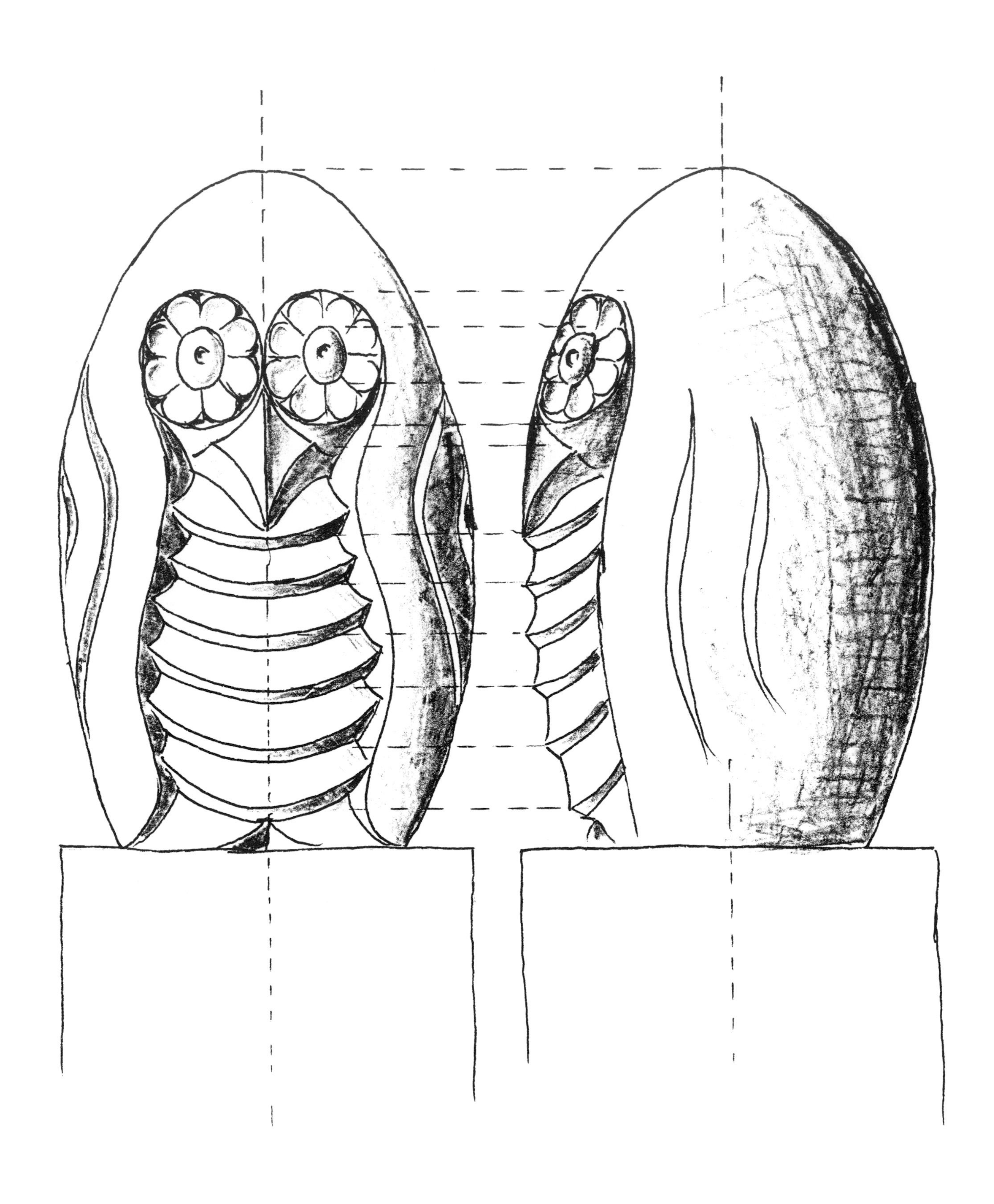

Plate 82

Part IV

A Few Pointers on Special Carving Techniques, Project Suggestions, and the Finishing Touch

Each exercise in Part III presented basic techniques of woodcarving. These methods should enable you to plan your own projects and to solve most common problems you are likely to encounter. Much is left to discover, however, and Part IV explores a few other aspects of this fascinating craft.

SPECIAL CARVING TECHNIQUES

Now that you have learned the carving basics, you might wish to become familiar with some special methods that will broaden your repertoire of carving skills.

Multiple Levels of Carving

When doing panel work, the relative depths are defined as follows:

Bas-relief (low relief, or surface carving) is a very shallow work that stays part of the surface (Plates 68 through 71).

Demi-relief (mid relief) denotes a work that looks as if it were superimposed on the background (Plates 72, 73, 92, and 123).

Haut-relief (high relief) is a very deep work that seems almost separated from the background. It may even be somewhat undercut to heighten the effect.

Rondebosse (carved in the round) indicates a form free of any background, such as statuary.

In deep carving, the following suggestions may prove helpful. First, establish a drawing of the whole on paper. This should be kept as a reference until the job is finished. Although the drawing can be transferred in its entirety onto the wood, it will soon become evident that portions of the tracing will vanish as cutting progresses. Thus, if you have templates of those vanishing parts on hand you can easily retrace them as needed later. Plate 85 illustrates this process. The templates are made of stiff material, such as tagboard, which permit accurate tracing of contours.

Appliqué, or Applied Carving

The points illustrated here have to do with the peculiar modes of holding pieces to be carved that cannot be held fast in the usual ways. (See Plate 86.) Often the design contour is first cut out, and the piece is then glued or nailed on to a larger board that can be clamped easily to the bench.

When you are using the gluing method, a not too thin piece of paper is put between the board and the carving. When you are finished, the job is separated from the board with the help of a chisel, and the back is cleaned up by scraping or sanding (Plate 87).

If nails are used, great care must be taken to ensure that the carving tools do not come into contact with the metal, and that the wedged nails enter the wood across the grain, to avoid splitting the wood (Plate 88).

Cutout, or Pierced Carving

Details are found in Plates 89 through 91. See also Photograph 2.

The Tudor Special

Details are found in Plates 92 and 93.

Ribbons and Bows

Details are found in Plate 94.

Of Scales and Feathers

Details are found in Plates 95 and 96. See also Photograph 3.

Gothic Tracery

The Gothic style originated in the twelfth century in the heart of France. There, in the abbey of Saint Denis outside of Paris, can be seen the first truly Gothic architecture. Known originally as French art, it owes nothing to the gothic invasions which put an end to the Roman world. Instead, to the men of the Renaissance period, enamoured of the culture of Greece and Rome, the term *gothic* signified that which was old, barbarous, and uncivilized. Lacking a better name, the appellation has persisted (Plates 97-99).

If you look carefully at the panel proposed as an exercise, you will notice two modes of treating the cusps. The left half illustrates the authentic *turning Gothic* form. The right shows the simplified, *flat Gothic*, which is easier to cut. Only the initiated will detect the difference.

Plates 99, 101, and 102 illustrate the treatment of the two modes. Plate 100 shows the tracing of the panel. For the step-by-step demonstration of Plate 103, the flat Gothic is used, with the exception of Step 11. For background finishing in the Gothic style, stippling is generally used. See Photograph 4.

The Fold

Details are found in Plates 104 through 107. See also Photograph 5.

The Grille System

Details are found in Plate 108. See also Photograph 6.

PROJECT SUGGESTIONS

You can use the following projects to further enhance your carving skills. Please remember that the carving patterns in Plates 109 through 122 and Photographs 7 through 10 are just suggestions. You are strongly encouraged to devise your own

Providing a base helps in holding

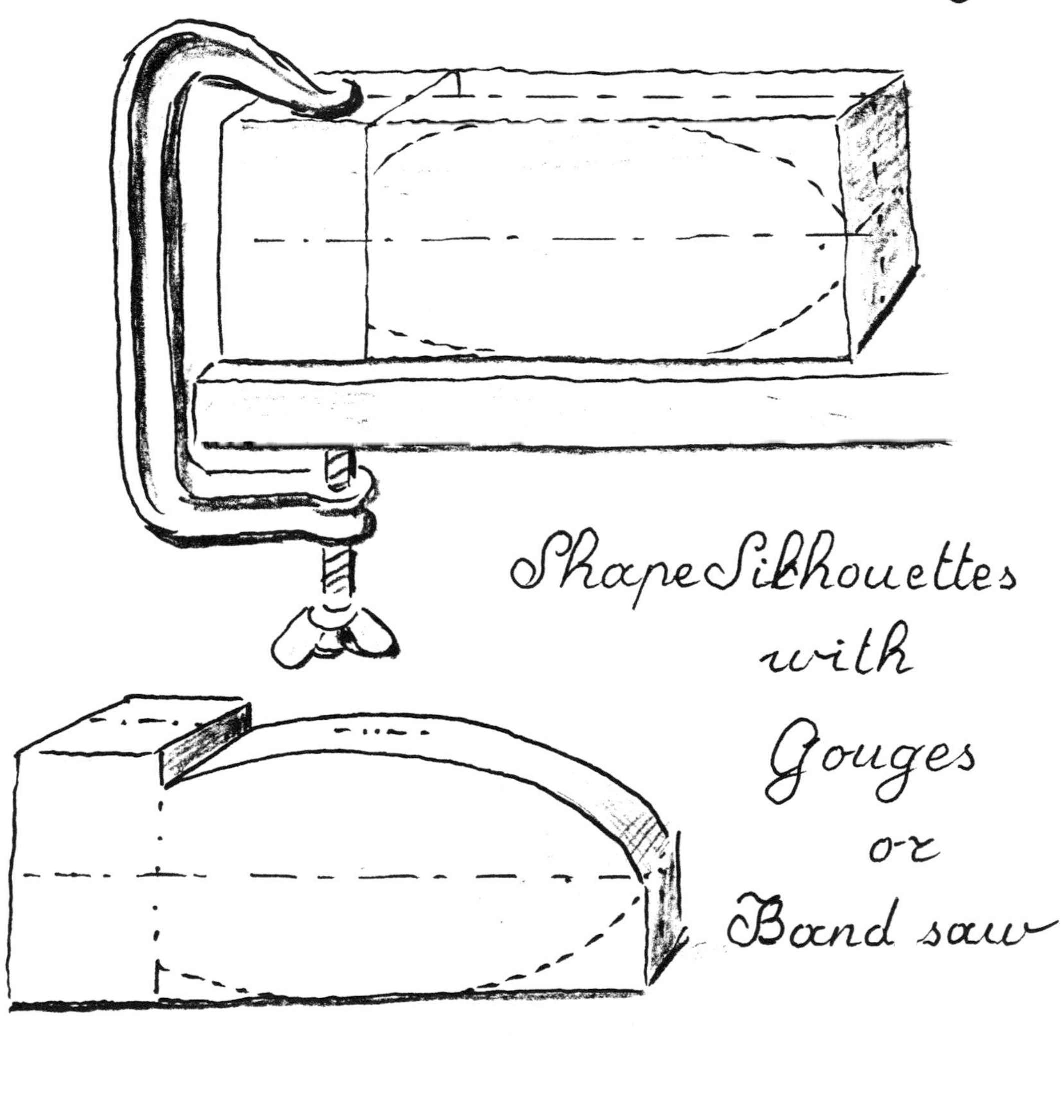

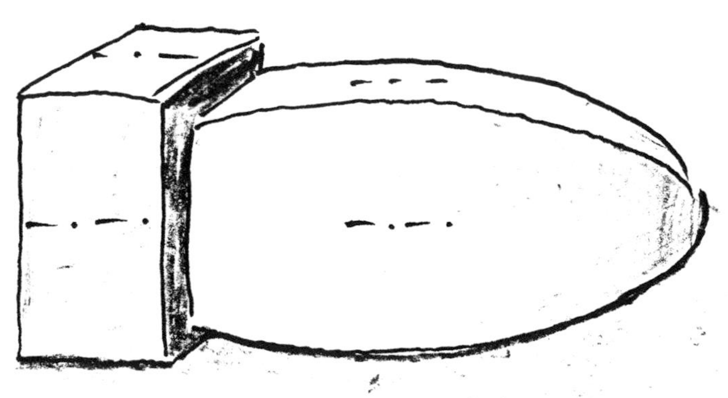

Plate 83

designs rather than follow those in the following pages. Copying is useful only to a point. If you have completed the preceding series of exercises, you have ample skill in carving to enable you to trust your own creative instincts.

THE FINISHING TOUCH

Once you have completed your carving, there are several finishing options open to you. You can leave the wood as is, sand it, or apply a protective coating of some type. Which method you select will depend on your own preference. This is also the time to attend to repairs in sections of a work which have been damaged during carving, although often repairs must be undertaken in the course of carving. See Plate 123.

Sanding

There is no hard and fast rule to follow when deciding whether or not to sand. Only the carver's good judgment and taste can give the answer. Tool marks often offer an attractive texture, especially on bland, uninteresting surfaces. On the other hand, when strong patterns of grain and color contrasts are present, the slick finish made possible by sanding may enhance the natural beauty of the material. Whatever the reason for sanding, however, there are strict rules to follow when using sandpaper.

- ☐ For the tools' protection, sanding must be done only after all cutting is finished.
- ☐ The sandpaper must be handled with the greatest care and discretion to preserve the sharp and crisp qualities of hand carving.
- ☐ Much damage can be done by using too coarse a paper, but too fine a grit will have no appreciable effect on raw wood. For the softer woods, use a #80 paper for rough sanding, and #100 for finishing. For harder woods #80 to #100 papers are best for rough sanding, and #150 for finishing work.
- ☐ When the work is finished, it must be thoroughly dusted using a clean brush with long, soft bristles. Sheets of sandpaper can be recut into sections of 2 3/4 × 4 1/4 inches. When folded in three, these make convenient pads for surface work. The three fold will also prolong the life of the sandpaper. When you wrap paper around your finger to reach inside concave cuts, however, use one layer of paper.

Coloring and Protective Coatings

Once a carving is completed, you may wish to apply a colored or clear protective coating. I have outlined the characteristics of the most common types of finishes in Tables I and II. Wax is probably the most practical type of clear finish to work with. It can also be applied over a painted surface to provide additional protection. Regardless of which finishing method you select, finishing work is best done in an airy room free of flying dust. Cleaning your brushes will be easier if you do not allow paints and varnishes to set.

Varnishes, oil paints and stains suspended in mineral spirits after brush cleaning will solidify in a few days. The clean liquid then can be transferred gently to a clean container and reused.

All varnishes come in gloss or satin finish and may be slightly colored. Ordinary varnishes tend to foam and leave air bubbles when dry. They are all oil based and clean as oil paints.

Rough out round Shapes with gouges, then finish with Rasp and File.
Trace Details and cut out

Plate 84

Table I. Coloring Agents: Paints and Stains

Paints	Solvent	Drying Time	Remarks
Poster paint	water	2 hrs.	Use brush; keep moist; clean in water.
Acrylic	water	fast	Keep brush moist; clean without delay.
Oil	mineral spirits	slow	Brush or spray; clean in thinner first, then in tepid, soapy water.
Urethane	mineral spirits	4 hrs.	Same as oil; gives a very slick finish.
Lacquers	lacquer thinner	fast	Brush or spray; clean in lacquer thinner.
Stains			
Water	water	2 hrs.	Little used; will raise the grain.
Alcohol	alcohol	instantly	Little used; many brilliant colors available; tricky to spread evenly; clean in denatured alcohol.
Oil	mineral spirits	slow	Most popular; clean as with oil paints.

Antiquing and Special Effects

Antiquing and special effects are used to bring out the highlights on stained light wood. First lightly sand the protruding parts with fine sandpaper. Then dust the work and apply the protective coating.

To accentuate outlines and shady spots, seal the wood with varnish or white shellac. Apply a darker stain all over and allow it to become tacky. Then use a soft, clean rag to wipe off the stain from the protruding parts. Leave the remaining color to dry and seal it in with varnish or wax.

Some antiquing toners can be brushed on a finished work and will not rub off after drying.

TIPS ON MINOR REPAIR WORK

In the course of carving, accidents happen. You should always have a simple equipment kit on hand to make quick and clean repairs. The kit should contain the following supplies:

Wood glue and a 1/2-inch glue brush.

2 small sticks, about 6 inches × 3/16 inch × 3/16 inch, one with a long sharp point, the other with a long, sharp, bevelled end.

Water, to clean glue from tools before it sets.

Waxed paper, to prevent glue from sticking where you do not want it to be.

Small metal weights, lead if possible.

A number of small, light, metal or wood clamps. Clothespins are a great help, too, as are rubber bands.

Effective placing of pressure weights, clamps, or rubber bands may tax the ingenuity of the carver. In difficult cases, it is good practice to run a dry test before you apply the glue. Then, once the glue has been applied, you should not resume carving on the damaged spot until everything is dry and solid. When a small crack appears, use the small sticks to introduce a bit of glue to repair it.

If a chip is broken away, it should be retrieved and glued exactly in its position. If lost, make a replacement piece of the same kind of wood, taking into ac-

Plate 85

Table II. Protective Coatings: Oils, Waxes, Lacquers, and Varnishes

	Drying Time	Remarks
Oils		
Boiled linseed oil	Slow	To soak outdoor work before applying spar varnish. Apply with brush, washed thoroughly in paint thinner after use.
Crushed nut and vegetable oils	Slow	Rubbed on wood to soak in oil. Used mostly on bowls and dishes. May get rancid in time.
Tung oil	Slow	Very toxic. Gives beautiful, thin finish.
Waxes		
Floor and bees' wax	Slow	Applied with rag wad. In paste form. Easily applied with brush or clean wad. Easy to repair. Pleasant satin finish. Will sink in raw wood. May require a few coats for best finish.
White shellac	Very fast	Used as sealer to speed up waxing process. Clean brush in denatured alcohol.
Lacquers and Varnishes		
Spar	Slow	For exterior work after linseed oil is dry. Two or three coatings may be required.
Urethane plastics	4 hrs.	Dries free of bubbles. Two or three coats are recommended.
Lacquers	Fast	Recommended for spray. Dries water-clear. Should not be used on oil-treated surfaces.

count the direction of the wood grain. First of all, however, smooth out the rough surfaces left by the accident. Then shape a new part to fit the excavation perfectly. For safety's sake, this part can be cut at the end of a larger piece and carefully separated when ready.

To remove a minor indentation caused by a shock (i.e. when the wood is not missing but simply pushed in) place a wet cotton pad on the injured spot and leave it a while to soak the wood. Then apply a hot iron. This creates steam which then raises the grain. Be very careful, however, to avoid burning the wood.

There are products available to fill in slits and crannies, or even to replace missing parts. Oil-based putties take a long time to set and dry. Plastic wood dries fast but does not take stains nicely. Water wood putty will dry fairly fast and is said to be suitable for carving, but when it dries it becomes brittle and somewhat crumbly and is no friend to the keen edge of tools. Finally, a paste made of slightly moistened, fine sawdust and water-based glue will serve nicely as a filler.

Bornons ici cette carrière,
Les longs ouvrages me font peur.
Loin d'èpuiser une matiere,
On n'en doit prendre que la fleur.

Jean de La Fontaine *FABLES*
Epilogue, Livre VI

Aplied Carvings

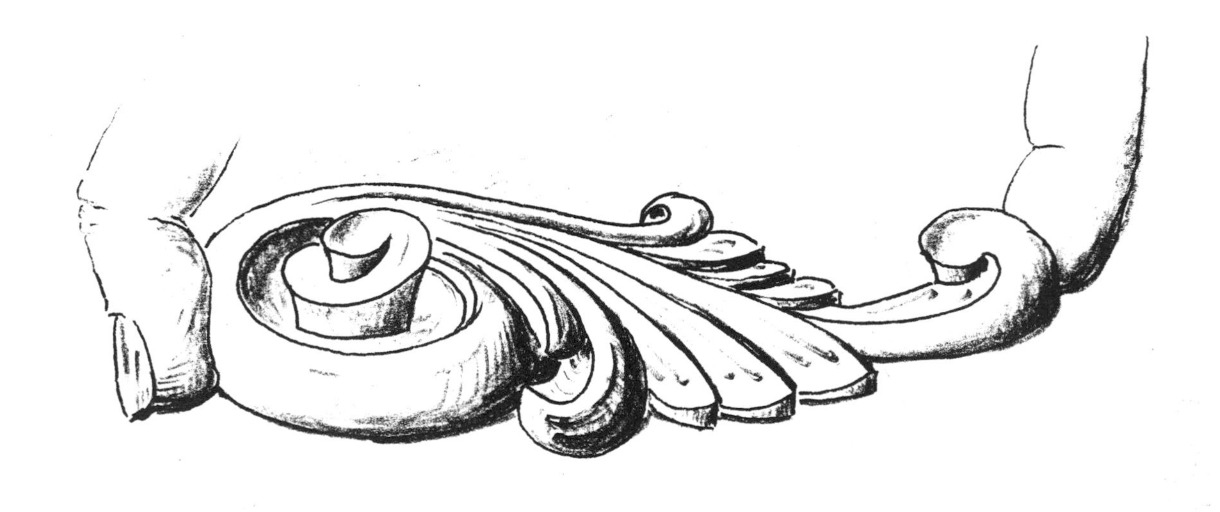

Plate 86

Glueing Method uses Paper

Lifting finished Carving with Chisel

Plate 87

Holding with Nails

Trace Outline ~ Locate Nails carefully

File Nails to cut Carving across Grain

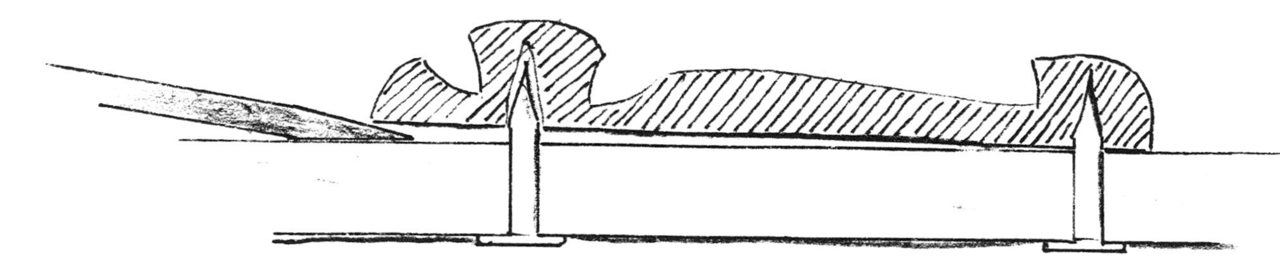

Plate 88

Plate 89

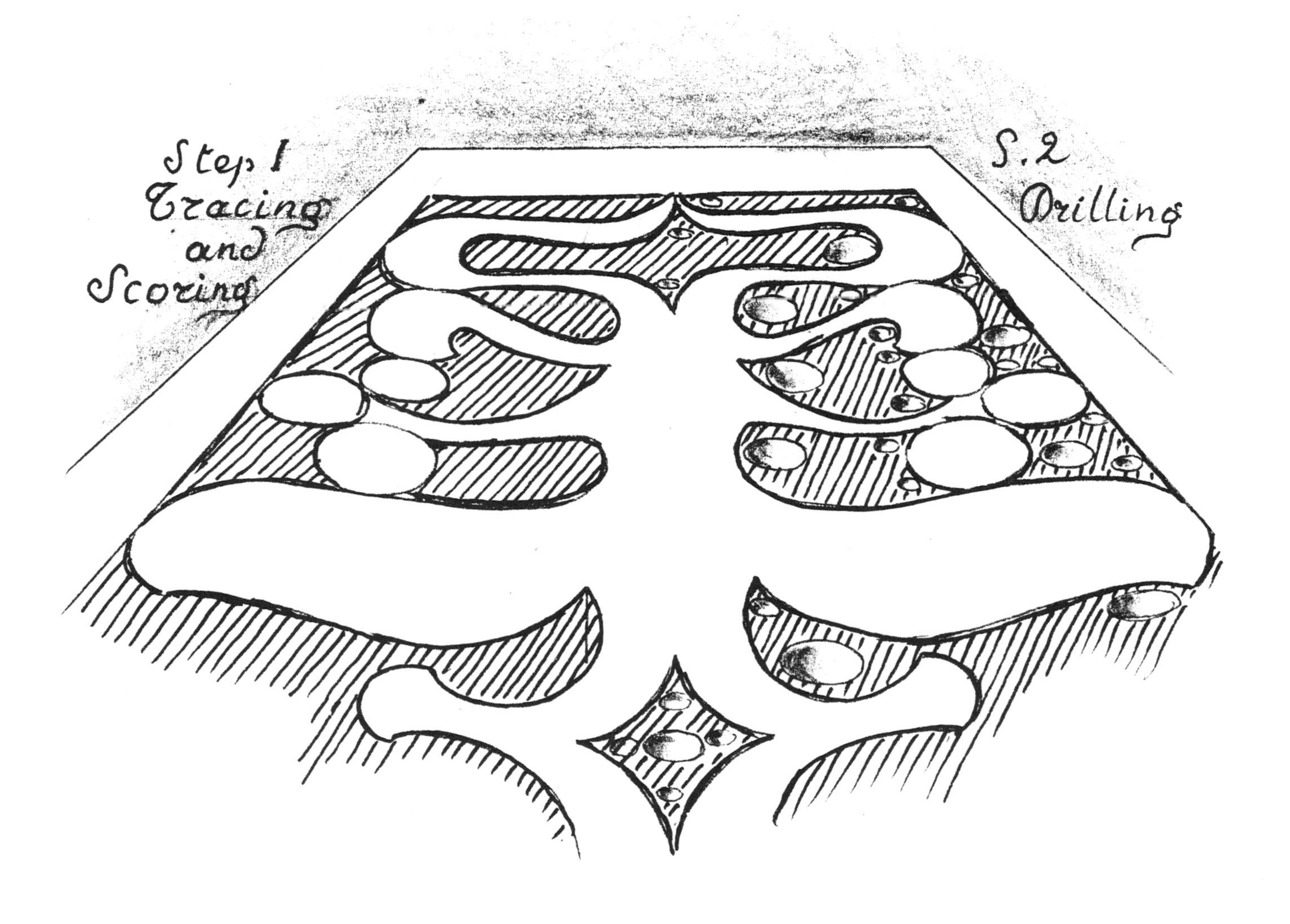
Step 1
Tracing
and
Scoring
S.2
Drilling

Plate 90

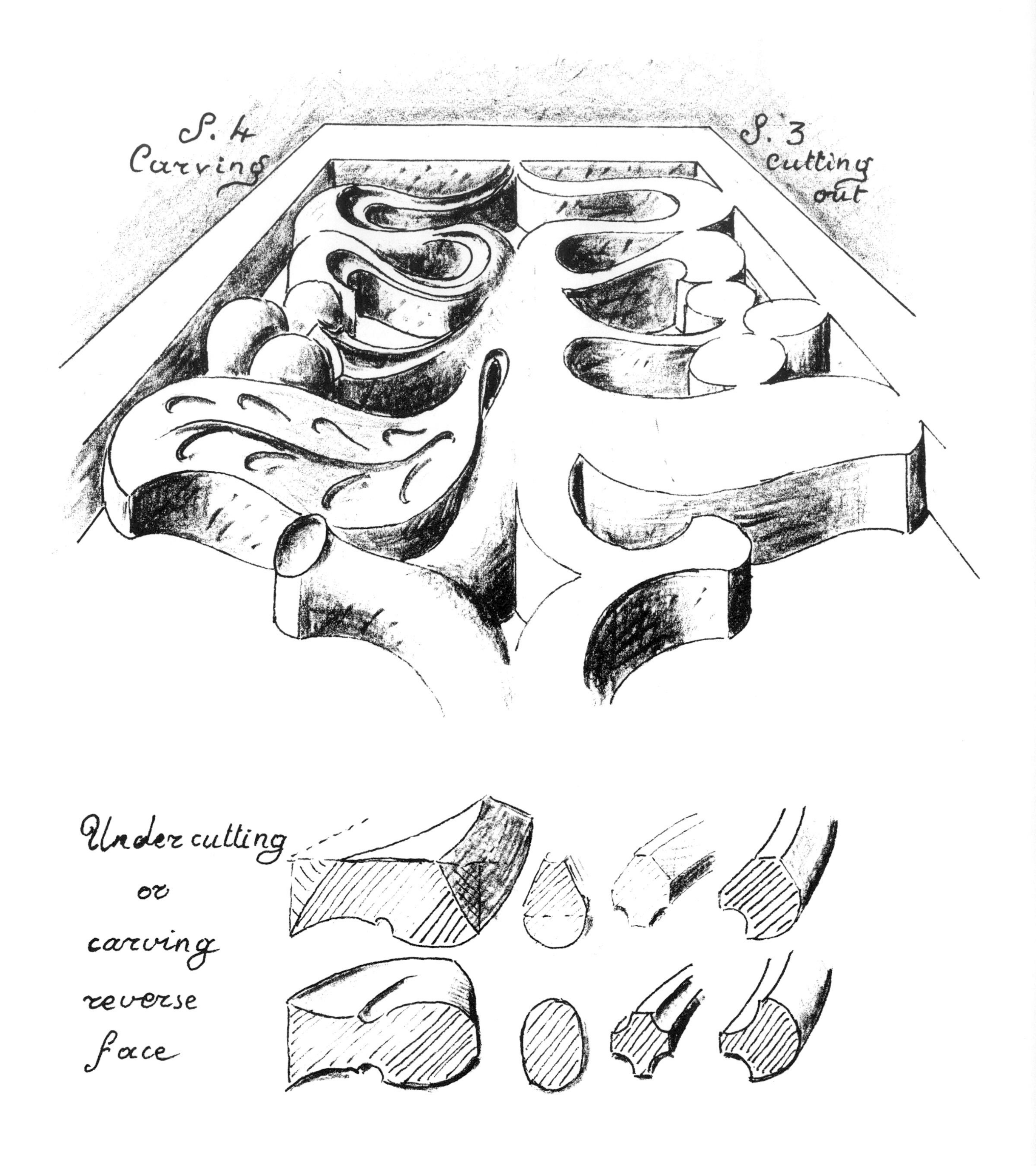
S. 4
Carving
S. 3
cutting
out
Undercutting
or
carving
reverse
face

Plate 91

Photograph 2

The Tudor Special

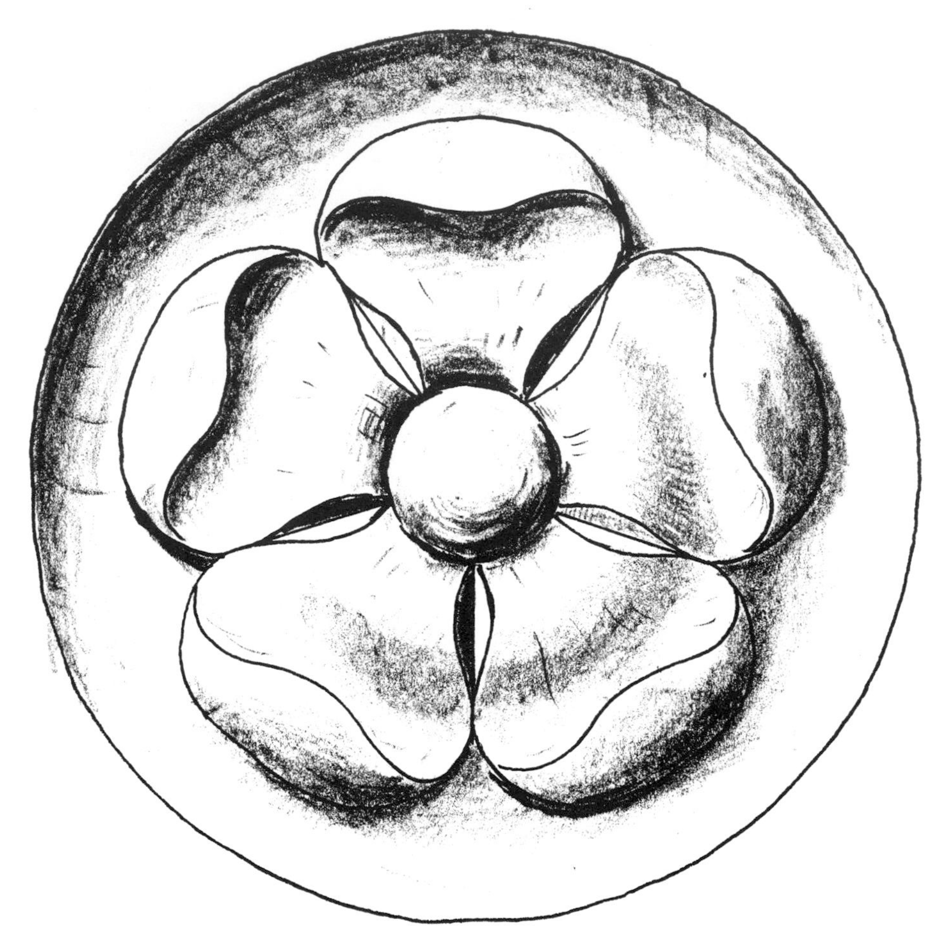

Working Profile

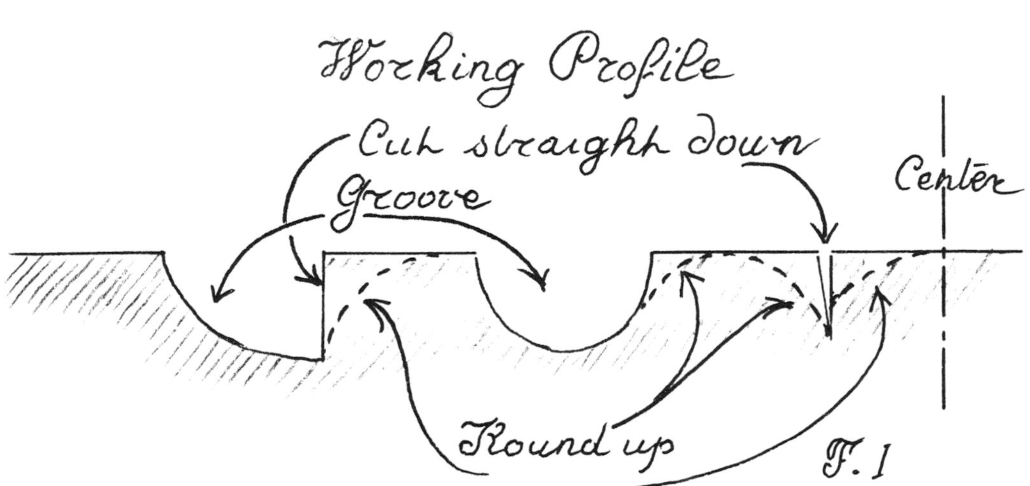

Plate 92

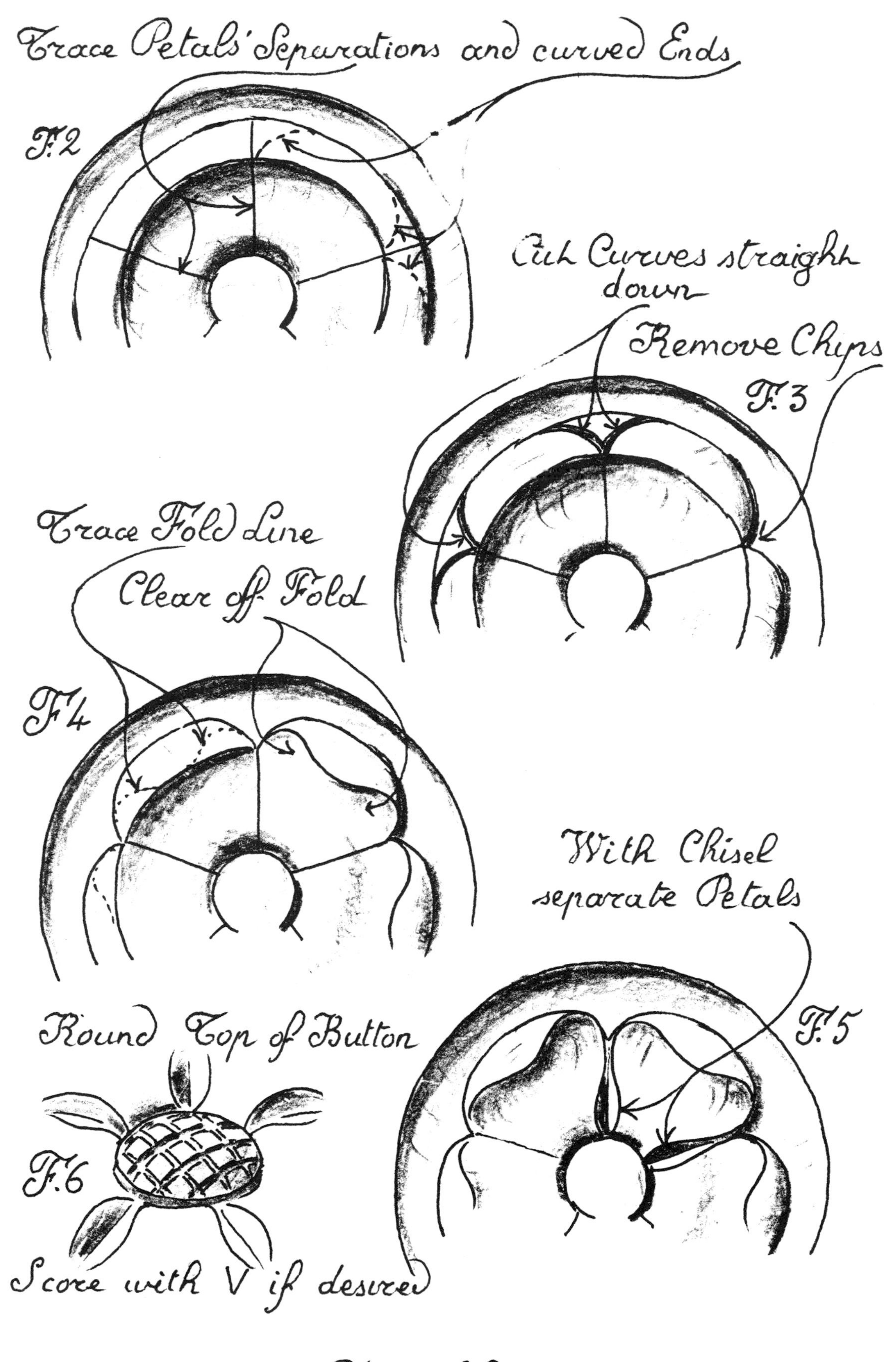
Trace Petals' Separations and curved Ends
F.2
Cut Curves straight down
Remove Chips
F.3
Trace Fold Line
Clear off Fold
F.4
With Chisel separate Petals
F.5
Round Top of Button
F.6
Score with V if desired

Plate 93

Plate 94

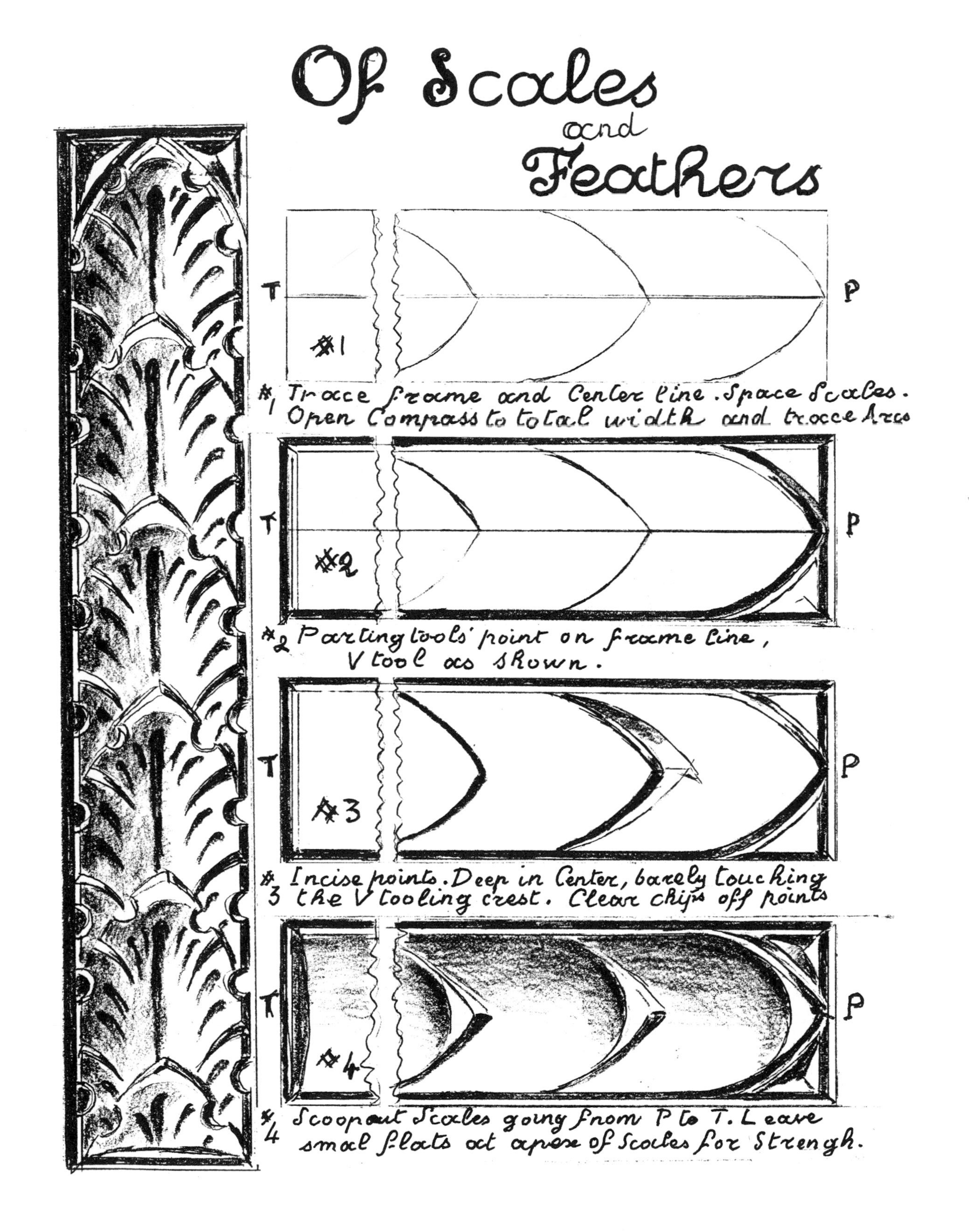
Of Scales and Feathers
T
P
#1
#1 Trace frame and Center line. Space Scales. Open Compass to total width and trace Arcs
#2
#2 Parting tools' point on frame line, V tool as shown.
#3
#3 Incise points. Deep in Center, barely touching the V tooling crest. Clear chips off points
#4
#4 Scoop out Scales going from P to T. Leave smal flats at apese of Scales for Strengh.

Plate 95

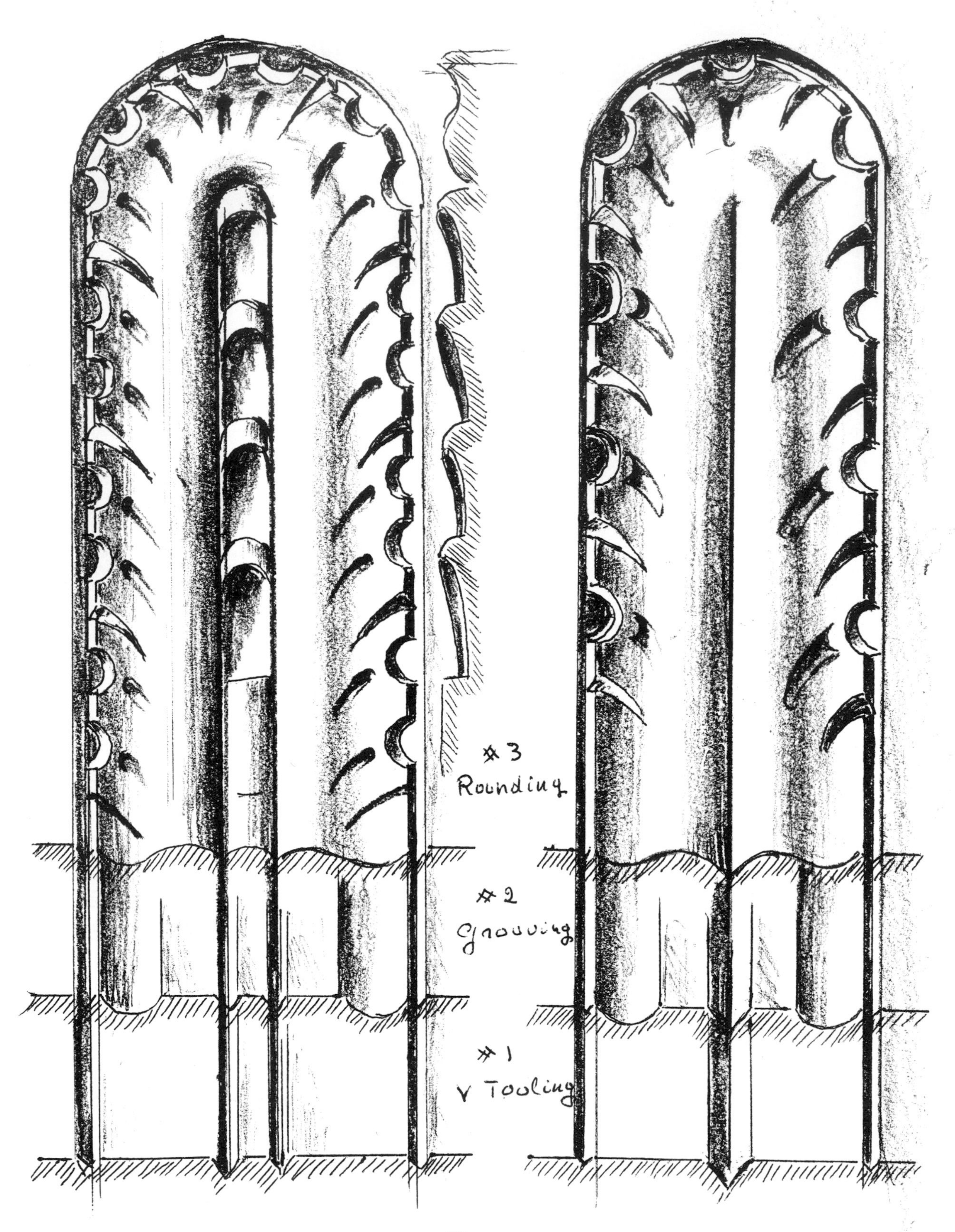

Plate 96

Photograph 3

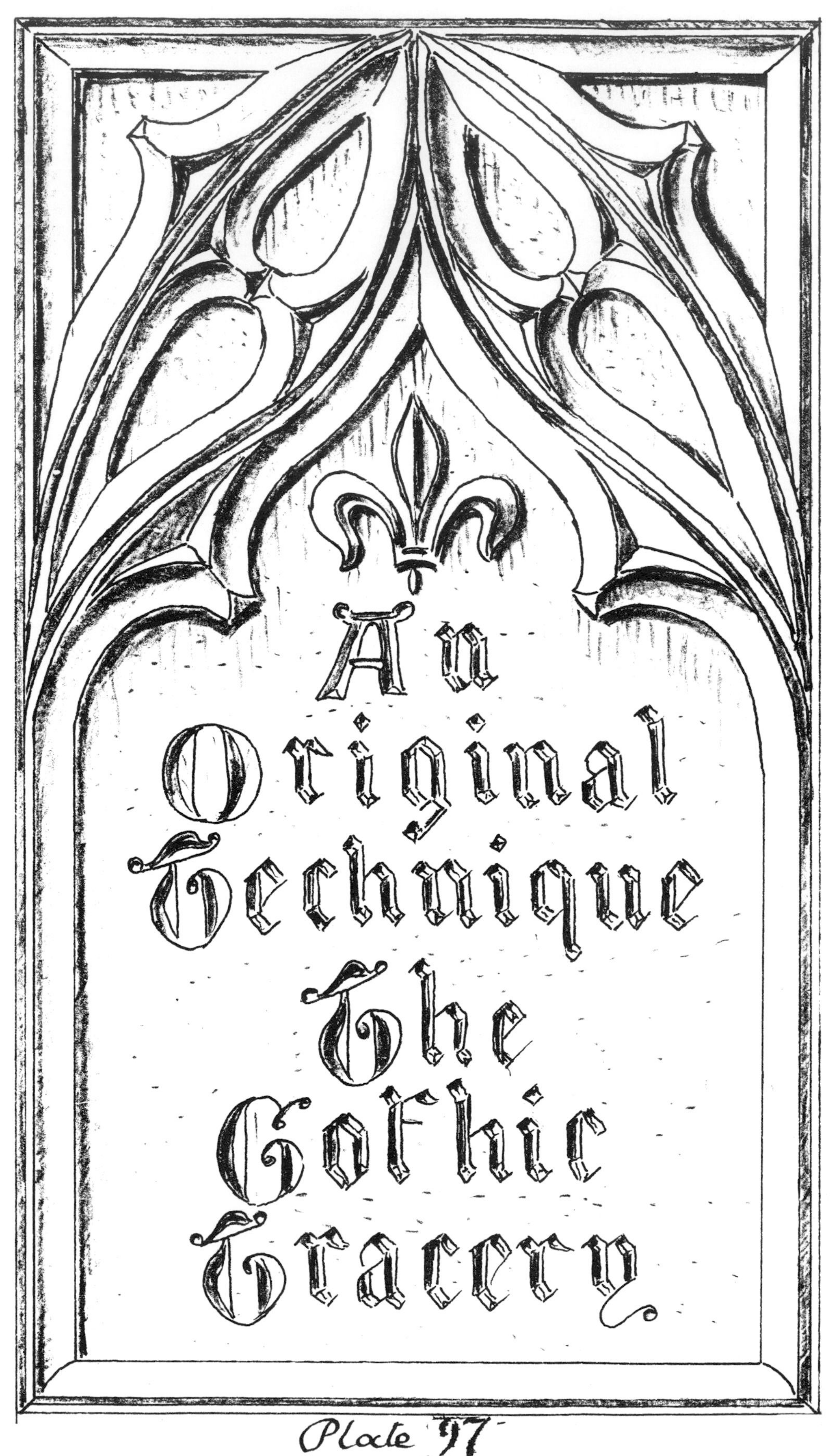

Plate 97

Suggested variations in the foliation of Gothic tracery and interpretation of supporting Lancettes

A few Words for the Gothic buff

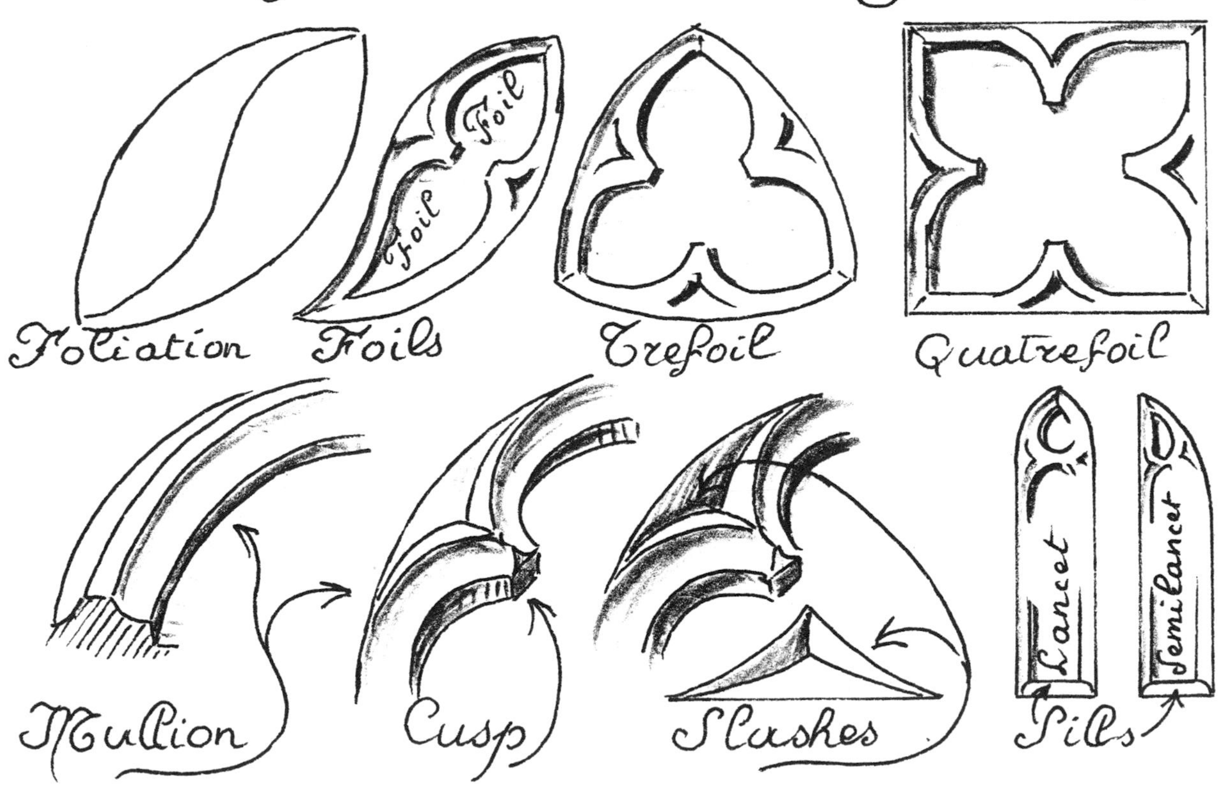

Plate 98

Plate 99

Tracing a Gothic Panel

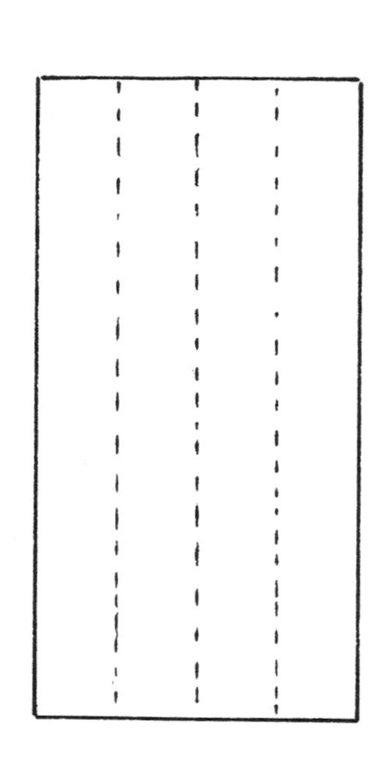

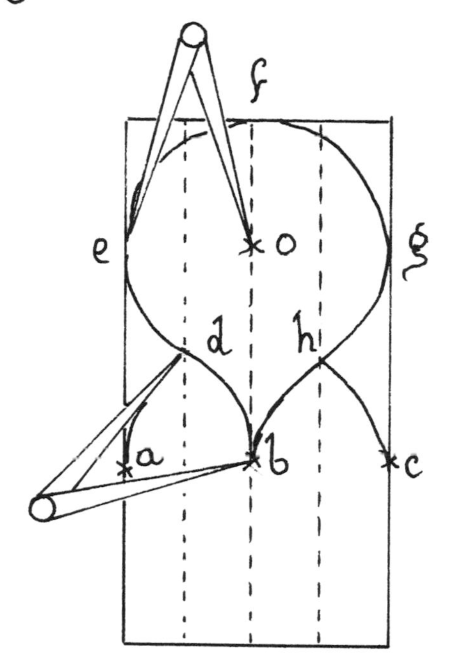

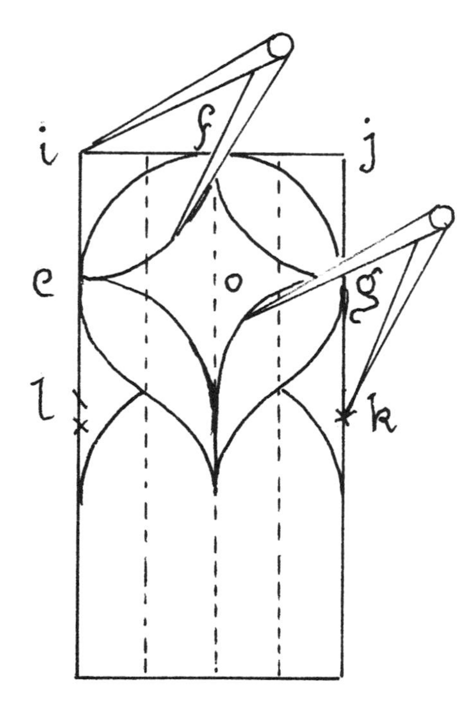

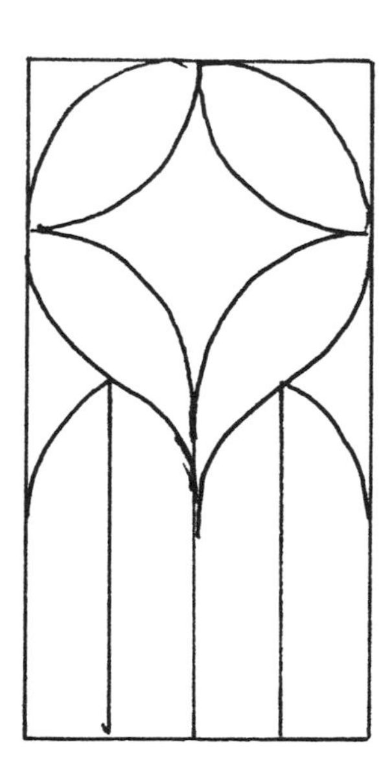

Plate 100

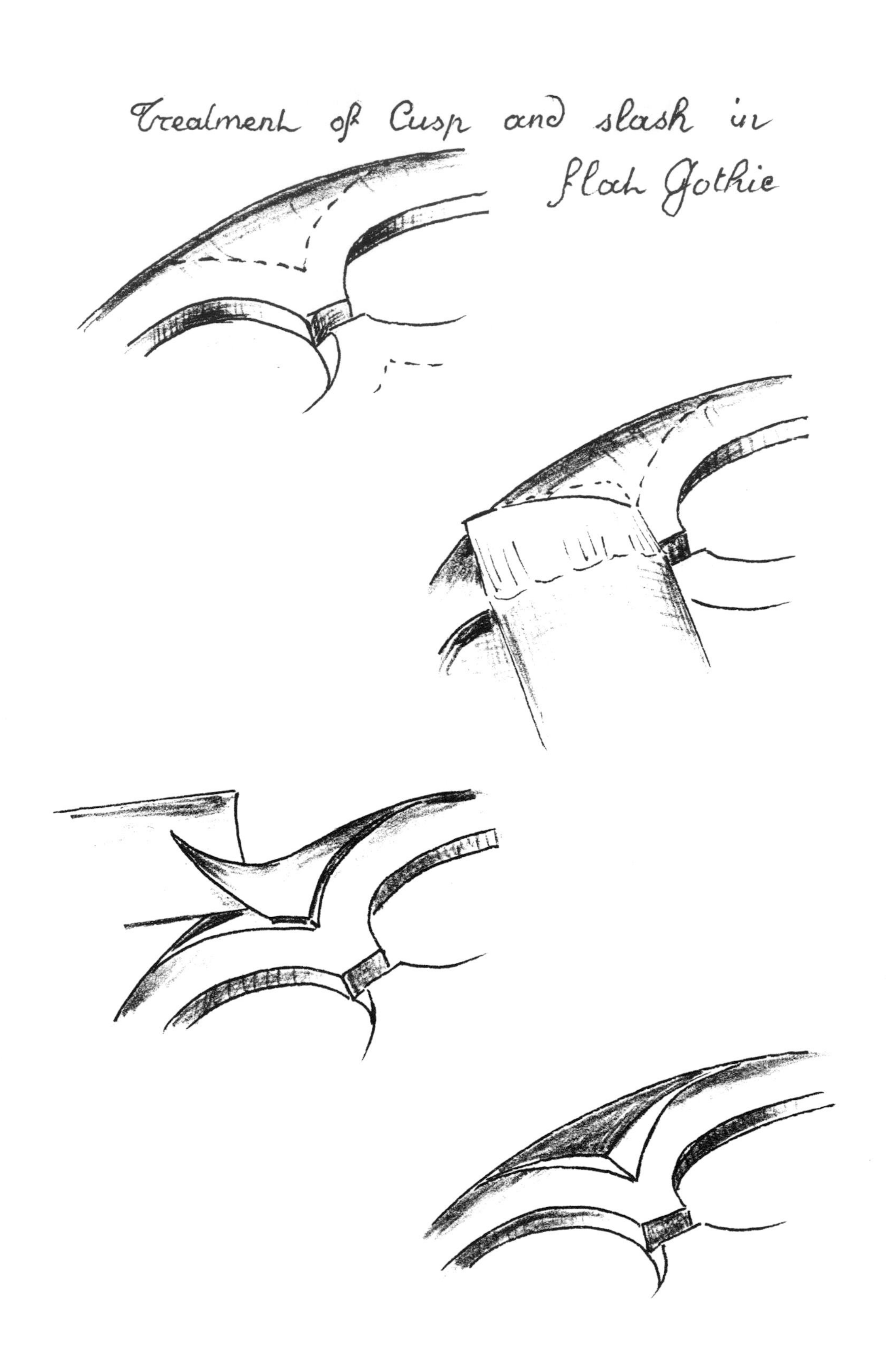

Treatment of Cusp and slash in
flat Gothic

Plate 101

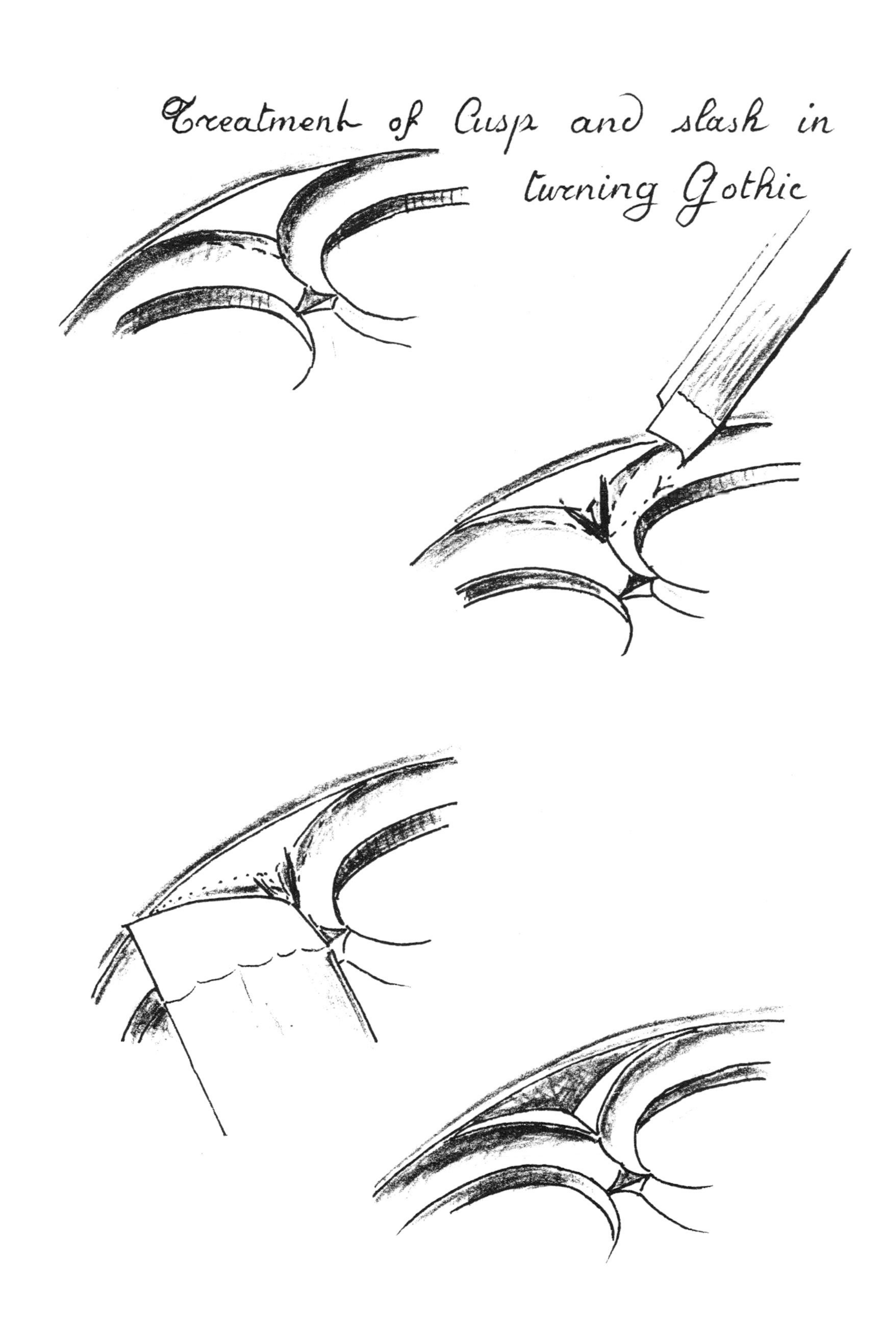
Treatment of Cusp and slash in
turning Gothic

Plate 102

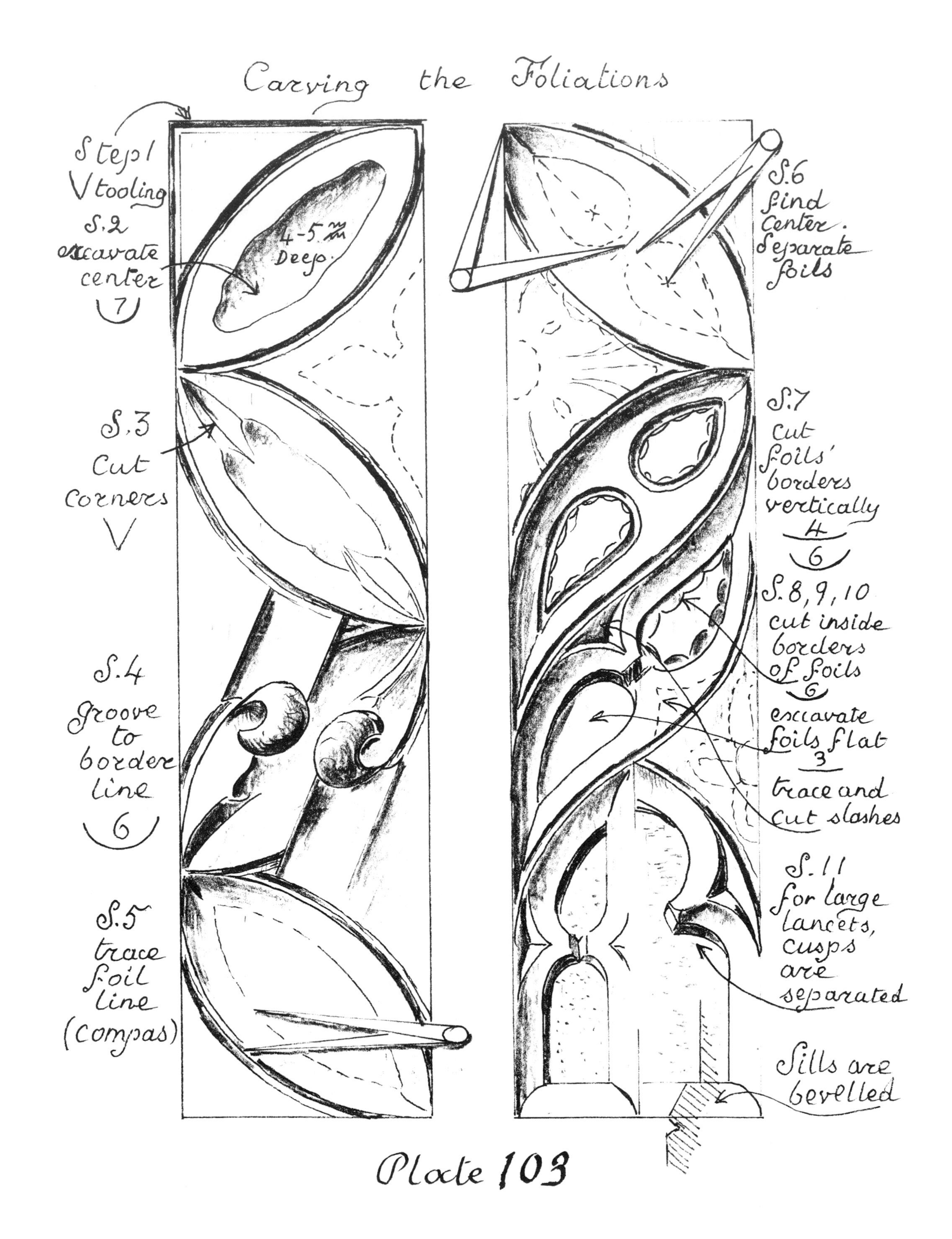
Carving the Foliations
Step 1
V tooling
S.2
excavate
center
7
4-5 m/m
Deep
S.3
Cut
Corners
V
S.4
Groove
to
border
line
6
S.5
trace
foil
line
(compas)
S.6
find
Center.
Separate
foils
S.7
Cut
foils'
borders
vertically
4
6
S.8, 9, 10
cut inside
borders
of foils
6
excavate
foils flat
3
trace and
cut slashes
S.11
for large
lancets,
cusps
are
separated
Sills are
bevelled
Plate 103

Photograph 4

Plate 104

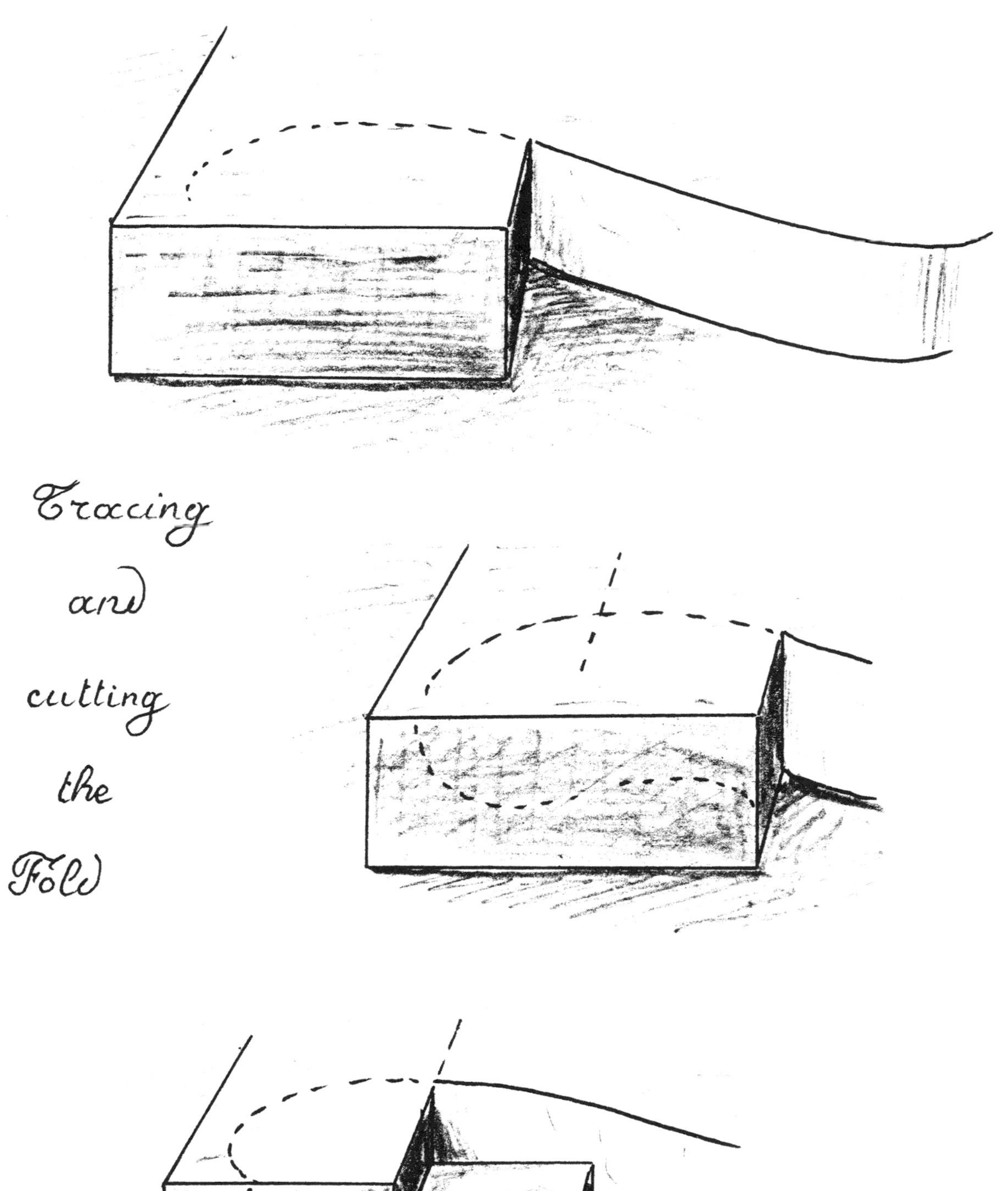
Tracing
and
cutting
the
Fold

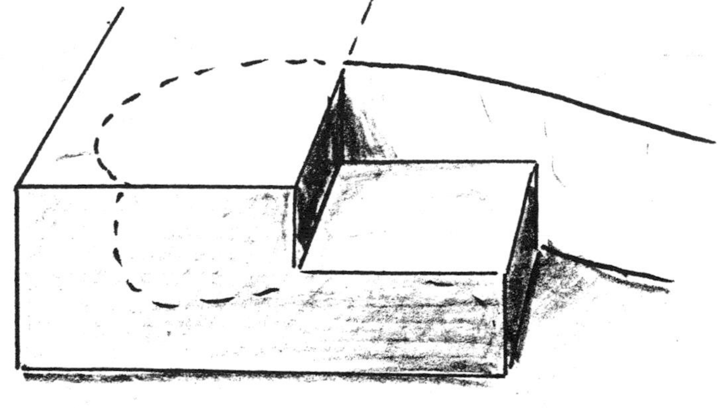

Plate 105

Cutting the Fold

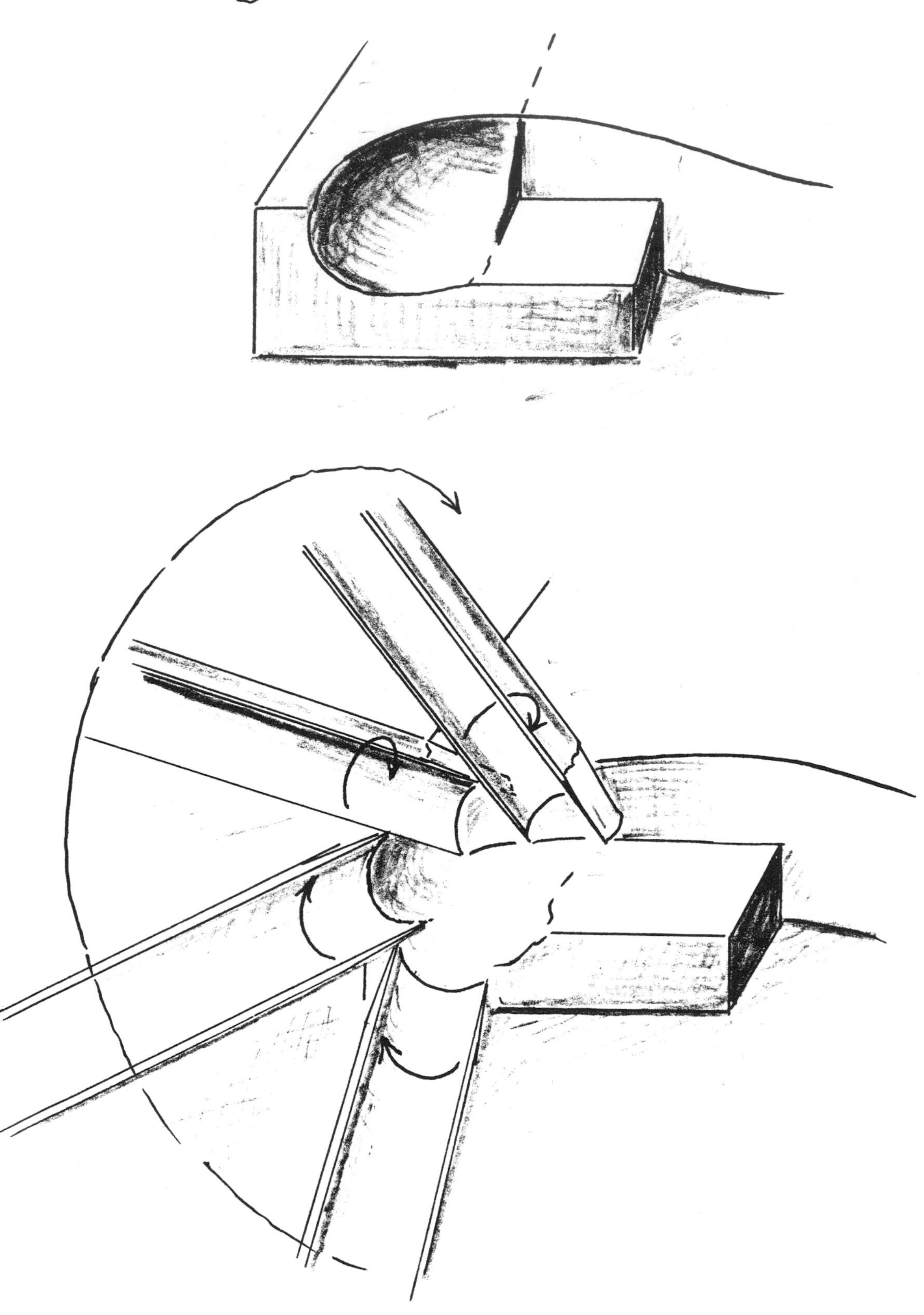

Plate 106

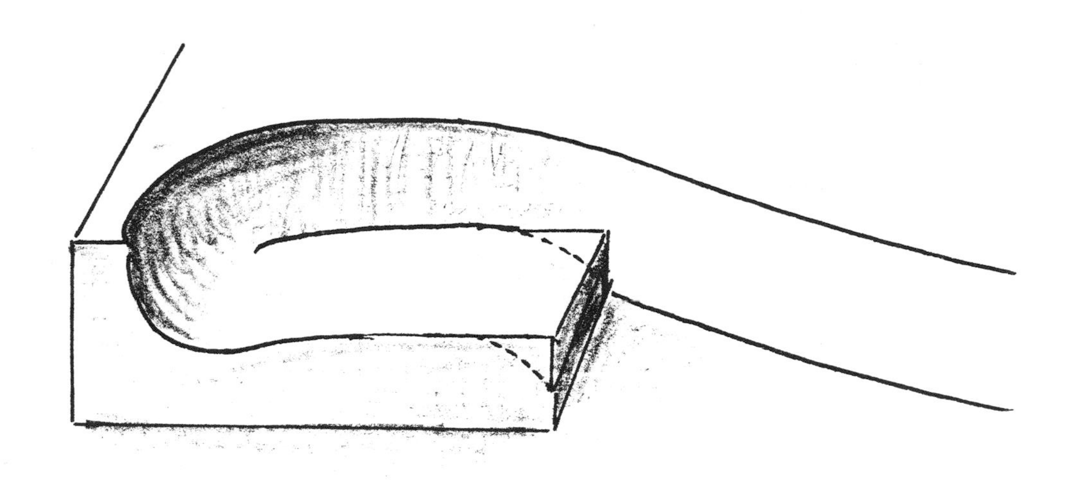

Finishing the Fold

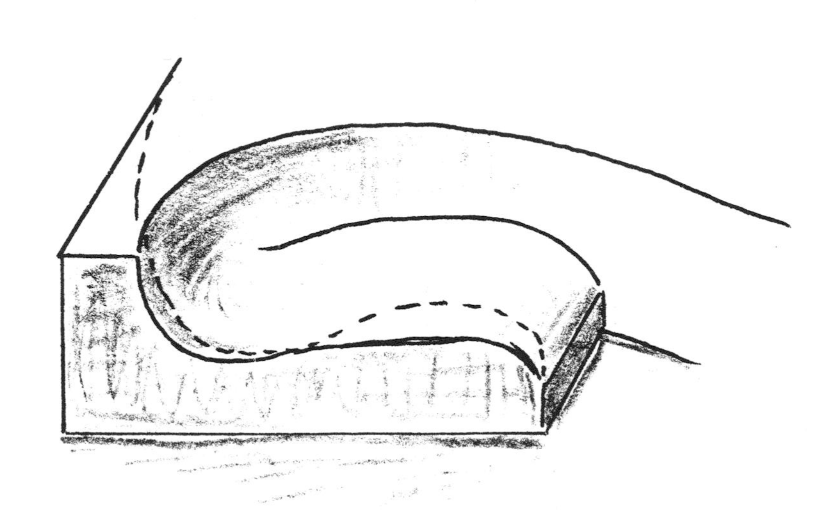

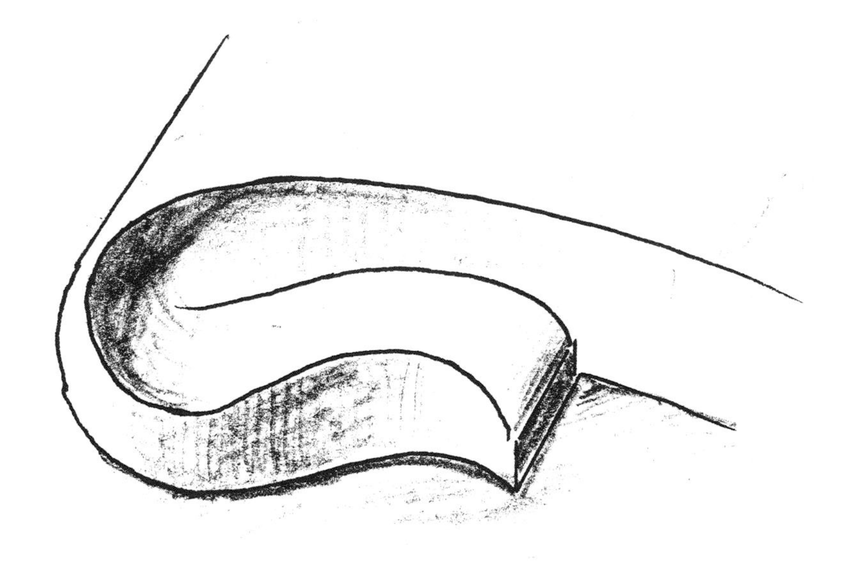

Plate 107

Photograph 5

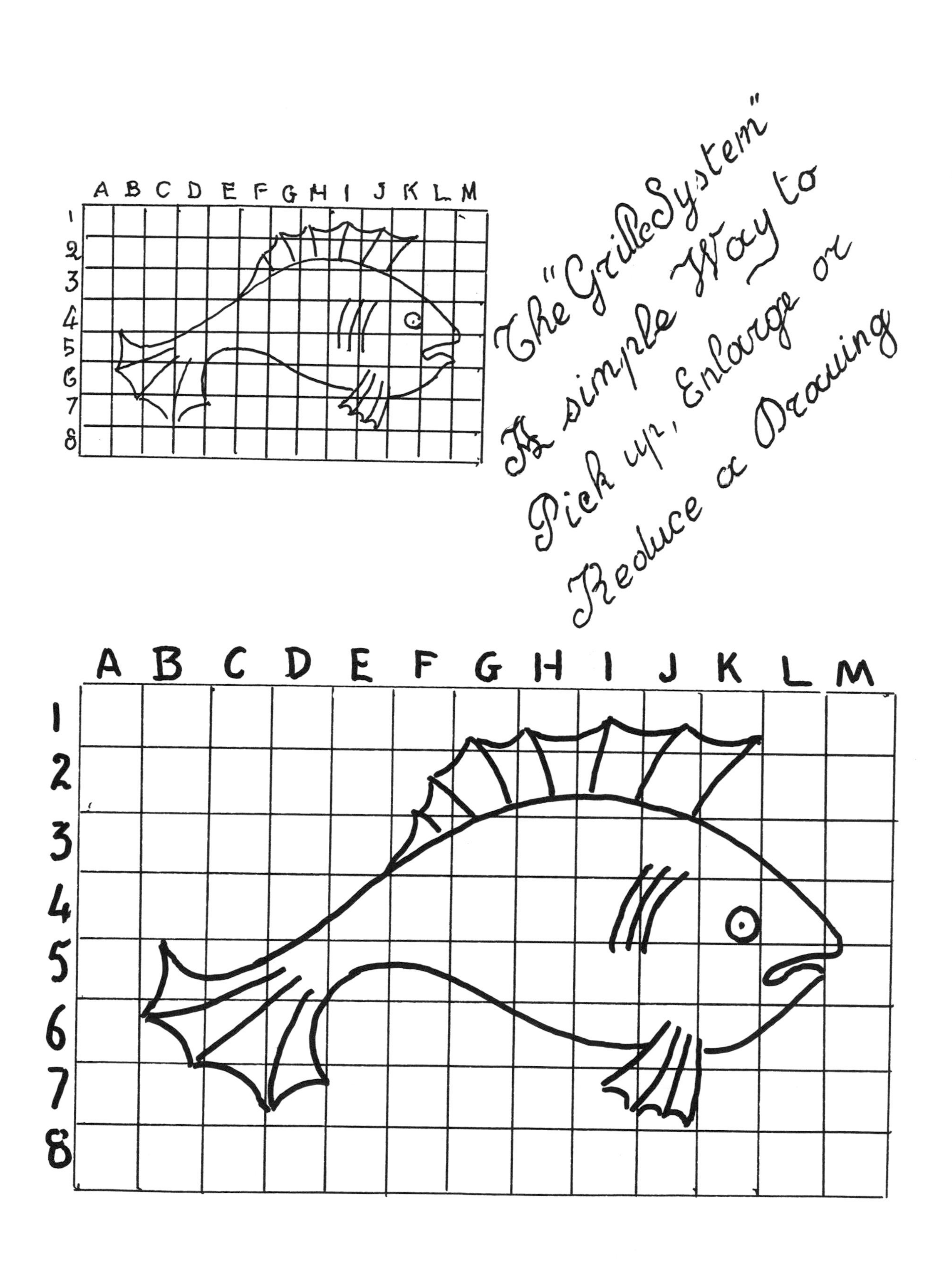
A B C D E F G H I J K L M
1 2 3 4 5 6 7 8
The "Grille System"
A simple Way to
Pick up, Enlarge or
Reduce a Drawing
A B C D E F G H I J K L M
1 2 3 4 5 6 7 8

Plate 108

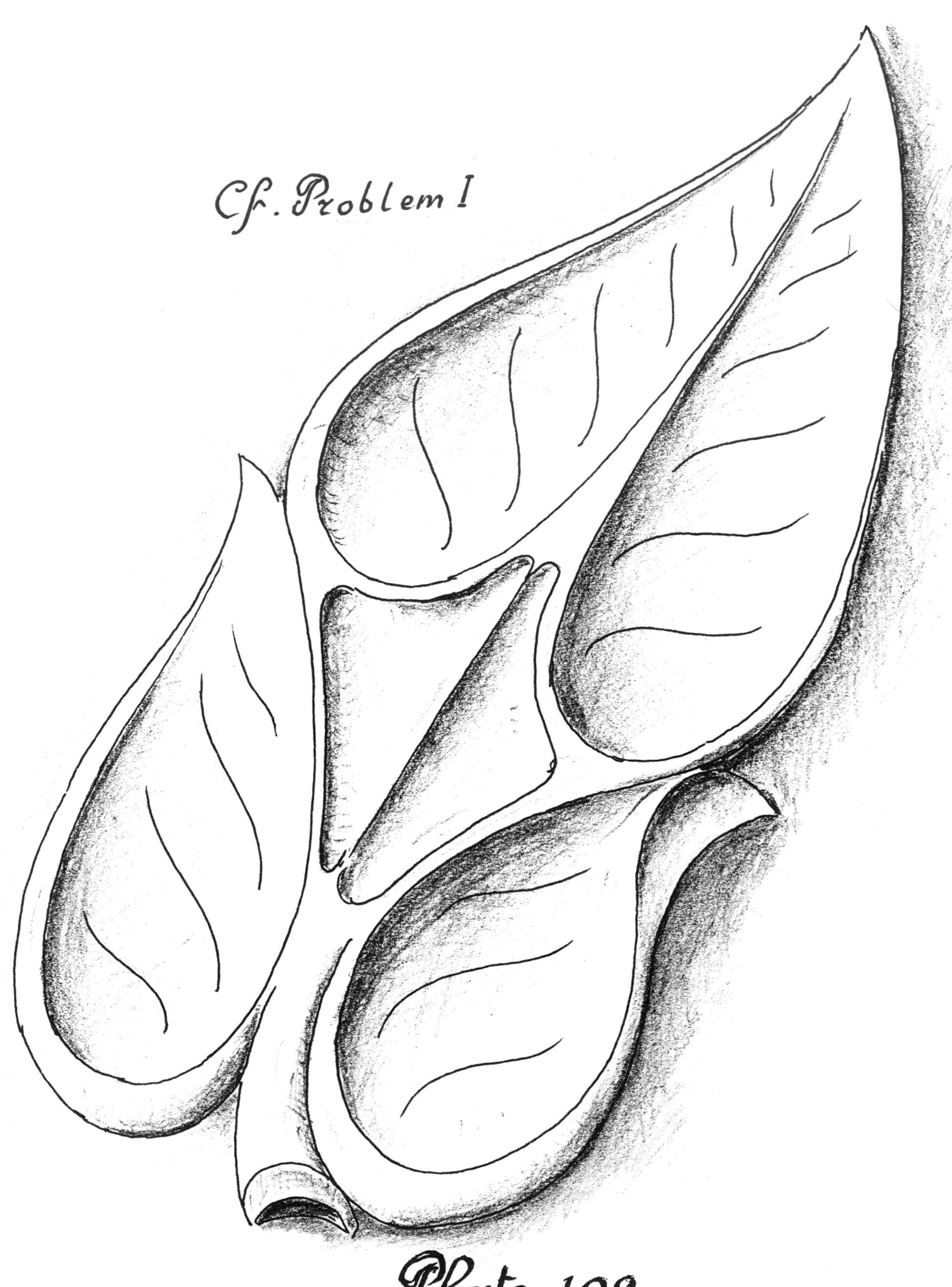

Plate 109

Photograph 6

Plate 110

Plate III

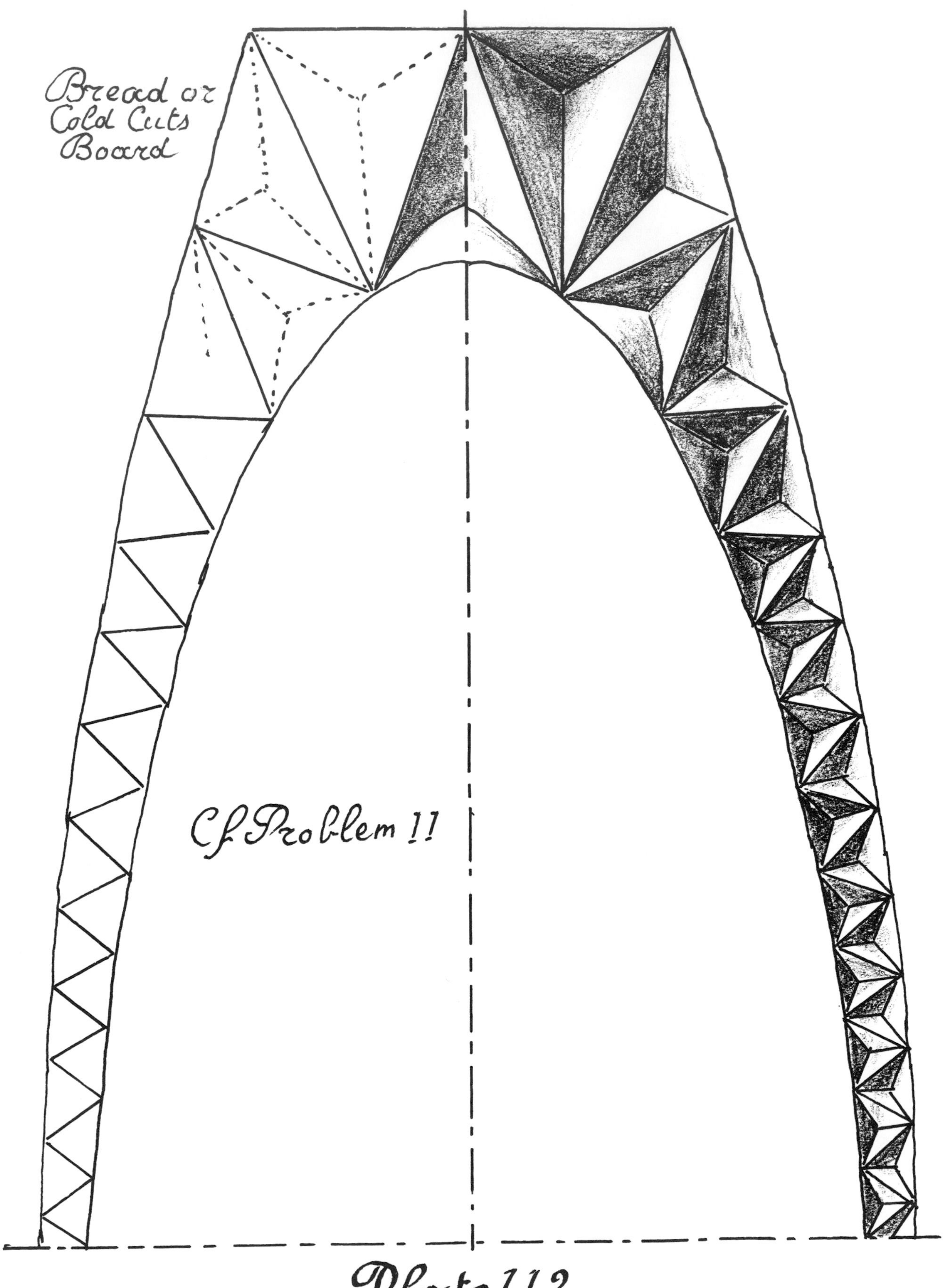
Bread or
Cold Cuts
Board
Cf. Problem 11

Plate 112

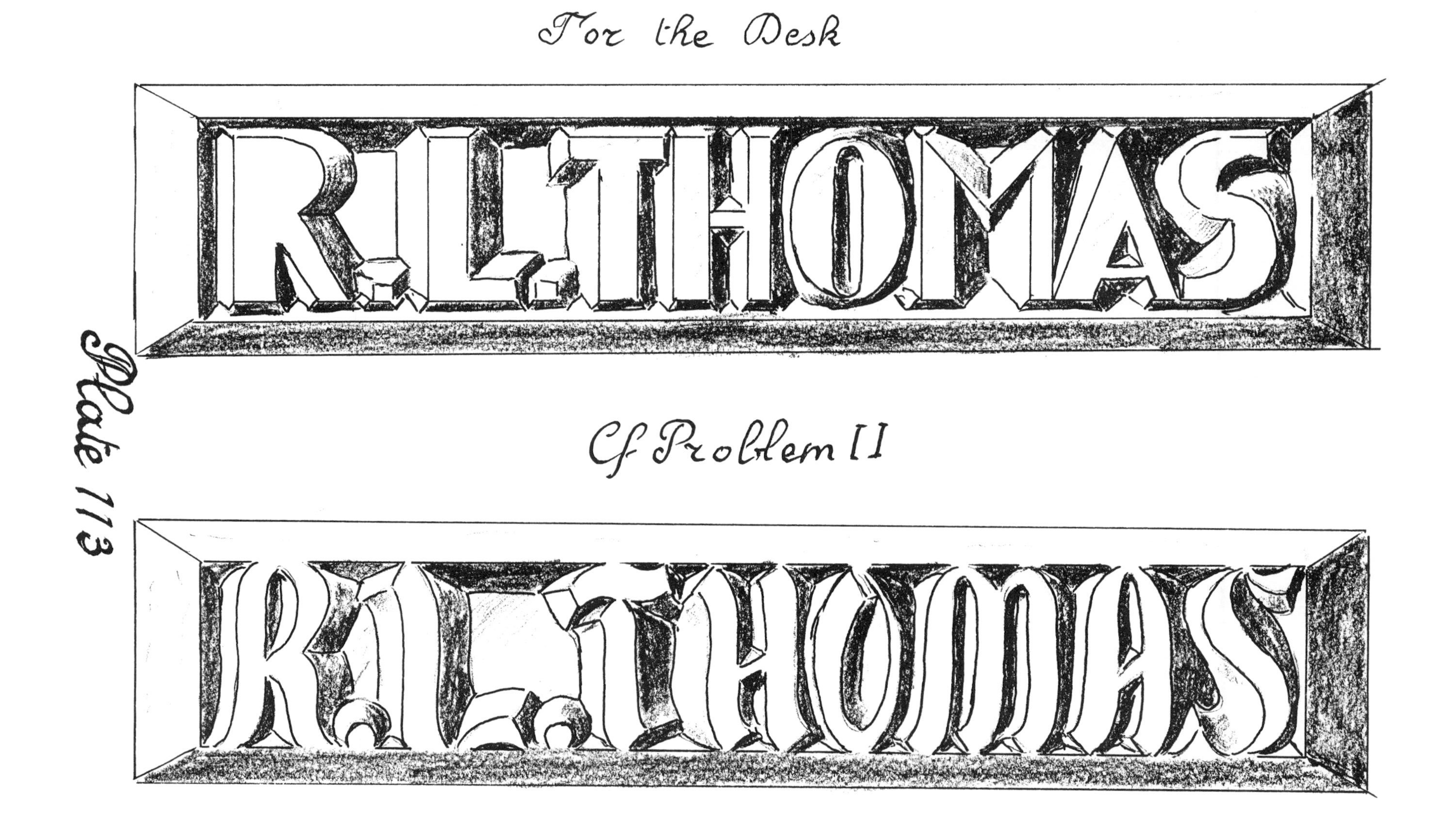

Plate 113

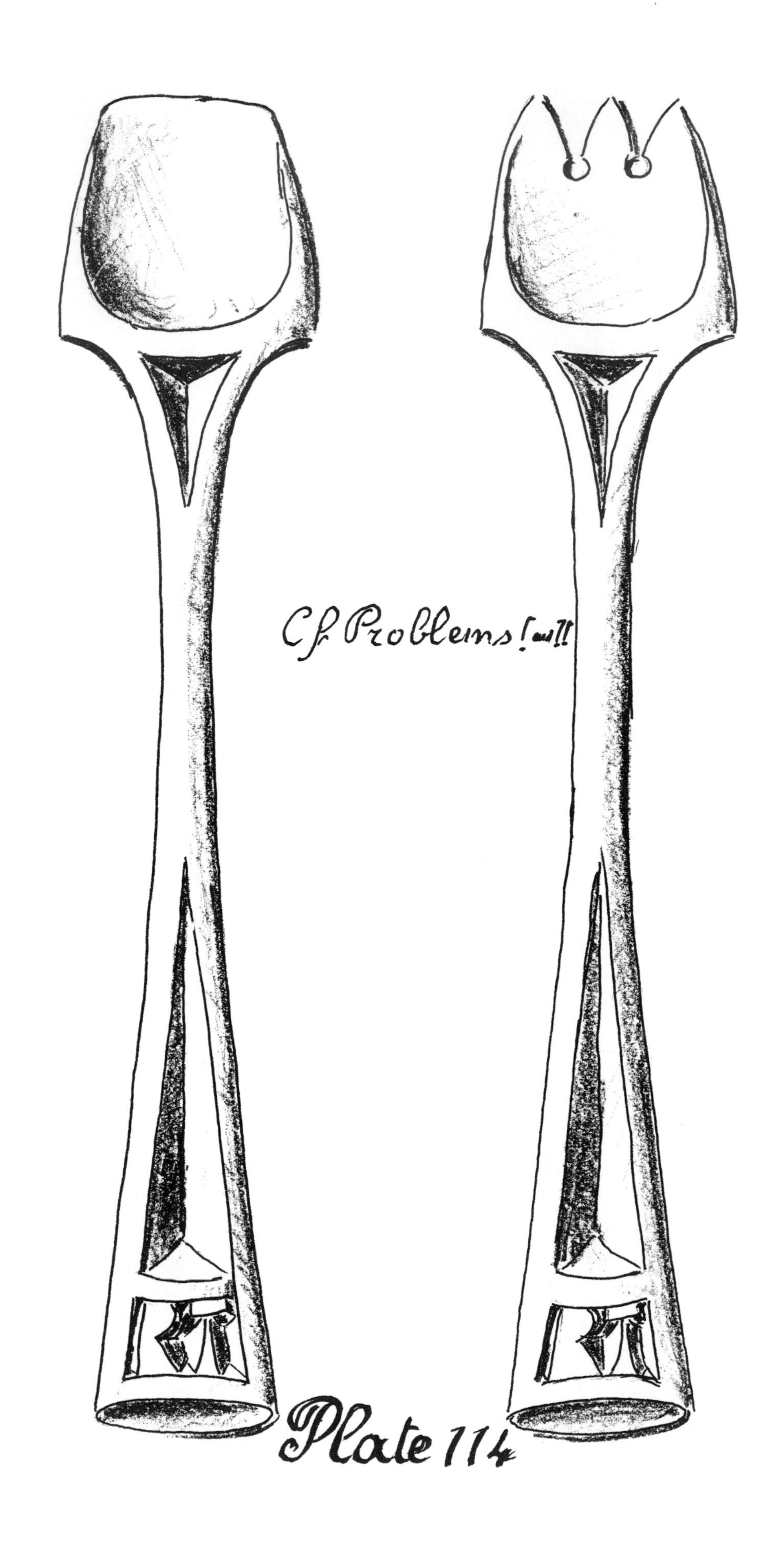

Plate 114

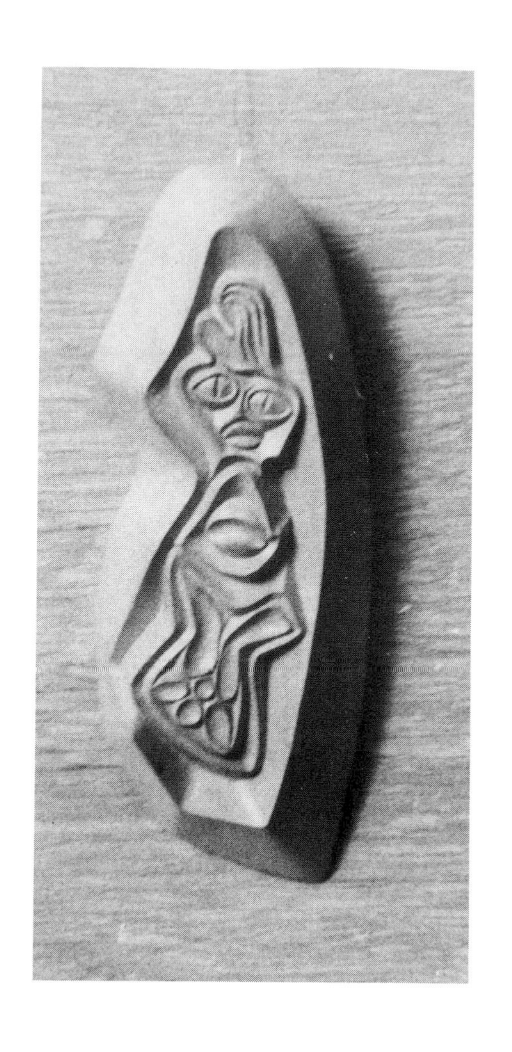

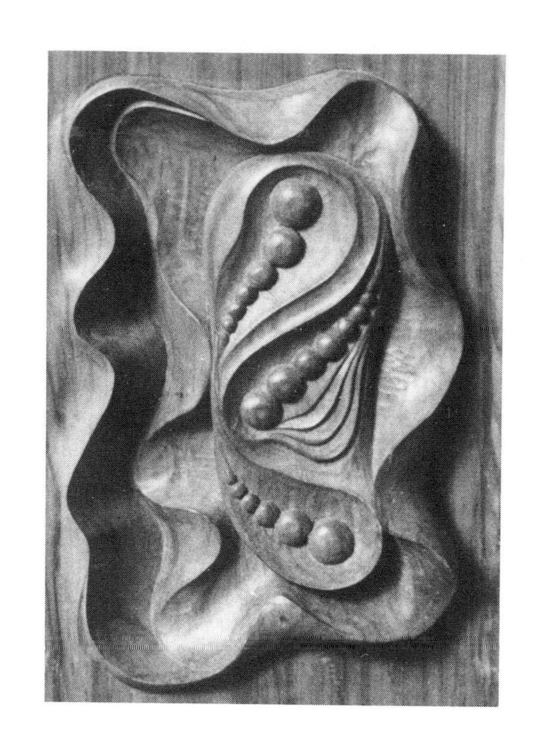

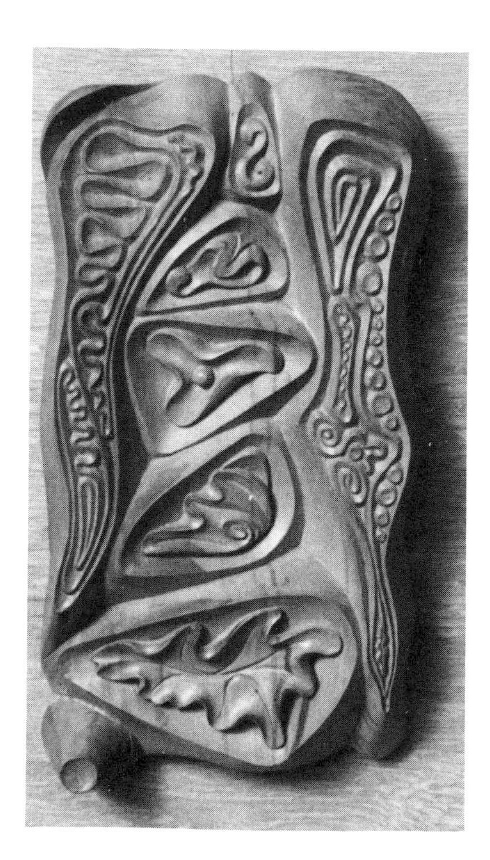

Photograph 7

Plate 115

Plate 116

Cf. Problem IV

House Number

Cf. Problem V

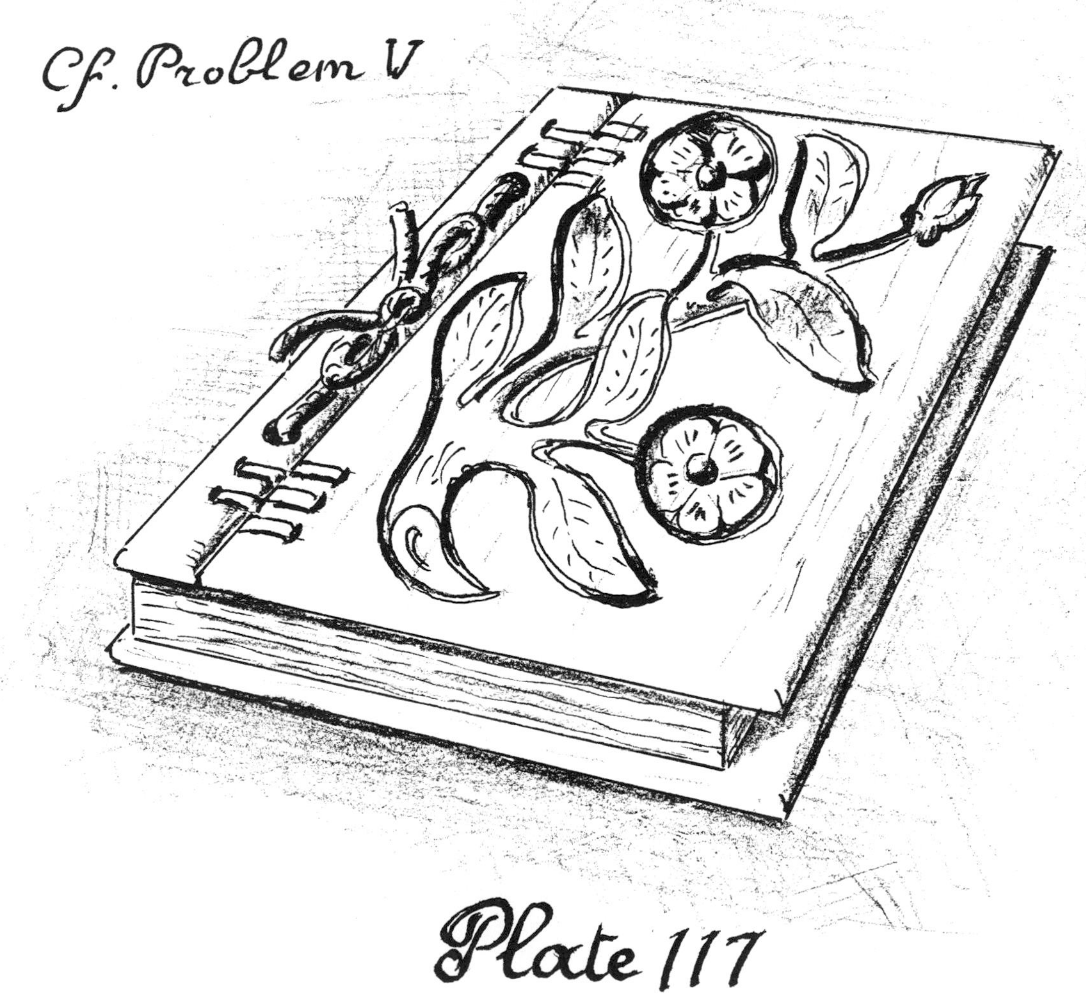

Plate 117

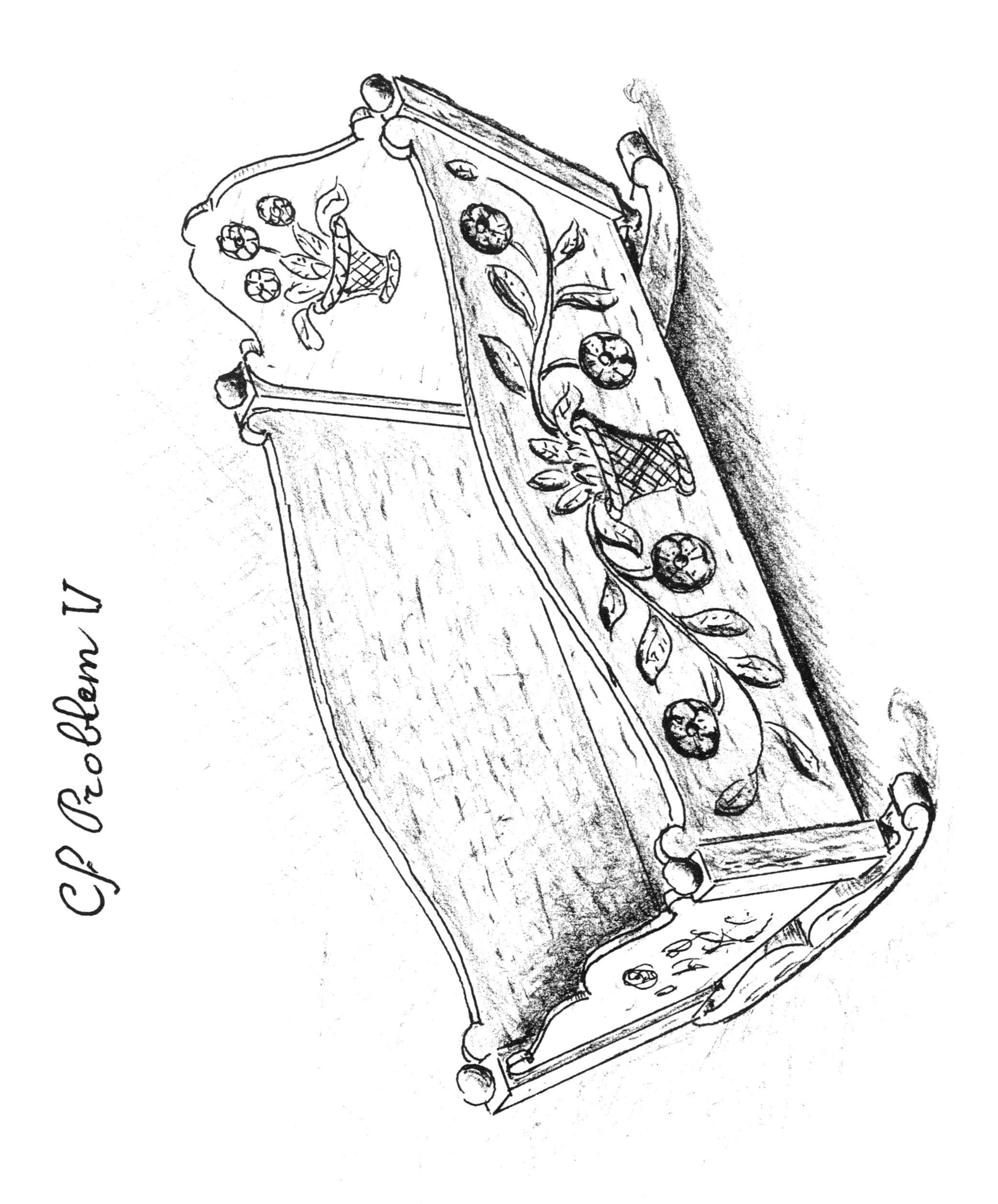

Plate 118

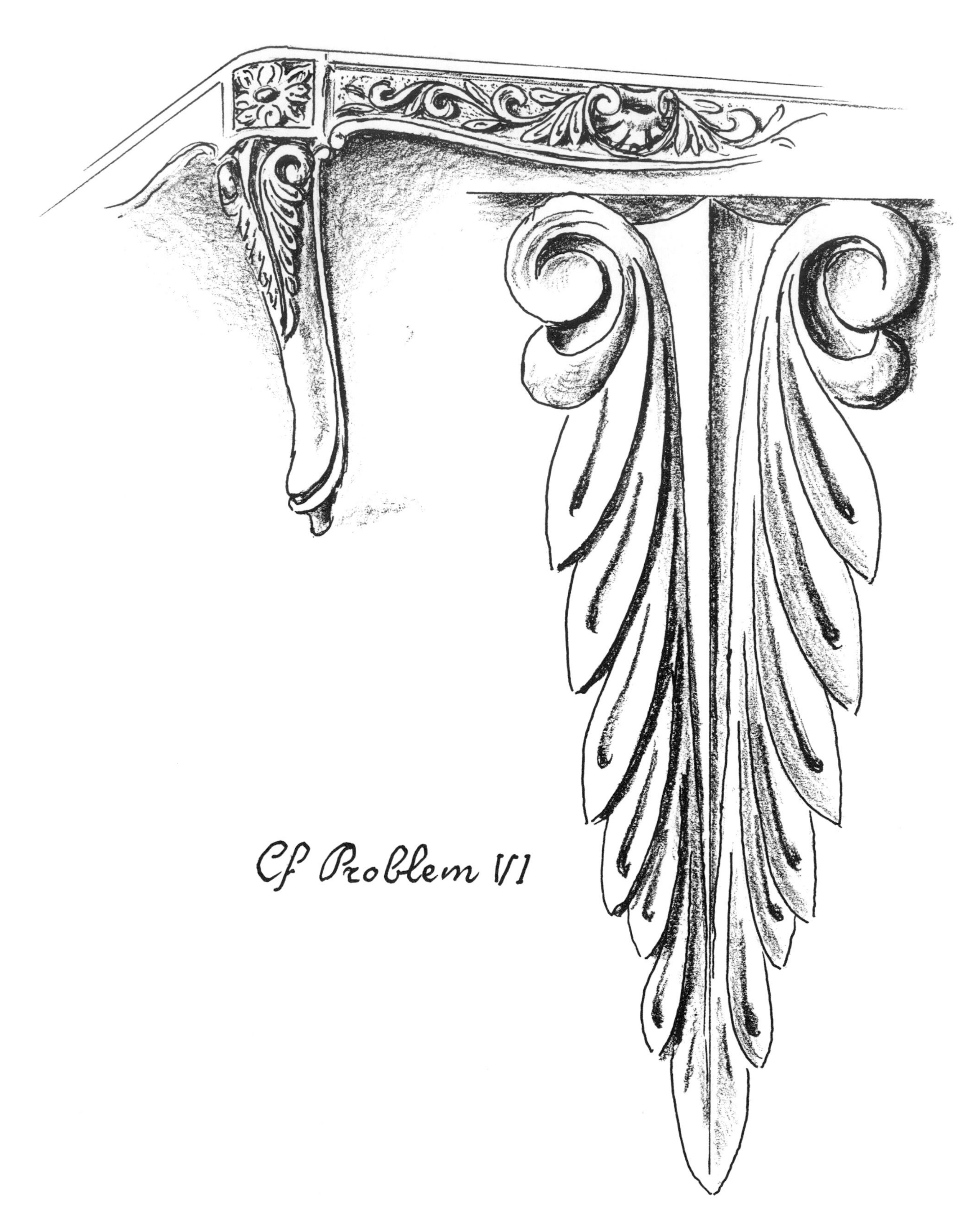

Plate 119

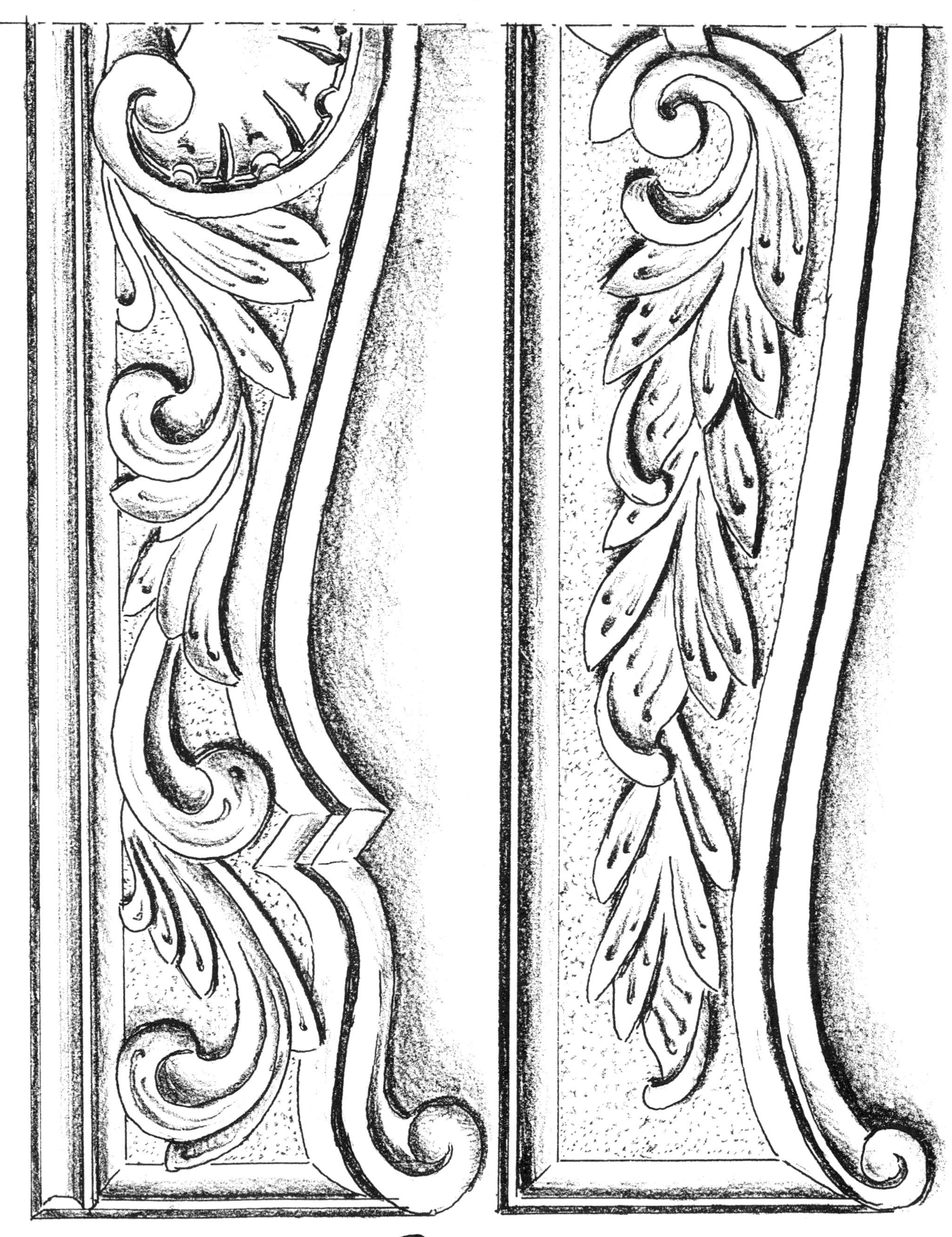

Plate 120

Cf. Problem VI

Plate 121

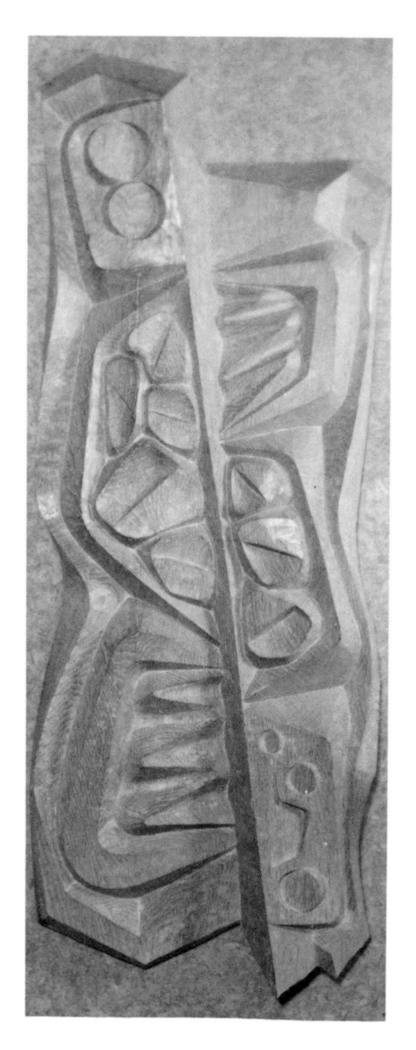

Photograph 8

Plate 122

Photograph 9

Photograph 10

Plate 123

Index

Index

Edited by Suzanne L. Cheatle